# ITALIANS IN CHICAGO, 1880–1930

# THE URBAN LIFE IN AMERICA SERIES

RICHARD C. WADE, GENERAL EDITOR

STANLEY BUDER
PULLMAN: An Experiment in Industrial Order
and Community Planning, 1880–1930

ALLEN F. DAVIS
SPEARHEADS FOR REFORM: The Social Settlements
and the Progressive Movement, 1890–1914

LYLE W. DORSETT
THE PENDERGAST MACHINE

MELVIN G. HOLLI
REFORM IN DETROIT: Hazen S. Pingree and Urban Politics

KENNETH T. JACKSON
THE KU KLUX KLAN IN THE CITY, 1915–1930

ZANE L. MILLER
BOSS COX'S CINCINNATI: Urban Politics in the Progressive Era

JAMES F. RICHARDSON
THE NEW YORK POLICE: Colonial Times to 1901

PETER SCHMITT
BACK TO NATURE: The Arcadian Myth in Urban America

HUMBERT S. NELLI
ITALIANS IN CHICAGO, 1880–1930: A Study in Ethnic Mobility

# ITALIANS IN CHICAGO
## 1880–1930

### A Study in Ethnic Mobility

HUMBERT S. NELLI

NEW YORK

OXFORD UNIVERSITY PRESS

*For Florence and Humbert Orazio Nelli*

# Foreword

Surely no one needs to be reminded again that the United States is a country of immigrants, or a "nation of nations" as Walt Whitman phrased it. The theme is now a conventional one, thanks to a generation of able scholars who have examined this great migration and assessed its significance in our national history. Moreover, we no longer see the process simply in the immigrant's impact on American society, but also in the way which this country transformed the immigrant as well. If the reaction to older residents was complex, so too was the response of newcomers to a strange land.

Yet, though we know a good deal about this general process, we know much less about its specific workings or its local variations. In *Boston's Immigrants,* Oscar Handlin brilliantly portrayed the acculturation of that city's most important, indeed ultimately dominant, group. But other studies handle many groups of newcomers or, like William V. Shannon's *The American Irish,* seek to encompass the whole national experience of one group over the sweep of American history. In this volume, Humbert Nelli makes an intensive examination of what happened to Italian immigrants when they came to Chicago. The story begins in the mid-nineteenth century and comes down to the Great Depression.

The choice of Chicago is a happy one. Few other cities had so large a proportion of immigrants and none so rich a mixture, "a compost of men and women of all manner of language," as William T. Stead put it in 1894. The Italians never became the dominant group, though their numbers mounted rapidly in the thirty years before the shutting off of immigration. Hence a portion of this story contains the relations of Italians with other ethnic groups as well as the more familiar theme of newcomers in a world of native Americans. But there were enough Italians to leave a clear mark on the midwest metropolis.

Mr. Nelli deals with the acculturative process in two ways. First, he sees the Italians joining other immigrant groups in "colonies" in the central city. Here the emphasis is on the initial settlement and the problems of acceptance and adjustment. Housing and jobs were crucial; there could be no future without them. However, the author also deals with the outward trek of Italians after the first concentrations had been established. Those who were modestly successful very quickly sought better conditions and more pleasant surroundings in neighborhoods farther away from downtown. Unlike other books which deal almost exclusively with immigrant "ghettoes," Mr. Nelli emphasizes the dual nature of the experience —both in concentrated settlements and the dispersal to other communities throughout the metropolis.

Indeed, mobility is Mr. Nelli's constant theme. Not only did Italians move away from the early "colonies" in large numbers, but they also continually changed residences within the old neighborhoods. A skillful use of the census, school reports, voting lists, and city directories permits the author to reconstruct this persistent migration. While outsiders always thought of the immigrant blocs as stable and unchanging, the evidence reveals precisely the opposite. Unlike Italians in the old country whose lives were likely to be bound up with the village of their birth, newcomers very quickly opted for American mobility.

Throughout the period of accommodation, Italians developed institutions to ease the transition to a new society and identify their relationships with older Americans. The church, of course, had been central in Italy, but its role was modified by conditions in Chicago. Mutual benefit societies expanded their importance, and the newcomers invented such institutions as the immigrant bank and the "colonial press" for which there was no old world analogue. Mr. Nelli is especially persuasive when he handles the ambiguous position of the Italian editor who had to interpret America to his readers without destroying their connection with the homeland.

One of the most compelling parts of this volume is the analysis of Italian predominance in the criminal field in Chicago. Mr. Nelli notes that actually Italians were newcomers to organized crime. The doubtful credit for the founding father of the underworld belongs to an Irishman, Michael Cassius McDonald. In the 1870's his organization entered the field through political manipulation. With virtual control of City Hall secured in the 1880's, McDonald invented Chicago's first "syndicate" and perfected many of the techniques which Italians would adopt forty years later. Except for the violence, little was added.

In fact, James Colosimo, the Italian pioneer in the field, served his apprenticeship with those two doughty rascals, "Hinky Dink" Kenna and "Bathhouse John" Coughlin in Chicago's notorious First Ward. But it was Prohibition, that peculiarly American experiment in reform, that provided the opportunity for more businesslike and powerful organized activity. Before the decade was finished, the gangs, mostly Italian, had established control of the city. Al Capone proved to be the most resourceful and successful (indeed, at 32 years old he became the town's youngest "mayor"), and Chicago and gang warfare became inextricably linked in the popular imagination. Neither Chicagoans nor Italian spokesmen liked the image, and Mr. Nelli details with low-keyed irony the attempts of the Italian community to claim that the linkage did not exist at the same time that it sought means of evading it.

In a period of renewed inerest in ethnicity, Mr. Nelli's volume has a particular relevance. Scholars have been re-examining the old "melting pot" notion with the conclusion that ethnicity persists even after long periods of assimilation and nearly fifty years after the closing of the historic policy of open immigration. Those concerned about civil rights have questioned whether the immigrant experience can serve as a useful guide to public policy toward black Americans who now comprise such a large proportion of the nation's urban residents. The *Italians in Chicago,* by an intensive study of one ethnic group in a major city, illumines the historical process of acculturation and provides a framework for viewing contemporary problems.

RICHARD C. WADE

GENERAL EDITOR

URBAN LIFE IN AMERICA SERIES

*Chicago, Ill.*
*June 1970*

# Preface

In the decades between 1880 and World War I, European immigrants and their children formed the major populations of the large industrial cities of the East and Middle West. According to the 1910 census, for example, first- and second-generation newcomers accounted for 77 per cent of Chicago's inhabitants, 78 per cent of New York's, and 74 per cent of Detroit's, Cleveland's, and Boston's. Thus the arrival of migrants, their efforts to assimilate, and the reaction of native Americans to them and the problems they created made up a large part of the story of urban America during this period.

Contemporaries expressed a deep concern over the influx of this alien horde—composed, many claimed, of criminals, paupers, ignorant peasants, and illegal contract laborers—who would inevitably inundate American cities, aggravate existing problems, and undermine the American character. As a rule, extremely undesirable conditions of life and labor typified areas of immigrant settlement. Books, articles, and numerous governmental reports examined community features, including filthy, substandard and overcrowded housing; crime; delinquency; exploitation of newcomers by their compatriots and native Americans; corrupt politicians; and overworking of immigrant women and children by American businessmen. Authors noted the tendency of successful members of the group, those who had moved away from the immigrant colony and identified with the American middle class, to ignore the needs of their original community. These characteristics appear to be the price paid by each new group in its adjustment to American urban life.[1]

Like most of the later immigrants, Italians seemed to move outward from the city's core more slowly and reluctantly than had Irish, German, and other older groups, which had settled in Chicago and other northern cities considerably earlier than did most Italians, eastern European Jews, Poles, Lithuanians, and Greeks. In actuality, while contemporaries did not recognize the extensive amount of residential mobility among Italians and other latecomers, from the first years of settlement, movement occurred not only inside colonies and from one district to another, but also from the early, centrally located neighborhoods toward outlying areas of the city and even into suburbs. By the 1920's the suburban trend was noticeable and significant. World War I and the immigration laws of 1921 and 1924 closed new sources of immigration, and Italian districts, lacking newcomers to fill vacancies left by former residents, began to decline.

Even at the height of immigration from the Kingdom of Italy, Chicago, like other cities, had few solidly Italian blocks or neighborhoods. A residue of immigrants remained when the composition of a colony changed, but most of an earlier group moved eventually from the central city, partly to escape encroaching businesses and partly to avoid contact with incoming residents new to urban life.

Neither the immigrants nor the receiving society recognized the values and benefits of the ethnic colony. Yet the community of the immigrant generation fulfilled an important function, for it served as a "beachhead" or staging ground where new arrivals remained until they absorbed the new ideas and habits that facilitated their adjustment to the American environment.[2] It appears that—within the limits of individual abilities and aspirations—conditions and opportunities in the receiving country (rather than old-world back-ground) determined the economic activities of newcomers. The new urban surroundings profoundly affected other traditions and viewpoints, although immigrants themselves believed that in America they were re-creating homeland village life. In the process they created a myth that they have nurtured to the present.

Most of Chicago's Italians came from that area of the Kingdom lying south of Rome (especially the provinces of Aguila, Campo-basso, Avellino, Potenza, Cosenza, Reggio, Catanzaro, and Bari) and the western portion of Sicily. Immense differences in history, geography, and language among and within these regions promoted loyalty to the native village rather than to the Kingdom of Italy.[3] Homeland or *paese* meant village of birth, outside of which lived strangers and enemies. Residents of other towns or provinces, regarded as foreigners, became objects of suspicion or contempt. This narrow perspective broke down in American cities, where new patterns and institutions influenced habits and outlooks. Of necessity, immigrants joined together in benefit societies, churches, and political clubs; they lived and worked in surroundings crowded with non-Italian strangers; their children attended schools filled with "outsiders." They read the same Italian-language newspapers, and they came to regard themselves as members of the Italian group. Thus, in contrast to the situation in the Kingdom itself, Italian-Americans from the area south of Rome can be described in group terms. In the text they will be identified as "Southerners," and their home provinces as the "South."

The five decades following 1880 comprised the years of major establishment, of pattern formation, of dynamic growth, and—after World War I—of group dispersion and the decline of core-area colonies. The purpose of this study is to describe and analyze the experience of Chicago's Italian community during this period.

H.N.

*Lexington, Kentucky*
*June 1970*

# Acknowledgments

I am grateful to the many Chicagoans who facilitated my research and who made my visits to their city a pleasant experience. I owe a special debt to Father Gino Dalpiaz of Our Lady of Pompei Church, who gave unrestricted use of his parish records and introduced me to priests in other Italian churches of the city; to Anthony Sorrentino for permitting me to xerox his unpublished autobiography; to Richard J. Jones of the Policemen's Annuity and Benefit Fund and to my good friend Archie Motley of the Chicago Historical Society for providing me with primary materials.

Grants from the American Association for State and Local History, Fordham University, and the University of Kentucky Graduate School made possible a number of research trips to Chicago. Summer teaching appointments in 1966 and 1967 at the University of Illinois at Chicago Circle speeded the collection of primary sources. Not the least of my obligations to Chicago Circle stems from the unlimited use of research assistants and departmental facilities, especially xeroxing equipment, provided during those two valuable summers. Summer grants in 1968 and 1969 from the University of Kentucky Research Foundation permitted me to devote my full attention to writing.

My thanks go to the editors of the *American Journal of Sociology*, the *Journal of American History*, *Labor History*, and the *International Migration Review*, for their permission to use material which appeared originally in those periodicals, although in somewhat different form.

A number of friends helped me to clarify and refine my ideas. Among those who graciously gave of their knowledge and time were Donald Klimovich and Melvin G. Holli of the University of Illinois at Chicago Circle; Robert D. Cross, then Professor of History at Columbia University and now President of Swarthmore College; Mark H. Haller, Jr. of Temple University; and Spencer Di Scala of the University of Massachusetts.

Two people deserve special thanks. Richard C. Wade of the University of Chicago guided my doctoral work on the role of the immigrant press in Chicago's Italian community, and aided the writing of this book with his advice and suggestions. My wife, Elizabeth, the only person able to decipher my handwriting, served as chief typist and editorial assistant from the first rough draft to the final galley proofs, and somehow combined these jobs with the supervision of a household and our three active sons.

# Contents

# Maps

# Tables

# ITALIANS IN CHICAGO, 1880–1930

# 1

# From Rural Italy to Urban America

Between 1880 and 1914, the period of large-scale emigration from Italy to the United States, some Italians went overseas to evade military service or to find religious freedom (as Waldensian Protestants); a few departed because of political considerations; and criminals fled to avoid punishment or to take advantage of greater opportunities elsewhere. Generally, such travelers intended their absences to be permanent, but in numbers they never amounted to an important total. Most emigrants were motivated by economic factors. Some felt driven by the desire to escape a vicious system of taxation, but the majority were attracted by the hope of bettering their income through seasonal or temporary labor abroad (or elsewhere in Europe).[1]

The flow of Italian transoceanic emigration varied according to the relative economic opportunities available in the various receiving countries. The large-scale movement of Italians to the United States in the years after 1880 formed the second great shift from the homeland to the new world. The first population movement, which lasted throughout most of the nineteenth century, surged to Latin America, and especially Argentina and Brazil.[2]

3

The allure of Latin America decreased toward the end of the century, and the decline continued into the twentieth century, partly because of unsettled political and financial conditions in Brazil and Argentina. Economic opportunities for immigrants in South America diminished at the same time that expanding American industry demanded unskilled laborers. Transportation to the United States cost less than that to Latin America, and more money could be earned in North America—two simple but important facts.[3]

Italians still felt drawn to Argentina and Brazil, but by the time these countries had solved their immediate political and economic problems, the mainstream of Italian immigration had been diverted to the United States. Larger numbers of Italians went to North America than had ever reached the Latin American countries. Rarely did a yearly total of Italian newcomers exceed 100,000 in Argentina or Brazil; after 1900, this figure was a yearly *minimum* for the United States.[4]

The shift in destination coincided with another change: the central source of Italian emigration gradually moved from the north to the south of the Kingdom. Although living conditions in the "South" reached depths of misery and degradation equaled nowhere else in Italy, emigration started from the north. "Southern" traditions and adherence to old ways had deep roots. Under the monarchy, however, when the area received treatment more appropriate for a colony or appendage, earlier resistance to movement began to crumble. In the late 'eighties, Baron Sidney Sonnino reminded parliament that during its more than twenty years of existence the Italian government had not produced one effective measure to improve living and working conditions for impoverished toilers of the "South." Diplomat and historian Luigi Villari, in a book published after the turn of the century, echoed this sentiment: "The North has made a great advance in wealth, trade, and education, while the South is almost stationary."[5]

Before the 1890's, Italians who entered the United States came chiefly from the northern and economically more advanced areas of Genoa, Tuscany, Venetia, Lombardy, and Piedmont. The flood from the "South" began in the 1880's, reaching its peak after the turn of the century. Between 1899 and 1910, some 372,668 Italians entered the United States from northern Italy; 1,911,933 came from the "South." These totals, however, include immigrants who entered and reentered the United States. Of the numbers given, 15.2 per cent (or 56,738) of the northerners and 13.7 per cent (262,508) of the "Southerners" had previously been in the United States.[6]

Migration did not flow evenly from all parts of the "South." It came for the most part from those areas that had experienced the breakdown of the old feudal system of class stratification, without compensating working-class organizations such as trade unions and cooperatives. According to demographer J. S. McDonald, a mixed system of property distribution developed, which provided the basis for an individualistic, open-class society. In 1901 British historians Bolton King and Thomas Okey described the "South" as suffering from an "individualism [which] runs riot; there is little mutual trust or cooperation, and industry goes limping in consequence . . . . The masses have small sense of cohesiveness or hope or effort." Political scientist Edward C. Banfield, in a study widely accepted by immigration scholars and students of Italian history, described a Sicilian-southern Italian society dominated by amoral familism. Banfield found peasants and gentry alike unable to act "for any end transcending the immediate, material interest of the nuclear family." If this analysis is accurate, it is reasonable to conclude that community and group consciousness among "Southerners" in the United States did not cross the Atlantic, but developed in the new homeland. Within the Italian system, emigration offered an important means of upward mobility and contributed toward the breakdown of feudal class distinctions. Dissatisfaction with economic conditions, aggravated by the absence of alternate group remedies (labor unions and the like) able to deal effectively with these problems resulted in high emigration rates. McDonald claimed that emigration "was related to the extent of participation and identification outside the nuclear family."[7]

While old-world habits and attitudes never disappeared entirely,

the American urban environment profoundly and pervasively influenced newcomers. One leader of a predominantly Sicilian colony
in Chicago described his neighborhood as having "unusual unity
and strength." He claimed to discern "the same kind of warmth,
friendliness, and intimacy in our community life that was to be
found in the small towns of Sicily from whence our parents came."
This neighborliness in Chicago, in fact, contrasted sharply with
nuclear family loyalties in the Kingdom, where "outsiders" were
not to be trusted, where village life remained relatively fixed and
stable, where conduct was based on face-to-face relationships, and
where custom and tradition controlled and influenced most aspects
of day-to-day living. The process of re-creating the homeland did
not, and could not, take place in the Chicago environment of
mobile population, absence of tradition, impersonal relationships,
and acceptance of change. Ironically, the old-world community
intimacy that Italians in America "recalled" so nostalgically originated in the new world as a response to urban surroundings.[8]

## II

William H. Keating, a geologist and the historian of Major Stephen
H. Long's expedition to the source of the St. Peter's River, passed
through Chicago in 1823. He found the climate inhospitable, the
soil sterile, the landscape flat and uninteresting, the few huts "low,
filthy and disgusting," the inhabitants a "miserable race of men."
Perhaps fifty people lived in the settlement by 1830. Chicago's
rapid growth began only after the dispersal of the Blackhawk
Indians in 1832, and especially after the completion of the Illinois-
Michigan Canal in 1848. The community's 350 inhabitants organized a town government in 1833. Four years later the town obtained a charter, and the first local census showed a population
of 4170. Despite a setback during the depression of the late 'thirties, some 4470 people lived in Chicago by 1840. The city's population exploded to 298,977 by 1870. By 1880, Chicago contained
503,185 residents, and after that date the number of inhabitants
increased approximately 500,000 each decade until 1930. (The

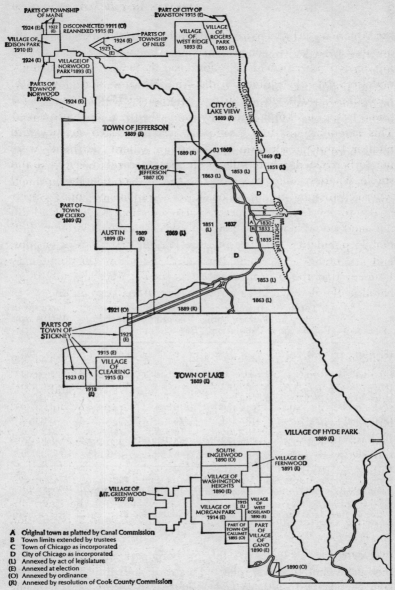

PARTS OF TOWNSHIP
OF MAINE

1924 (E) | 1922 (E) | DISCONNECTED 1911 (O)
REANNEXED 1915 (E)

PART OF CITY OF
EVANSTON 1915 (E)

VILLAGE OF
EDISON PARK
1910 (E)

1924 (E) | 1924 (E) | PARTS OF
TOWNSHIP
OF NILES

1923 (E)

VILLAGE
OF
WEST RIDGE
1893 (E)

VILLAGE
OF
ROGERS
PARK
1893 (E)

1924 (E)

VILLAGE OF
NORWOOD
PARK 1893 (E)

PARTS OF
TOWN OF
NORWOOD
PARK

1924 (E)

CITY OF
LAKE VIEW
1889 (E)

OLD SHORELINE

TOWN OF JEFFERSON
1889 (R)

1889 (R) | (L) 1869

1869 (L)

VILLAGE OF
JEFFERSON
1887 (O)

1863 (L) | 1853 (L)

1851 (L)

PART OF
TOWN
OF CICERO
1889 (E)

1851
(L)

1837

D

C
B | 1830
A | 1833
B | 1835
C

OLD PIER SHORE LINE

AUSTIN
1899 (E)

1889
(R)

1869 (L)

D

1853 (L)

1863 (L)

1921 (O)

PARTS OF
TOWN OF
STICKNEY

1921
(E)

1915 (E)

VILLAGE
OF
CLEARING
1915 (E)

TOWN OF LAKE
1889 (R)

1923 (E)

1918
(E)

VILLAGE OF HYDE PARK
1889 (R)

SOUTH
ENGLEWOOD
1890 (O)

VILLAGE OF
FERNWOOD
1891 (E)

VILLAGE OF
WASHINGTON
HEIGHTS
1890 (E)

VILLAGE OF
MT. GREENWOOD
1927 (E)

1915
(L)

VILLAGE
OF
WEST
ROSELAND
1890 (E)

VILLAGE OF
MORGAN PARK
1914 (E)

PART OF
TOWN OF
CALUMET
1895 (O)

PART
OF
VILLAGE
OF
GANO
1890 (E)

1890 (O)

A  Original town as platted by Canal Commission
B  Town limits extended by trustees
C  Town of Chicago as incorporated
D  City of Chicago as incorporated
(L) Annexed by act of legislature
(E) Annexed at election
(O) Annexed by ordinance
(R) Annexed by resolution of Cook County Commission

## 1. Growth of Chicago by Annexations, 1830–1930

Based on Edith Abbott, *The Tenements of Chicago, 1908–1935* (Chicago, 1936), 12.

7

city's land area also expanded over the century from 1830 to 1930, growing from less than one half square mile to over 200 square miles.)[9]

The population increase came from three main sources: immigration, migration from other parts of the United States, and natural increase. While growth through births tended to expand over the years regardless of economic conditions, immigration totals bore a direct relationship to those conditions. Immigration played a large part in Chicago's population increases during the decades of 1860–70, 1880–90, and 1900–1910, but it had a much smaller role during the depression-dominated 1870's and 1890's.

### Table 1

SOURCES OF INCREASE OF CHICAGO POPULATION, 1830–1930

| Decade | Total Increase in Population | Increase in Foreign born Population | Increase in Negro Population | Increase in White Population from Other Parts of U.S. | Increase in Births over Deaths |
|--------|------|------|------|------|------|
| 1830–40 | 4,429 | | | | 400 |
| 1840–50 | 25,484 | | | | 2,000 |
| 1850–60 | 79,243 | | | | 10,000 |
| 1860–70 | 188,717 | 90,133 | | 63,000 | 30,000 |
| 1870–80 | 205,108 | 60,302 | | 95,000 | 50,000 |
| 1880–90 | 496,665 | 244,769 | 7,791 | 144,106 | 100,000 |
| 1890–1900 | 588,725 | 137,584 | 15,879 | 265,262 | 170,000 |
| 1900–1910 | 468,708 | 194,105 | 13,953 | 48,650 | 212,000 |
| 1910–20 | 525,422 | 24,165 | 65,000 | 236,257 | 200,000 |
| 1920–30 | 674,733 | 36,575 | 146,000 | 259,158 | 233,000 |

Source: Homer Hoyt, *One Hundred Years of Land Values in Chicago: The Relationship of the Growth of Chicago to the Rise in Its Land Values, 1830–1933* (Chicago, 1933), 284.
Note: Before 1860 no accurate data is available for increase in foreign born population.

Over the years Chicago's foreign born population, like that of the whole United States, reflected a steady shift in national origin. Newcomers from northern and western Europe predominated before 1890, especially those from Germany and Ireland. After that year, southern and eastern Europeans (particularly Poles and Italians) came in increasing numbers, although important exceptions existed. A large proportion of the city's Bohemians, for example, arrived prior to 1890, while the high point of Swedish settlement came after that time.

Whatever their place of origin, European immigrants and native Americans as well poured into the lake metropolis, lured by economic opportunities. The city offered work in packing plants, agricultural-implement works, stove factories, steel mills, electric-generating plants, mail-order houses, railroad shops, clothing shops, wholesale houses, building construction, breweries, distilleries, and retail stores. In sum, Chicago provided excellent job opportunities in manufacturing, transportation, the trades, and the professions.[10]

A number of questionable features accompanied the expansion. Chicago exhibited, until well into the twentieth century, many characteristics of a frontier town. It was vigorous, brash, lusty, optimistic, energetic. It also had labor violence, corruption in civic and business affairs, apathy toward poverty, inadequate housing, unsanitary living conditions, vice, and organized crime. According to English journalist William T. Stead, who lived in the city for five months (until March 1894), "The first impression which a stranger receives on arriving in Chicago is that of the dirt, the danger, and the inconvenience of the streets." Stead found Chicagoans equally indifferent to the plight of the poor, to corruption in business and politics, and to Christian precepts. Chicago's citizens worshipped "a Trinity of their own"—Marshall Field, Philip D. Armour, and George M. Pullman. Stead concluded that Chicagoans, massed together and forming a veritable congress of "different nationalities, a compost of men and women of all manner of languages," recognized one common bond—money. They "came here to make money. They are staying here to make money. The quest of the almighty dollar is their Holy Grail." Lincoln Steffens characterized Chicago thus: "First in violence, deepest in dirt; loud, lawless, unlovely, ill-smelling, irreverent, new; an overgrown gawk of a village, the 'tough' among cities, a spectacle for the nation." This environment, with its unparalleled economic opportunities, optimism, mobility, corruption, filth, and violence, received increasing numbers of "Southerners" in the years after 1880.[11]

The city's materialism, its impersonal character, and its vast size shocked and repelled the newcomers. They resented the miserable conditions of life and labor that they were obliged to accept as the latest arrivals in alien surroundings. In order to endure, immigrants created an idealized past, usually located in the village of their origin, to which they yearned to return.[12]

Many, in fact, did return. But there they found themselves disappointed with the vast changes which they believed had occurred in the months and years since their emigration. They did not recognize that they, and not the homeland, had altered. The easily identified *Americani* (the name given to those who returned) brought back to the homeland "new habits, new needs, new skills, a higher level of education, a greater sense of independence," and full awareness and knowledge of their rights as opposed to the interests of employers and governmental authorities. Many found old-world conditions and opportunities appallingly limited and depressing.[13]

Remembering the benefits of life in the United States, a number of *Americani* relinquished their illusions of "remembered" pleasantness and idyllic village life and returned as quickly as possible to America. One second-generation Italian recalled in the late 1920's how much his immigrant father had changed since his arrival in the city in 1895, "especially in regard to his preference for this country." His new homeland dissatisfied him the first few years, until he had "made a visit to the old hometown. He said in a letter to me while he was over there, 'Things have changed so much here . . . that it makes me quite homesick [for Chicago].' After he came back he was quite satisfied with Chicago and has given up forever the idea of returning to Italy to spend the remainder of his life." Many descendants of the immigrant generation recounted similar experiences.[14]

Ethnic colony residents thought they looked, talked, and behaved just as they had in the old world; native Americans shared this view. Newly arrived immigrants, however, noticed pronounced differences. John Foster Carr, a Protestant minister who worked among Italians in New York, asserted that repeatedly Italians tried to convince him that "for a long time after landing they could not distinguish between an Italian who had been here four or five years and a native American." Carr suggested that "a different life breeds different habits, and different habits with American [urban] surroundings effect a radical change in the man." For most immigrants this process of adapting to America took place, or at least began, in the ethnic community.[15]

## III

At the turn of the century, living conditions in the various communities inhabited by Italians (and generally other new groups) typically exhibited unhealthy, unpleasant, and socially demoralizing features. Beginning as early as the late 1880's and continuing into the 1920's, Italian-language journals and American newspapers described and discussed home and job environments in Italian quarters of Chicago. These topics also provided material for articles and books by Italian visitors and native-born social workers, of city and federal government reports and official Italian documents, and of studies by university professors and graduate students. The American press tended to employ colorful and intensely critical language in picturing conditions in Italian districts, ascribing the filth, squalor, and misery of the inhabitants to ethnic characteristics. On July 17, 1887, the *Chicago Herald* stated, for example, that "it is not abject poverty which causes such nasty and cheap living; it is simply an imported habit from Southern Italy."[16]

Italian-language papers admitted the justice of much American criticism, particularly in reports of neighborhood slum conditions and the willingness of newcomers to accept lower pay than Americans, although they usually replied with emotional outbursts, rationalizations, and irrelevant arguments. In their reactions, city papers and their Italian counterparts satisfied the needs of their particular audiences. Readers of American tabloids desired sensation, titillation, and scandal; they also enjoyed reading about people or groups less fortunate than themselves. Italian journal readers, on the other hand, craved spokesmen and apologists— roles played by their press. This vociferous, belligerent, generally defensive element of the Italian community, it must be noted, did not consist of hard-core residents of the ghetto (who were indifferent to American attitudes), but rather of that segment of the immigrant group which had left the slum or was in the process of departing, or hoped to leave some day. This element included publishers and editors of the Italian-language press as well as businessmen who promoted the solvency of the newspapers through advertising funds.[17]

Studies by government agencies, private associations, social workers, and scholars operated on another plane, and worked toward different objectives. Investigators generally intended to gather accurate and complete information on which to base remedial action. The belief that full and reliable data would obliterate public apathy, overcome official indifference, and end undesirable housing conditions and attendant evils provided motivation for the writing of *Hull House Maps and Papers,* the Department of Labor Studies, and the "Chicago Housing Conditions" series. Social reformers like Jane Addams, Robert Hunter, and Grace and Edith Abbott considered environmental factors, not heredity, to be responsible for the crime, misery, poor hygiene, and collapse of family life found in slum areas. They feared the establishment of a cycle of poverty. "No one who becomes a part of the life of these tenements [in the area bounded by Polk, Twelfth, Halsted, and Canal streets] can escape their contaminated and corrupt atmosphere," Hunter warned in a report prepared in 1901 for the City Homes Association.[18]

Native Italians, writing for consumption in the homeland, published official reports and studies, books and articles; ambassadors, consular officials, special governmental agents, and investigators prepared factual studies, generally heavy with statistics, on current conditions and future trends in the various cities and countries to

which Italians came. These data helped to determine the Kingdom's emigration policies, since the Italian government, basing its
attitude on the provisions of national law, held that every emigrant
remained forever an Italian (even if he became a citizen of another
country), and endeavored to protect the interests of Italians
abroad. In addition, the government used the statistics gained
from these reports to provide accurate information for businessmen and others about economic situations and investment possibilities overseas.[19]

Numerous articles and books written by private Italians about
their experiences abroad complemented official publications.
Homeland residents craved information about immigrant life in the
new world, some because they had relatives or friends there, others
because they themselves planned or hoped to emigrate. Writers
of travel accounts ranged from former emigrants like Adolfo Rossi
(who later became Minister, Royal Emigration Department of
Italy) to musicians, actors, and playwrights (like Giuseppe Giacosa). In contrast to the factual, impersonal, and often dryly
written official publications, Italian visitors' accounts were colorful,
impressionistic, and personalized, emphasizing the writers' reactions to life in a foreign land.[20]

Despite differences in motivation, background, and objectives,
these various studies focused on, and documented, the poverty,
degradation, and unhappiness that existed in slum living. A survey
by the Commissioner of Labor in 1892–93, for example, studied
conditions in the district bounded by Halsted, Newberry, State,
Polk, and Twelfth streets, an area containing a large Italian element. The Commissioner reported serious overcrowding in tenements, high rents for inferior housing, barely adequate sanitary
conditions, and extremely poor social relationships. The City
Homes Association in 1901 found much tenement-house property
to be old and in need of repair, for many residences remained in
"a wretched and dangerous state of dilapidation." Inhabitants
often could not keep such houses clean; consequently, said the
report, filth and vermin were to be found everywhere. Crime,
squalor, poor hygiene, evil associations, and the collapse of family

life resulted from these conditions. "Thousands of Jewish, Polish and Italian children are growing up in tenements inhabited by the wretchedly poor, by drunkards, criminals, and immoral women. Almost every word these growing children hear, and every action they see, corrupts their minds, and destroys forever their purity of heart." [21]

In 1911 Edith Abbott and Sophonisba P. Breckinridge published the results of a survey of living conditions on Chicago's Near West Side. The purpose of the report was to determine the extent of changes that had taken place during the ten-year interval since the City Homes Association's Report of 1901. While the Abbott and Breckinridge study examined conditions in Italian neighborhoods, it focused primarily on the Polish, Bohemian, and eastern European Jewish colonies. The authors found only one striking improvement: "the removal of the noxious privy vault." Despite efforts of the City Homes Association, as well as the enactment of a tenement code and changes in administrative organization of the Health Department and Sanitation Bureau, the writers observed "the same overcrowded areas, alleys, tenements, dilapidated houses, oppressive density of population, families in outlawed cellar apartments, in dark and gloomy rooms, and in conditions of overcrowding which violate all standards of decency and health." [22]

Two years later Grace Norton conducted a study of two of the largest Italian districts in Chicago, one on the Near North Side and the other on Plymouth Court in the Loop. Miss Norton concluded that living conditions among these people compared unfavorably with the worst circumstances of other immigrant groups. "The Italian," she noted, "is paying a comparatively high rent for dilapidated, unhealthful quarters. He is living in illegally overcrowded rooms, in damp and gloomy apartments, and under conditions which . . . are acknowledged to be dangerous and demoralizing." [23]

In 1915 Natalie Walker reported conditions in the Near West Side Italian neighborhood around Hull House, the city's largest Italian colony. In the sixteen blocks covered by her survey, she found only a fifth of the houses to be in good repair, 1636 of

4564 occupied bedrooms rated as "overcrowded," and 1930 bedrooms classed as "gloomy or dark." In these blocks lived 10,125 people; "over 3,000 of these are little children, growing up in an environment which is full of menace to their health and to their future civic usefulness." Miss Walker clearly indicated that her purpose in writing the report—to bring about improvements in Chicago's housing conditions—inclined her to concentrate upon the worst possible situations. Her study, therefore, gave the impression that all Italians lived in filth and degradation, whereas many lived in pleasant and even well-to-do areas. Life in most Italian districts, however, and in all the larger ones, was unhealthy, unpleasant and socially degenerate.[24]

Giuseppe Giacosa found himself horrified by living standards among compatriots in the new world. "The only concern of Americans toward Italian immigrants is that of a sordid, degrading and insensible disinterest," he lamented. "The clothes, food and living quarters of the common Italian in New York and Chicago present a spectacle of such supine resignation to poverty, of an ascetic indifference toward life's pleasures that . . . one expects to find [only] among the Chinese." [25]

## IV

Americans concerned over slums and the effects that incoming European peasants might have in perpetuating miserable conditions and multiplying city problems believed that urban difficulties could be alleviated or even solved by encouraging immigrants to move out of the city to rural surroundings. Shifting "Southerners" into agriculture appeared to be "the natural solution of the probblem of Italian concentration in the slums," wrote Professor I. W. Howerth of the University of Chicago, in 1894. "Henceforth the tendency of Italians to congregate in large cities will decrease." In order to bring about this desired event, the Italian and American governments, individual states and private agencies (such as local Italian-American chambers of commerce) supported the establishment of agricultural colonies for Italian immigrants throughout the United States, and especially in Texas, Arkansas, Mississippi, Louisiana, and Alabama.[26]

Despite auspicious beginnings and official support, most rural ventures came to nothing. For example, Alessandro Mastro-Valerio (later editor of *La Tribuna Italiana Transatlantica,* and head of the Italian Chamber of Commerce's Agricultural Section) founded an Italian agricultural colony at Daphne, Alabama, in 1892. This enterprise received counsel and financial aid from Jane Addams and the residents of Hull House. Italian residents of Chicago avoided the colony, withheld moral and financial support, and indicated only apathy when it failed. Truck gardens near large urban centers of the East and Middle West, and in California, achieved a greater measure of success than did efforts to attract immigrants to rural colonies.[27]

Contemporaries wondered why more Italians did not move to farms. Some maintained that "new" immigrants, trapped in cities, lacked the strength, ability, and knowledge required to take advantage of the marvelous agricultural opportunities offered in the United States. According to this thesis, "old" immigrant groups had seized these opportunities and thus had proven themselves to be superior to "new" arrivals. In this vein, labor economist and historian John R. Commons observed that "in the immigrant stage [Italians] are helpless." In contrast, "immigrants from Northwestern Europe, the Germans and Scandinavians" had been from the start "the model farmers of America" because of their "thrift, self-reliance, and intensive farming." He added, "The least self-reliant or forehanded, like the . . . Italians, seek the cities in greater proportions than those sturdy races like the Scandinavians, English, Scotch and Germans." [28]

Commons believed that serious consequences would follow the massing of recent immigrants in American cities, because cities did not create the spirit of independence and initiative achieved by farm workers. He distrusted new immigrant groups and feared the phenomenal growth of urban areas and the changes being wrought there by technology and increasing populations. "The dangerous effects of city life on immigrants and the children of immigrants cannot be too strongly emphasized," he wrote. Foreigners in urban centers "are themselves dragged down by the parasitic and dependent conditions which they [cities] foster among the immigrant element." [29]

Others held similar views and expressed them in magazines, books and reports. "The illiterate races, such as the Hungarians, Galicians, and Italians, remain in the cities to lower the standards of the already crowded Atlantic territory," declared one. Said another, "The illiterate immigrants congregate chiefly in the slums of our great cities." [30]

Alessandro Mastro-Valerio reported to the United States Industrial Commission in 1901 that Italian immigrants wanted desperately to farm but did not know "how to get the land and the means to work it until it produces." Consequently, he said, they remained caged in cities. Because most of the immigrants had been engaged in farm labor in Italy, it seemed logical that they would want to settle on the land in America. As country people, "they should have been established in the country." Americans, he said, had a responsibility for moving immigrants out of cities and into agriculture. In the years between 1890 and the 1920's *L'Italia, La Tribuna Italiana Transatlantica,* and other Chicago Italian-language newspapers encouraged immigrants to move to rural areas.[31]

An Italian visitor to an early farming settlement in the American south indicated some reasons why immigrants crowded into cities rather than seeking rural "opportunities":

> The colony lives in poorly constructed houses, made of wood, without the most elementary precautions against the weather; frequently . . . the dwellings are really tents, where members of the colony sleep together without distinction as to age and sex. . . . Hygiene is unknown. . . . Our people are eternally deeply in debt . . . and the current agricultural contracts, for sharecropping or renting, are not to the advantage of the Italians.[32]

Robert F. Foerster has shown that such factors as ignorance of opportunity, climate, or even cost of land were not the primary deterrents that kept Italians from farming in the United States. In

Argentina, Italians worked the land very successfully, adapting without difficulty to new world conditions, crops, soils, and markets. A more important factor contributing to immigrant distaste for rural settlements was that most Italians simply did not travel to America with hopes or intentions of farming.[33]

Like the majority of immigrants, "old" as well as "new," Italians arrived seeking economic opportunities. In the last decades of the nineteenth century and the early ones of the twentieth, prospects of financial gain existed in commercial and industrial centers of the north and east, and not in agriculture. This fact resulted in the failures of agricultural colonies such as the one at New Palermo, Alabama, as described in *L'Italia* of Chicago on May 21, 1904. The immigrants, reported the paper, "went with the delusion of finding riches," and instead "found nothing but misery." The United States Industrial Commission recognized the desire for economic betterment in its summary volume, published in 1902, where it examined the factors responsible for immigrant concentration in cities. The Commission noted first "the general movement of all modern industrial peoples toward urban life—a movement quite characteristic of the American people themselves." For the foreign born, additional factors reinforced this trend: (1) the isolation of farm life in the United States, in comparison with more crowded conditions in rural areas of Europe; (2) immigrant memories of "hardships and oppressions of rural life from which they are struggling to escape"; (3) ready employment in cities directly upon arrival and for higher wages than those paid farm laborers.[34]

In the period after 1890, as English historian Frank Thistlethwaite has pointed out, the great migrations proceeded "from farm to factory, from village to city, whether this meant from Iowa to Chicago, Silesia to Pittsburgh or Piedmont to Buenos Aires." Writing in 1906, demographer Walter F. Willcox found no evidence that "immigrants as a class or recent immigrants, or illiterate immigrants tend disproportionately toward cities." He claimed that newer immigrants showed no stronger tendencies to crowd into cities than had earlier groups. Nevertheless, during the years between 1890 and 1905, writers and speakers repeated the idea that immigrants—especially illiterate ones—clung to the slums of large cities. The American public accepted this view.[35]

In Italy, cities of the north underwent rapid growth in the period from 1880 to World War I. "Southerners" migrating to these cities faced problems similar to those encountered in American urban areas. Thus "to a peasant of Sicily, Milan would have been as much of an alien city as New York. In both towns the customs, the ways of life, to a certain extent even the language were equally strange to him." [36]

Significantly, Americans and Italians who encouraged agricultural colonies did so at least in part because of the conviction that foreigners would become assimilated more rapidly and completely in a rural setting than they could in a city. Commissioner-General of Immigration Frank P. Sargent maintained that "if, instead of crowding into our large cities," immigrants would go to rural areas, "there would be no cause to fear for the future." Probably the opposite was true.[37] As the experience of German agricultural colonies in Pennsylvania and the Middle West made clear, assimilation slowed or halted in rural environments where there existed only limited contacts with outside agencies and individuals. In sparsely populated areas, an ethnic community is forced in upon itself, or can maintain a desired isolation. In cities, on the other hand, contacts of one type or another were (and are) virtually inevitable.

Sociologist Robert E. Park, of the University of Chicago, observed in 1921 that the rural experience "is naturally in the opposite direction" to the urban. Country life "emphasizes local differences, preserves the memories of the immigrants, and fosters a sentimental interest in the local home community." An expert on foreign-language newspapers, Park cited the example of the "German provincial press, which is printed in a dialect no longer recognized by the European press, and which idealized German provincial life as it existed fifty years ago and still lives in the memories of the editors and readers of these papers." This comment paralleled an observation made several years before by John Foster Carr, who noted that by 1906 "only two poor fragments remain of the numer-

ous important German and Irish colonies" that had flourished in
New York City in the 1870's and 1880's. In contrast, "the ancient
settled Pennsylvania Dutch, thanks to their isolation, are not yet
fully merged in the great citizen body." Clearly, new arrivals faced
the basic problem not of escaping from a mythical urban "trap" or
of finding agricultural jobs, but rather of settling into their new
way of life, that of the city community.[38]

The cultural problem of adjusting to new living patterns, the
result of moving to an urban environment, constituted a key factor
responsible for immigrant difficulties in urban America. Contemporaries failed to recognize that adjustment would have been necessary had the villagers migrated to a city in Italy or to some other
European city rather than across the Atlantic. Americans of rural
background who moved to urban areas faced many of the same
problems encountered by Sicilians who journeyed to the new
world, to Milan, or to other cities in the Italian peninsula and
other parts of Europe.

## V

Willingly or unwillingly, individual newcomers began the process
of assimilation as soon as they arrived in the urban environment.
The immigrant colony and its institutions fulfilled their functions,
not of prolonging old world traits and patterns, but of providing
important first steps in assimilation, and they did so effectively.
Schools and settlement houses introduced many directly to middle-
class ideas and living patterns and in this way, as "outside" or
American agencies, they served the needs of the second generation
and of the more independently minded immigrants who felt no
need of colonial institutions. Economic achievement played a vital
role in furthering adjustment and in spurring movement out of
early ethnic districts. Over the years newcomers and their children
moved up the economic ladder, progressing from unskilled labor
into commercial, trade, and professional lines. Channels of progress also appeared within organized labor and politics, while

criminal activity provided a lucrative means of financial advancement, both within the settlement and outside it.

Like most recent immigrants, Italians appeared to move away from the urban core more slowly and reluctantly than had the Irish, Germans, and other older groups. The "old" elements arrived in Chicago and other northern cities considerably earlier than did most Italians, Russian Jews, Poles, Lithuanians, and Greeks, and had the opportunity of profiting economically and socially in cities that had not then developed rigid political or financial patterns. "The process of acculturation," noted sociologist Richard G. Ford, "has been going on considerably longer for the Swedish, German and Irish immigrants than for the Italians and Russians." [39] An additional factor, one that contemporaries overlooked, was the extensive amount of residential mobility among Italians and other late arrivals.

# 2

## Patterns of Settlement

Northern Italians (most of them from Genoa or Tuscany) founded Chicago's Italian community and dominated the rapidly expanding settlement until the 1880's. According to the federal census the city's Italian-born population grew from four in 1850 to 100 in the following ten years. The total increased to 552 in 1870. By 1884, when the movement from the "South" began to assume significant proportions, Chicago contained 4091 Italian residents. From that decade until World War I, most new arrivals were "Southerners." [1]

The early northern Italian group consisted largely of settled family units; some (according to the 1870 manuscript census schedules) had as many as thirteen children. The men generally worked at skilled and semiskilled jobs, or found employment in service and trade occupations. They became saloonkeepers and bartenders; fruit, candy and ice cream vendors; confectioners; clerks; barbers; hairdressers; and restaurant owners or employees. During these years few engaged in unskilled labor—30, according to the 1870 federal census, while Richard Edwards counted only 18 in his independently conducted (and incomplete) census the following year. Some owned considerable wealth. For example, saloon proprietor John Raggio, who lived at 110 North Clark

Street, possessed $18,000 in real estate and $2500 in personal property; carpenter Joseph Devoto of 125 West Van Buren Street, $4000 in real estate and $3000 in personal property; cigar manufacturer Samuel C. Raggio, 183 South Halsted, $5000 in personal estate; saloonkeeper Louis Gazzolo, 16 Dunn Street, $10,000 in real estate, $500 in personal property; confectioner Don S. Barboro, 30 West Randolph Street, $2500 in personal property; confectioner Louis Musto, 147 North Clark Street, and saloonkeeper Joseph Bossi, 217 North Clark, both with personal estates valued at $2000. Like the "Southerners" who arrived later, most immigrants from northern Italy had neither financial reserves nor ready cash. They augmented family incomes by withdrawing their children from school and either having them work as peddlers or charging them with household duties in order to free the mothers for outside jobs.[2]

These first immigrants usually settled in or near the center of the city. In 1870, for example, Italians resided in all of Chicago's twenty wards except the Seventh, but most lived in three general areas: immediately north of the Chicago River, where they clustered around Clark Street; south of the river in what became the central business district, or Loop; and west across the south branch of the river to Halsted Street, between Kedzie and Van Buren streets.[3]

The most populous area of settlement at this time was south of the river, between Randolph and Harrison streets, in the Loop. As this location evolved into the city's main business area, the accompanying leap in land prices forced Italians and other residents to relocate. On January 1, 1883, for example, choice retail-business property along State Street brought $3000 per front foot; bank and office property on La Salle and Washington streets, $2000; wholesale business on Wabash Avenue, $1500; while working-class residences of good quality, regardless of their locations, brought $40 per front foot, and cheap residential property, $20.[4] Another factor combined with real-estate prices to influence the location of Italians: the principal railroad depot for incoming trains from the Atlantic coast was situated in the area south of Van Buren Street. Most Italians entering Chicago came through the

Dearborn Station (at Polk and Dearborn streets) and remained at least for a short time in that general section of the city. As a result of these two factors—land cost and place of arrival—Italian residents had almost disappeared from the central business area by 1900.

The population of the once-thriving Italian colony located directly west across the river also declined rapidly. Independent retail-business enterprises, small factories, and warehouses selected that district for operation and expansion, and before the end of the century had pushed out nearly all Italian residents. Those who left generally moved northward, to the area of Chicago Commons Settlement House, or southward, to the Hull House community. In the Near North Side, Italians like Antonio Arado and George B. Cuneo bought property at least as early as 1871 (the Great Fire destroyed earlier property records). They purchased lots on Illinois between Franklin and Orleans streets. In following years other northerners bought extensively and in the 1880's formed the city's first Italian parish. Yet, before the end of the succeeding decade, the city's first discernible Italian colony was breaking up as economically mobile northern Italians moved away to more pleasant surroundings.[5]

Continuing the pattern set by their northern predecessors, "Southerners" who obtained the financial means also moved away from the colony. If migration from the ethnic settlement—a sign of financial achievement and desire for better housing and living conditions—did not take place in the first generation, it generally occurred in the second or third. Nevertheless, the continued presence of a number of neighborhood Italians led contemporaries to believe that immigrants, their children, and their grandchildren after them remained on the same streets and in the same tenements from the time they appeared in the city until they died. Americans further assumed that compact, unchanging settlements grouped according to place of birth. While this description might have fitted the initial phase of settlement, new relationships quickly formed, both with other Italians and with members of different nationality groups. The composition of Italian colonies (like that of other ethnic groups) remained in constant flux, a major cause of the inhabitants' continual forming and expanding of new relationships.[6]

Contrary to popular belief, Chicago, like other urban areas, contained few blocks inhabited exclusively by Italians, and even fewer solidly Italian neighborhoods. Between 1880 and 1920, only limited sections of certain Chicago streets held a 50 per cent or higher concentration of Italian immigrants and their children. The population density of Italians in the city's various Italian districts fell considerably below 50 per cent.[7]

## II

In 1884, when the Board of Education prepared a detailed breakdown of Chicago's ethnic population, the largest Italian concentration south of the Chicago River—and in the entire city—existed in the area bounded by Harrison and Twelfth streets (Twelfth Street later became Roosevelt Road), the south bank of the river, and State Street. Nearly one quarter (996) of Chicago's 4091 Italians lived there. Smaller contingents were located in nearby communities; one, with 126 Italians, was directly south, in the area bounded by Twelfth and Sixteenth streets, the river, and the lake. The other community, west of the river to Halsted Street between Van Buren and Twelfth streets, held a small but growing Italian element, numbering 172 in 1884. During following years, Italians poured into this area in such numbers that by 1898 it, rather than the lower Loop district, contained the city's heaviest Italian concentration.[8]

A similar pattern operated north of the river, where Italians moved from the original area of settlement around Clark Street. In 1884, when only 77 Italians resided in the district bounded by Clark, Franklin, and Ohio streets, and the river, the area directly west of Franklin to the north branch of the river (between Ohio on the north and the river on the south) housed a total of 455 immigrants from the Kingdom of Italy. In addition, 367 Italians had spread across the river to Halsted Street, between Ohio and Kinzie

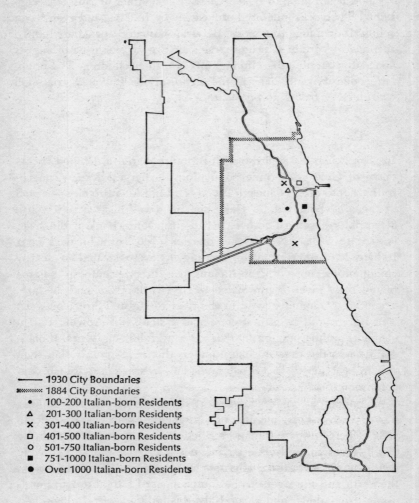

——— 1930 City Boundaries
※※※※※ 1884 City Boundaries
• 100-200 Italian-born Residents
△ 201-300 Italian-born Residents
✕ 301-400 Italian-born Residents
□ 401-500 Italian-born Residents
○ 501-750 Italian-born Residents
■ 751-1000 Italian-born Residents
● Over 1000 Italian-born Residents

2. Italians in Chicago, 1884

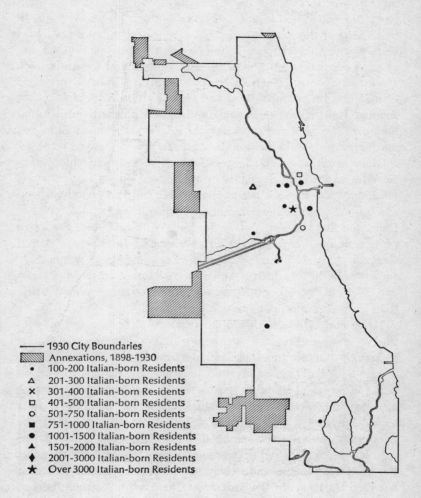

- ——— 1930 City Boundaries
- ▨ Annexations, 1898-1930
- • 100-200 Italian-born Residents
- △ 201-300 Italian-born Residents
- ✕ 301-400 Italian-born Residents
- □ 401-500 Italian-born Residents
- ○ 501-750 Italian-born Residents
- ■ 751-1000 Italian-born Residents
- ● 1001-1500 Italian-born Residents
- ▲ 1501-2000 Italian-born Residents
- ◆ 2001-3000 Italian-born Residents
- ★ Over 3000 Italian-born Residents

3. Italians in Chicago, 1898

streets, while others had scattered even farther west, to Western
Avenue.

Italians also lived south of Twelfth Street as far as Thirty-ninth
Street (which in 1884 formed the city's southern boundary) and
from Ashland Avenue as far east as Cottage Grove Avenue. In
most parts of this southern arc, immigrant groups were small and
widely separated, but two heavy concentrations existed. One, between Fourteenth and Sixteenth, and Morgan and Centre streets,
contained 130 newcomers. The other, with 317 Italians, stretched
from Thirtieth to Thirty-third and from Halsted Street to Stewart
Avenue. Italians resided in communities near northern and western
boundaries as well, in the vicinity of Fullerton Avenue (Chicago's
northern limit) and Crawford Avenue, the city's western edge.

Characteristically, in Italian settlements, newcomers seldom comprised a majority of residents in any area. In 1884, for example,
no district had an Italian majority; and in only one neighborhood
did Italians form the largest ethnic group. Thus 453 lived between
Clark and State streets, and Taylor and Twelfth streets (the lower
portion of the Loop, located directly east of Dearborn Station);
Germans and Irishmen, their closest rivals, numbered 362 and 99,
respectively. In this district, however, Italians accounted for about
one third of the total population of 1303. In other areas of the city,
they formed proportionately smaller groups.

These early patterns of mobility and ethnic concentration continued, in succeeding years, to operate among "Southerners" as they
had with the northern Italian community of the first period.
Throughout the 1880's and into the twentieth century, the neighborhood around Dearborn Station served new arrivals as an area
of first settlement. Its transient nature showed clearly in the character of the Italian population. Composed almost entirely of the
immigrant generation, it consisted mainly of bachelors or married
men whose families had not yet joined them. In 1898, for example,
the area west of Plymouth Court to the south bank of the river,
between Harrison and Twelfth streets, held a total of 1068 Italians,
only 16 of them American born.[9]

Examination of property records supports the view of the fluctuating nature of the lower Loop settlement. Few Italians owned land in the area; those who did were generally of northern Italian background—the Raggios, Cellas, Arados, and Lagorios, for example—who had settled in Chicago as early as the 1850's and 1860's, and who had acquired, over the years, both money and property in various parts of the city. More recently arrived "Southerners" leased land, usually a portion of a lot, for a limited time.[10]

In 1912 Grace P. Norton, of the Chicago School of Civics and Philanthropy, discussing a survey of housing conditions in this Italian settlement, characterized it as "a polyglot territory." At the Jones Elementary School (at State and Harrison streets), Miss Norton found that "probably more nationalities are represented than in any other school in Chicago." The heaviest Italian concentration lived opposite Dearborn Station on Plymouth Court, between Taylor and Polk streets. On this block Italians made up 118 of 119 heads of households (the other was a Negro). Reviewing the findings and conclusions of investigations conducted in city tenement districts during the preceding 28 years by University of Chicago faculty members and graduate students, Edith Abbott in 1936 noted that "no block in any of the other Italian districts was so exclusively Italian as this Plymouth Court block," at least in the years prior to World War I. After the war, conversion of the area to business use forced Italians to move out.[11]

The movement southward continued after the turn of the century. By 1920 nearly 4800 foreign-born Italians resided between Twelfth and Thirty-ninth, and State and Halsted streets. The heart of the community, which included more than 2000 Italian immigrants, lay in the area bounded on the north by Twenty-second Street, on the south by Twenty-fifth Street, on the east by the Chicago, Rock Island and Pacific Railway tracks, and on the west by the south branch of the Chicago River and by Wallace Street. Here was one of Chicago's twelve Italian parishes, Santa Maria Incoronata. Originally located in 1899 at Eighteenth and Clark streets, the church moved five years later to Alexander Street (between Twenty-second and Twenty-third) near Wentworth Avenue. The location of parishes and the year of founding indicate the

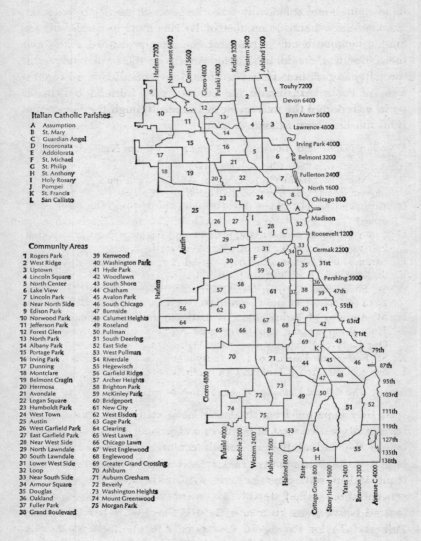

Italian Catholic Parishes

A   Assumption
B   St. Mary
C   Guardian Angel
D   Incoronata
E   Addolorata
F   St. Michael
G   St. Philip
H   St. Anthony
I   Holy Rosary
J   Pompei
K   St. Francis
L   San Callisto

Community Areas

1   Rogers Park
2   West Ridge
3   Uptown
4   Lincoln Square
5   North Center
6   Lake View
7   Lincoln Park
8   Near North Side
9   Edison Park
10  Norwood Park
11  Jefferson Park
12  Forest Glen
13  North Park
14  Albany Park
15  Portage Park
16  Irving Park
17  Dunning
18  Montclare
19  Belmont Cragin
20  Hermosa
21  Avondale
22  Logan Square
23  Humboldt Park
24  West Town
25  Austin
26  West Garfield Park
27  East Garfield Park
28  Near West Side
29  North Lawndale
30  South Lawndale
31  Lower West Side
32  Loop
33  Near South Side
34  Armour Square
35  Douglas
36  Oakland
37  Fuller Park
38  Grand Boulevard

39  Kenwood
40  Washington Park
41  Hyde Park
42  Woodlawn
43  South Shore
44  Chatham
45  Avalon Park
46  South Chicago
47  Burnside
48  Calumet Heights
49  Roseland
50  Pullman
51  South Deering
52  East Side
53  West Pullman
54  Riverdale
55  Hegewisch
56  Garfield Ridge
57  Archer Heights
58  Brighton Park
59  McKinley Park
60  Bridgeport
61  New City
62  West Elsdon
63  Gage Park
64  Clearing
65  West Lawn
66  Chicago Lawn
67  West Englewood
68  Englewood
69  Greater Grand Crossing
70  Ashburn
71  Auburn Gresham
72  Beverly
73  Washington Heights
74  Mount Greenwood
75  Morgan Park

4. Chicago's Community Areas and Italian Catholic Parishes

areas of settlement judged by the Archdiocese of Chicago to be large enough and sufficiently stable to support a separate national church. While a sizable number of Italians lived in the Dearborn Station neighborhood, its transient character precluded a location there. By 1920, on the other hand, the Near West Side contained three Italian parishes: Holy Guardian Angel, founded in 1899; Our Lady of Pompei, 1910; and San Callisto, 1919. Formation of these parishes reflected the movement of Italians through the West Side from the Dearborn Station district.

Founding Date and Location of Chicago's Italian National Parishes

A. Assumption, 1886; Illinois near Orleans Street
B. St. Mary of Mount Carmel, 1892; Sixty-seventh and Page streets, moved in 1915 to 6722 South Hermitage Avenue
C. Guardian Angel, 1899; 178 Forquer Street (renumbered 717 in 1909)
D. Santa Maria Incoronata, 1899; Clark and Eighteenth streets, moved in 1904 to Alexander Street near Wentworth Avenue
E. Santa Maria Addolorata, 1903; Grand Avenue and Peoria Street
F. St. Michael, 1903; Twenty-fourth Place near Wentworth Avenue
G. St. Philip Benizi, 1904; Gault Court and Division Street, moved in 1914 to Oak Street and Cambridge Avenue
H. St. Anthony of Padua, 1904; Kensington and Prairie avenues
I. Holy Rosary, 1904; 249 (later 612) North Western Avenue
J. Our Lady of Pompei, 1910; 1224 Macalister Place
K. St. Francis de Paula, 1911; Seventy-eighth Street and Ellis Avenue
L. San Callisto, 1919; Polk and De Kalb streets

Source: *The Official Catholic Directory* (for the years from 1886 to 1920).

As they departed from the lower Loop settlement, most Italian immigrants settled west of the river on the Near West Side, which, before the end of the nineteenth century, contained Chicago's largest Italian community. This area continued to hold the dominant Italian settlement beyond 1920, although the population concentration shifted steadily westward. In 1898 the colony was located between the river and Halsted Street, in a band between Polk and Taylor streets. In its report of 1901, the City Homes Association mistakenly labeled the blocks between Polk and Twelfth, Canal and Halsted streets, "The Italian District." This

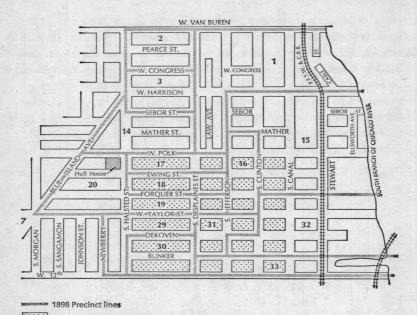

**5. Near West Side Italian District, 1898 and 1901**

Based on City of Chicago, Board of Election Commissioners, Nineteenth Ward, Election Precincts for 1898; and Robert Hunter (for the City Homes Association), *Tenement Conditions in Chicago* (Chicago, 1901), 12–13, 55–56.

description distorted the actual situation; for although Italians represented a majority of residents in part of the area surveyed by the Association, they formed a minority element elsewhere. Furthermore, in not one block of the entire area did Italians comprise the only ethnic group.[12]

The Near West Side contained some of the worst housing in the city. Structures facing the street (most of them brick and three stories high) were unsoundly constructed, inadequately lighted, poorly ventilated and dangerously overcrowded. Owners and managers utilized all available space for living purposes. Each floor

## Table 2

### NEAR WEST SIDE ITALIAN DISTRICT POPULATION IN 1898, BY PRECINCT

| Precinct | Italians | | Non-Italians | | Total | | Principal Non-Italian Groups |
|---|---|---|---|---|---|---|---|
| | Foreign born | American born | Foreign born | American born | Foreign born | American born | |
| 1 | 239 | 121 | 379 | 663 | 618 | 784 | Irish, German |
| 2 | 1 | 5 | 297 | 600 | 298 | 605 | Irish, German |
| 3 | 10 | 2 | 430 | 483 | 440 | 485 | Irish, German |
| 14 | 10 | 12 | 377 | 671 | 387 | 683 | Irish, Russian |
| 15 | 349 | 306 | 276 | 361 | 625 | 667 | Irish, German, Greek |
| 16 | 706 | 450 | 346 | 387 | 1052 | 837 | Irish, German |
| 17 | 850 | 614 | 178 | 221 | 1028 | 835 | Irish, German |
| 18 | 730 | 482 | 182 | 186 | 912 | 668 | Irish, German, Greek |
| 19 | 544 | 365 | 376 | 575 | 920 | 940 | German, Russian, Irish |
| 20 | 202 | 239 | 664 | 671 | 866 | 910 | Irish, Russian, German |
| 29 | 124 | 150 | 825 | 1005 | 949 | 1155 | Polish, Russian, German |
| 30 | 9 | 3 | 1283 | 1044 | 1292 | 1047 | Bohemian, Polish, German, Russian |
| 31 | 66 | 92 | 491 | 546 | 557 | 638 | Bohemian, Russian, Polish, German |
| 32 | 202 | 162 | 759 | 844 | 961 | 1006 | Russian, German, Irish |
| 33 | — | 12 | 994 | 894 | 994 | 906 | Russian, Bohemian, German, Irish |

Source: City of Chicago, Board of Education, *Proceedings, July 13, 1898, to June 28, 1899* (Chicago, 1899), 187–89.

(including the basement) generally contained two apartments of four rooms each, although the district also provided many one- and two-room apartments. Each apartment, in turn, housed one or more families, and frequently lodgers or boarders as well, who shared kitchen and bedroom facilities. Inhabitants often ate and slept in shifts.[13]

The presence of two buildings, and sometimes three, on a single lot compounded the problem of overcrowding. The rear tenement, a serious problem in all Chicago slum areas, typically consisted of a one- or two-story wooden structure, of deservedly bad reputation. Writing in 1895 in the *Hull House Maps and Papers,* Agnes Sinclair Holbrook noted that "rear tenements and alleys form the core of the district, and it is there that the densest crowds of the most wretched and destitute congregate." Six years later Robert Hunter reported (using as his basis studies conducted by City Homes Association investigators) that "sickness, epidemics, high death-rates, are universally more common in rear tenements than in other dwellings. In fact, almost all insanitary conditions are found in and about rear tenements." Not unreasonably, he concluded that "rear tenements make the worst possible dwellings for human beings." [14]

Italian residents no less than investigating middle class reformers recognized the unpleasantness and undesirability of housing in the area—front tenements as well as rear dwellings. Residents showed a reluctance to buy or even lease property along streets east of Morgan, in sharp contrast to their readiness to buy in neighborhoods farther west. It should be noted that the purchase of property formed a principal objective of Italians and other "new" immigrants, and a major reason for their emphasis on putting all family members to work. Social worker Sophonisba P. Breckinridge observed (in a book published in 1921) that to immigrants of the prewar era, land ownership carried with it an important degree of social prestige. She recognized that in Chicago and, by implication, other American cities, "Bohemians, Lithuanians, Poles, and Italians . . . bend every energy toward this end." [15]

In 1893 United States Department of Labor investigators, di-

6. School Section Addition, Blocks 33 and 34

Note: Lots 8 and 9, Block 33, are divided into four sublots.
Lot 15 and the west half of Lot 16, Block 33, are divided into five sublots.
Lots 14 and 15, Block 34, are divided into five sublots.

rected by Hull House resident Florence Kelley as Special Agent
Expert, collected information on social and economic conditions
in the Near West Side for comparison with slum areas in Baltimore,
New York, and Philadelphia. The Department published this information, its *Seventh Special Report*, in 1894. The raw data,
copies of which Hull House retained, served as the basis for maps
and comments on the area in *Hull House Maps and Papers*, prepared the following year by residents of the social settlement.[16]

By the early 1890's the area bounded by Polk, Desplaines,
Taylor, and Jefferson streets (School Section Addition, Blocks 33
and 34) contained a large Italian element. Italians bought prop-

erty here as early as the 1880's, but in each case sold the land to non-Italians before the end of the decade. In 1893, at the time of the U.S. Department of Labor investigation, Italians owned only two lots and portions of six others in Block 33, and portions of two lots in Block 34. Of the land on which Italians resided in 1893–94, they owned only the following: Block 33—west half of lot 3 (until 1900); sublot 3 of lots 8 and 9 (until 1916); lot 11 (until 1916); east half of lot 12 (until 1903); sublots 3 and 4 of lots 15 and 16 (to the 1940's and 1920's, respectively); undeveloped half of east half of lot 16 (until 1904); Block 34—west half of lot 3 and west half of lot 5 (to the 1920's). Italians owning land purchased most of it after 1900 and held it for only limited periods of time; it changed hands frequently and soon passed to non-Italians.

Although deteriorating and unpleasant, property in the area was nevertheless expensive. In 1913, for example, land east of Morgan Street sold at prices ranging from $200 to $300 per front foot. The rise in land values is seen in the fact that property located at Jefferson and Ewing streets, which sold for $100 per front foot in 1899, by 1913 brought $250. Although businessmen and manufacturers could afford to buy, the average immigrant could not. As a result, before 1900 railroad tracks, warehouses, and small industrial plants cluttered the section between the river and Canal Street, and in following years industrial buildings spread rapidly westward.[17]

Italians departed from the Canal Street, Ewing Street, and Jefferson Street tenements largely because of the encroachment of industry, the desire for a more pleasant environment in which to raise families, or the appearance of newer arrivals from overseas (unless they welcomed relatives or friends, settled Italians viewed recent arrivals from the "South" as only slightly less intolerable than newcomers from Russia, Greece, or Mexico). These masses of adjusting "Southerners" who moved into housing between Morgan Street and Western Avenue and beyond, forced earlier German and Irish residents to locate themselves still farther away from the city's center in the hope of escaping contact with such "highly undesirable" elements.[18]

The area beyond Morgan Street held many attractions for Italians. Housing seemed better than any with which they had come into contact during the group's westward trek from the lower Loop district across the river to Halsted Street. The new neighborhood appeared to be middle class, with many one- and two-family detached frame houses, which contrasted favorably with the tenements just vacated by the immigrants. Land values also played an important role. Property cost less than in tenement and business districts to the east. Thus residential property located between Morgan Street and Racine Avenue in 1913 was valued from $50 to $125 per front foot, while that between Racine and Ashland avenues went for $40 to $90, except for the choice block of Macalister Place facing directly on Vernon Park (where Nineteenth Ward political boss John Powers lived); it sold for $100 per front foot.[19] As a result, Italians spread rapidly westward from the area of major settlement, which in the 1890's and early 1900's was in the vicinity of Ewing and Jefferson streets. After 1905 they began to buy extensively in the blocks between Morgan and Racine, and after 1910 along streets west of Racine. By the end of World War I they were buying homes on Hoyne, Leavitt, Oakley, and Western. While Italians settled throughout the area and owned extensive amounts of land, nowhere were they the only ethnic element; nor did they own all the property on any block.

Examination of real estate conveyances indicates that the most solidly Italian block on the Near West Side—and in the entire city—was that bounded by Vernon Park Place on the north, Polk Street on the south, and Sholto and Aberdeen on the east and west. Prior to 1920, Italians eventually owned 23 of 26 lots in that block, although the land changed hands frequently over the years, with non-Italians sharing in the transactions. Italians owned half the lots (14 of 28) between Harrison and Flournoy streets, and Racine Avenue and Lytle Street, an area only three blocks west and one block north of Vernon Park Place and Aberdeen Street. Italians obtained approximately three quarters of the property along Taylor Street, from Sholto westward to Loomis. (This figure does not include the block between Arthington and Taylor streets,

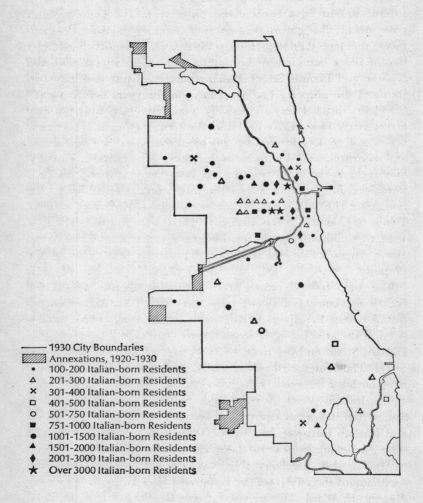

1930 City Boundaries
Annexations, 1920-1930
• 100-200 Italian-born Residents
△ 201-300 Italian-born Residents
✕ 301-400 Italian-born Residents
□ 401-500 Italian-born Residents
○ 501-750 Italian-born Residents
■ 751-1000 Italian-born Residents
● 1001-1500 Italian-born Residents
▲ 1501-2000 Italian-born Residents
♦ 2001-3000 Italian-born Residents
★ Over 3000 Italian-born Residents

7. Italians in Chicago, 1920

and Lytle Street and Ada Avenue, which from 1872 to 1908 be-longed to the Seminary of the Sacred Heart, from 1908 to 1935 to the Chicago Hebrew Institute and later the Jewish Peoples Institute, and in 1935 became the property of the United States government; the government located a public housing development, the Jane Addams Houses, on this and surrounding land.) On the block bounded by Arthington and Taylor streets, and Ada Avenue and Loomis Street, Italians purchased just less than two thirds of the property (20 of 33 lots) in the years before 1921.[20]

Italians did not buy extensively along streets between Robey Street (later Damen Avenue) and Western Avenue until the early 1920's. Of 58 lots located in the block between Hoyne Avenue and Harrison, and Flournoy and Robey streets, Italians owned only eight in the years before 1921. Between 1921 and 1924, they purchased fifteen other lots in the block, but never obtained the remaining thirty-five lots, which non-Italians continued to own. While Italians did not purchase property here in the years after 1924, they did buy land in surrounding streets until the end of the 1920's. In no block did they own more than two thirds of the property.[21]

The 1920 federal census tract population figures reflect the Italian movement westward from the earlier district of concentration along the river. In that year 2753 foreign-born Italians lived in the area bounded by Van Buren and Twelfth streets, and Halsted Street and the river, while 741 remained east of Jefferson Street. The center of the community, however, had shifted to the neighborhood between Halsted and Marshfield, where there were 13,279 Italians. West of Marshfield, Italian population reached a smaller but still significant peak concentration between Winchester and Leavitt, Harrison, and Taylor, then decreased to Kedzie, with diminishing numbers beyond Kedzie to the city limits.[22]

Another shift paralleled the movement of Italians through the west side of the city from the vicinity of Hull House in Chicago's Nineteenth Ward. This movement was the exodus from the Chicago Commons district in the Seventeenth Ward toward the western city limits, between Kinzie Street and Chicago Avenue. In a

1915 housing survey of Seventeenth Ward Italians, Chicago Department of Public Welfare investigators noted the large-scale movement from the area around Chicago Commons, which "has been growing stronger every year." Investigators found that "Italians, when they grow more prosperous, do move out of the Italian district." As a result, the slum colony contained "only the comparatively *recent* immigrants," a qualification that applied to other slum colonies as well.[23]

The early Near North Side community between the river and Ontario Street continued in existence, but its population and importance diminished after the turn of the century, as the southern portion of the area converted to industrial and business activities and as the composition of the colony changed. Italians began to move north of Chicago Avenue where formerly, in the 1880's and early 1890's, few Italian residents could be found. During the following decades, immigrants secured a beachhead along Gault Court and Milton Avenue between Chicago Avenue and Division Street. Between 1900 and 1920, Italians pushed across Division Street to North Avenue, and spread outward to Wells Street on the east and Halsted Street on the west. Earlier populated by Germans, Irishmen, and Swedes, the area soon became identified as "Little Italy." Although mainlanders (most of them from south of Rome) also settled on these streets, the majority of the Italian residents came from the island of Sicily. "Southerners" bought land here in the years after 1900, but they, like residents of other so-called "Italian districts" in the city, seldom remained in the same place for very long.[24] The early location of Italians in core areas and their dispersal outward through the city was not unique to that group, but also characterized elements contemporary with Italians as well as earlier ethnic groups.

## III

Chicago was an immigrant city long before Italians, Poles, Jews, and Greeks inundated the area. The federal census of 1850 showed that 52 per cent of Chicago's 29,963 inhabitants were born outside the United States. In these early decades, Germans, Swedes, Norwegians, and Irishmen arrived in ever-increasing numbers, and clearly identifiable immigrant settlements appeared in the city. (English, Welsh, and Scottish newcomers comprised a sizable element, over 8 per cent of the city's total population in 1850; but kinship with native Americans in speech, religious beliefs, and cultural heritage eased their process of assimilation and speeded up the movement of members into the native community.)[25]

On the city's Near North Side, Germans settled in the area bounded by Kinzie, Ohio, Clark, and Franklin streets. Some middle-class Americans resided there, and during the 1850's a few northern Italians drifted in; but the nucleus of the neighborhood remained German for many years. Here the migrants built churches and meeting halls, foremost among them Deutsche Haus. They organized athletic clubs, singing societies, and fraternal organizations, and attended dances, theatrical performances, and operas. During the same period Swedes and Norwegians located themselves in the area bounded by Indiana Avenue (later renamed Grand Avenue), Erie and Orleans streets, and the north branch of the Chicago River—the area then referred to as "Swedentown." In 1860 nearly all of Chicago's 816 Swedes resided in this Near North Side colony. Norwegians originally settled in the same area and intermingled with the Swedes, but by the middle 1850's most had moved across the north branch of the river where they organized their own community. Another immigrant enclave, Kilgubbin, stretched along the river northward to Kinzie Street, bounded on the east by Clark Street and on the west by the north branch of the Chicago River. In its heyday, this Irish settlement boasted a reputation as unsavory as that accorded by later generations to Italian colonies along Gault Court in the Near North Side, and Jefferson Street in the Near West Side. A contemporary described Kilgubbin thus: "The population of this collection of shanties reached to the number of several thousand at one time, and it became the terror of constables, sheriffs, and policemen in the days of its glory. Large droves of geese, goats, pigs, and fowls were everywhere to be seen; it was a refuge for criminals of all descriptions, the police not venturing to invade its precincts, or even to cross its borders without having a strong reserve force at hand." [26]

These highly concentrated German, Irish, and Swedish settlements disintegrated as residents adjusted economically and moved away to more desirable locations in the city. Ethnic elements new to urban life took their place—among them Poles, Italians, Greeks, Turks, Mexicans, and Negroes. By the decade 1910–20, Vivien M. Palmer, in a study prepared for the United Charities of Chicago, found that newer elements—Assyrians, Syrians, and Armenians— were "forming distinct settlements, using this old battered area as a stepping stone to something more desirable." [27]

The "old battered area" was, of course, far from unique in serving this necessary function. Other early settled districts of the city and, in fact, the core area in general, fulfilled this purpose for successive waves of newcomers. Thus the district directly west of "Swedentown," centering on Grand Avenue and Morgan Street (the location of Chicago Commons Settlement House), formed "the shore on which many a group of poor, ambitious pilgrims found a first foothold, from whence they gradually fought their way to the comforts of the well-to-do," in the words of a 1915 Department of Public Welfare survey. Originally settled by native Americans, the neighborhood in the southeastern section of West Town underwent its first nationality transformation during the 1850's as Irish immigrants displaced their native American predecessors. Former inhabitants moved in order to escape contact with what appeared to be a highly objectionable and unassimilable element. In the following decades there emerged a pattern that would be repeated with other incoming groups; by 1915 this area (noted as once having housed "many of the now most prominent Irish in Chicago") had few Irishmen. As early as the 1870's they had begun to drift westward, although many families remained in the vicinity for years after the main body of the group had moved away. Norwegians became the predominant group during the 1870's; they mingled with native American and Irish holdovers from earlier days, and small numbers of Germans, German Jews, and northern Italians. In turn, Norwegians began their trek farther west to the Logan Square and Humboldt Park districts in the years after the Columbian Exposition. Improved economic conditions and better transportation facilities made this movement both feasible and possible, while the influx of "Southerners" hastened its speed. Although a few northern Italian families had resided in the area by the 1870's, a general movement from Italy (and this largely from the "South") did not take place until twenty years later. By about 1905, Italians constituted the dominant group in the district. Ten years later a noticeable change in ethnic composition again took place as Poles began to displace "Southerners," who (in the words of a contemporary) "have been moving west and to other parts of the city." [28]

A similar pattern emerged in other community areas, including the Near West Side, Armour Square, and the Near South Side. Americans living in the neighborhood of Hull House in the Near West Side gave way, in the years following the Great Fire of 1871, to Irishmen and Germans, who in turn departed as Jews from eastern Europe and Italians moved in. These latest newcomers moved on as Greeks and Bulgarians arrived in large numbers during the years between the turn of the century and 1914. During and after World War I, Mexicans and Negroes began to crowd into the district, pushing out members of earlier waves of residents. In Armour Square and the Near South Side, Germans, Czechs, Swedes, and Irishmen displaced original native Americans, and were followed by Croatians, Italians, Chinese, Mexicans, and Negroes.[29]

Newcomers in each immigrant wave shifted from central-city areas toward peripheral residential communities at the same time that they moved upward economically and socially. Sociologist Paul Frederick Cressey tested the validity of this process, known as population succession, by measuring the movement of eight ethnic groups (Germans, Irishmen, Swedes, Czechs, Poles, Italians, Jews, and Negroes) in Chicago during the period from 1898 to 1930, using census-tract data for 1910, 1920, and 1930, and the detailed Chicago School Census of 1898. Cressey concluded that "the distribution of these various groups reflects . . . a regular sequence of settlement in successive areas of increasing stability and status." On its arrival in Chicago, an immigrant group settled "in a compact colony in a low-rent industrial area usually [but not always] located in the transitional zone near the center of the city" where newcomers perpetuated "many" old world traits. After years of residence in a congested area, "the group, as it improves its economic and social standing, moves outward to some more desirable residential district, creating an area of second settlement. . . . Subsequent areas of settlement may develop in some cases, but the last stage in this series of movements is one of gradual dispersion through cosmopolitan residential districts." This last stage marked "the disintegration of the group and the absorption of the individuals into the general American population." While Cressey found northern European groups to be highly mobile during the period from 1898 to 1930, he viewed Poles and Italians as exhibiting the opposite tendency. Indeed, "until 1920 the Italians were even more compact and immobile than the Poles." [30]

This illuminating, but incomplete, picture of Italian mobility has become widely accepted. An acute present-day observer of American political behavior declared that "in Chicago, for example, the Italians were a static, immobile force until 1920." Richard G. Ford accepted and elaborated on Cressey's description of "patterns of succession" in Chicago in the period to 1930. He described the process to 1940, taking for granted that a "regular and orderly pattern of cultural succession [functions] in a large heterogeneous city." [31]

While acceptable in a general sense, significant qualifications must be placed on the validity of population succession as a measure of group adjustment. Superficial examination leaves the erroneous impression that an orderly, logical process took place. It did not. Tenaciously clinging to inferior housing in slum communities, many immigrants resisted any change in location even after members of a succeeding ethnic wave had inundated the neighborhood. Ethnic colonies did not quickly, readily, or willingly disintegrate. While many economically and socially mobile members moved to more fashionable and desirable residential areas, others remained behind and sought to perpetuate familiar and accepted patterns of living. Only the large-scale invasion of a new, different, and unacceptable group, or the conversion of the district to industrial or commercial use, could eliminate the hard core of earlier inhabitants. Many Irishmen remained in Kilgubbin on the Near North Side, for example, until the location of industrial concerns (particularly metal-working plants) in the area forced them out after 1900. Long before this year, prosperous members of the Irish group had settled throughout the city's Far North Side as well as in upper-income suburbs.

Closely related to this mixed character of immigrant communities was the fact that—except for Negro districts—Chicago had no areas occupied exclusively by one ethnic group. Not only did remnants of earlier ethnic elements remain, but members of other "new" immigrant groups also resided in neighborhoods that contemporaries labeled "Italian." Large numbers of Germans, Irishmen, Poles, Jews, and Bohemians, for example, lived in the Near West Side tenements. On the Near North Side, investigators under the direction of Grace Norton in 1912 found Italians (especially "Southerners") barely predominating in a five-block area lying directly north of Chicago Avenue between Sedgwick Street and Gault Court, the very heart of "Little Italy." Of 1438 heads of households located in the area, 743 (or 53 per cent of the total) were Italian. A medley of nationalities, including Scandinavians, Irishmen, and Germans, composed the remaining 47 per cent (695 heads of households).[32]

Another feature of the ethnic experience that violated the "population succession" theory was the formation of communities in sections of Chicago far from the central-city colonies, at an early date in the group's settlement in the city. During the 1850's, for example, when the center of German cultural, social, and economic life began to revolve around the primary settlement bounded by Kinzie, Clark, Ohio, and Franklin streets, a flourishing German colony developed above North Avenue and west of Sedgwick

Street, in an area annexed to the city in 1853. Large and important Irish communities emerged not only in the area immediately north of the Chicago River, but also several miles to the south along the line of the Illinois and Michigan Canal in the Bridgeport community area.

During the 1890's Italians formed several settlements miles away from the colonies located near the central business district. These Italian neighborhoods were not composed of immigrants and their children who had entered the middle class—that is, who had escaped central-city ghettoes—but consisted of laboring classes living near factories, railroad yards, and other places of employment. In 1898 more than 400 "Southerners" of the first and second generation lived within the triangle of land formed by Chicago Avenue, Western Avenue, and the Chicago, Milwaukee and St. Paul railroad tracks. Although about two miles west of the large Chicago Commons community in the Seventeenth Ward, and four miles from the Loop, this colony lay only a short distance from the railway yards where the men worked. During this same period, Italians—largely from the northern part of the peninsula—began to move in among Germans, Swedes, Irishmen, and Bohemians along blocks bounded by Twenty-fourth Street, Blue Island Avenue, Western Avenue, and Leavitt Street. Residents here lived within walking distance of several industrial plants. The most important of these was the giant International Harvester Works, which provided employment for most of the area's Italians. This colony grew so quickly that in 1903 St. Michael's Church opened on Twenty-fourth Place, between Western and Oakley avenues.[33]

On the Far South Side, Italians (most of them "Southerners") settled in large numbers in the West Englewood, Grand Crossing, Roseland, Pullman and West Pullman community areas. They worked in railway yards and streetcar barns, in the building trades and in factories, including the Pullman Company. The early and large scale movement into these districts is reflected by the location of churches. In 1892 Chicago's first South Side Italian parish, St. Mary's of Mount Carmel, also the second Italian parish in the city, opened in West Englewood at Sixty-seventh and Page streets (and later, in 1915, moved to Hermitage and Sixty-seventh streets). In 1904 St. Anthony of Padua began services for residents in the Roseland-Pullman-West Pullman areas, and seven years later St. Francis de Paula opened its doors in Grand Crossing. By 1920 each community area held a significant number of Italians, many of them property owners, although in none did these newcomers constitute the dominant ethnic element.[34]

The heaviest concentration of South Side Italians resided in the vicinity of St. Anthony of Padua (216 Kensington Street), between 111th and 119th streets, State Street, and Lake Calumet. A total of 6014 immigrants lived there, of whom 1591 were Italian by birth, largely from the Kingdom's northern provinces. Although Italians formed the largest single ethnic contingent, fourteen other groups each contributed over a hundred residents:[35]

| | | | |
|---|---|---|---|
| Poland | 981 | Canada (French and British) | 198 |
| Lithuania | 546 | Netherlands | 189 |
| Sweden | 522 | England | 167 |
| Germany | 396 | Scotland | 131 |
| Russia | 245 | Austria | 129 |
| Greece | 241 | Hungary | 111 |
| Ireland | 198 | Czechoslovakia | 105 |

Not only did Italian colonies flourish in various parts of the city, but also Italians exhibited a great deal of mobility throughout the period from the 1890's to 1920. Original sources do not support the contention that they formed an immobile element in the years prior to 1920 and that they suddenly showed movement during the decade of the 'twenties. A district might contain a sizable Italian element over a period of years, but within that group there operated a continual turnover of individual residents. Among contemporary sources that substantiated this fact was the 1915 City Department of Public Welfare survey of the Seventeenth Ward's Italian district. Investigators found that nearly one half of the community's residents changed their dwelling place each year, sometimes within the same area but often to other districts. Unskilled laborers moved frequently in search of work and with the hope of improving their lot in life. If it appeared impossible to achieve these goals in Chicago, they moved elsewhere in the United States or returned to the home village in Italy. Source materials make abundantly clear that adjusting Italians also exhibited geographic mobility, shifting constantly throughout the city and its nearby suburbs.[36]

Although the manuscript population schedules of the federal census for 1890 no longer exist and those for 1900 to 1920 are not open to public use, two available primary sources shed light on individual mobility.[37] One—precinct lists—records the location of Italians by house and street of residence from year to year. The other—city directories—permits the researcher to focus upon individuals and to trace their movements over the passage of years.

Precinct lists provide an invaluable, although largely unused, source of information concerning not only voting patterns but also residential locations of registered Italians. Registering to vote required time, effort, and some degree of interest and involvement in community political life—requirements that immigrants who did not intend to remain in the new world had no intention of fulfilling. In order to vote a newcomer had to become an American citizen and had to reside in the nation, the state, and the city for specified lengths of time. Political bosses violated these requirements whenever possible; but by the 1890's, because of efforts of the Municipal Voters League and other reform groups, they found subterfuge increasingly difficult. Limitation of corrupt election methods took place, it should be noted, during the early stages of the large-scale movement of "Southerners" to the United States and to Chicago. Not all immigrants registered to vote; and ward organizations made no attempt to place all of them on record books. Newcomers who sought a stake in the American system, or who expected to realize certain advantages from politics, registered and voted. Among these were laborers employed in patronage jobs, ethnic colony businessmen seeking exemptions from city ordinances or hoping to gain contracts or other benefits from the municipality, and the politically ambitious, who sought elective or appointive office.[38]

The steady turnover of registered voters in Italian districts during the years prior to 1920 took place not only in the transient area around Dearborn Station, but also in colonies that appeared to be stable and unchanging. Of 34 men who in April, 1897, listed their place of residence as 416 South Clark Street (located two blocks west of Dearborn Station), only nine remained two years later. Included among these were future vice lord James Colosimo and his prospective lawyer, Rocco De Stefano. By 1902, however, both Colosimo and De Stefano had moved elsewhere and only one of the 1897 residents, Charles Pellettiere, remained. This trend held true for other buildings in the vicinity. The 31 structures between 354 and 422 South Clark Street in 1899 contained 231 registered voters, 151 of them Italian. Only 21 men, including 10 Italians, remained at the same addresses in both 1899 and 1902. While some moved to adjoining or nearby houses, most left the area (Precinct Fifteen of the First Ward) in the intervening three years.[39]

The turnover of registered voters reached a sizable total on the Near West Side, in the Nineteenth Ward, although it never approached the proportions attained east of the river in the First Ward. Of the residents on streets with heavy Italian concentrations in 1900—Forquer, Desplaines, Jefferson, Polk, Taylor and Ewing—fewer than 50 per cent remained at the same address just two years later. While Italians comprised most of these people, many non-Italians also stayed. Thus of the 53 registered voters residing at buildings from 109 to 130 Forquer Street at the turn of the century, 26 remained in 1902; and of these, five were non-Italians. A heavy turnover took place in the years between 1902 and 1918. By the latter year fewer than one sixth of the voters registered in 1902 lingered at the same address. A small element of non-Italians, especially Irishmen, formed a part of this immobile core. Thus Vincenzo Di Giovanni remained at 69 Ewing Street (later renamed Gilpin Place) and Tomasso Parrillo and Vito Tortoriello at 99 Ewing, Frank Sesso at 140 Taylor, Luigi Mondo at 163 Taylor, John Pech at 152 Forquer, and Brian Cooley at 119 Polk Street throughout the sixteen years following 1902.[40]

Many of the Italians who left their place of residence after 1902
—perhaps as many as half—remained within the general limits
of the expanding West Side Italian colony, even though some
moved frequently. Usually they settled along a street located between Morgan and Western Avenue (an area which, to a former
resident of Ewing or Jefferson Street, appeared to be middle class
and highly attractive). Those who departed from the Near West
Side settled throughout the city as well as in Cicero, Melrose Park,
Chicago Heights, and other nearby industrial suburbs. The experience on the Near West Side paralleled that of the Seventeenth
Ward, Grand Crossing, Gault Court-Milton Avenue, Pullman, and
other established Italian colonies elsewhere in the city.

The Near North Side community along Franklin, Illinois and
Indiana streets, the oldest established Italian colony in the city,
appeared to be the most stable of all Italian settlements.[41] Appearances deceived contemporaries and later investigators alike. In
1897 the following buildings along three streets contained a total
of 114 registered voters: Franklin Street—Nos. 62, 66, 68, 72, and
76; Illinois Street—Nos. 64, 65, 66, 67, 68, 69, 70, 75, and 77; Indiana Street—Nos. 70, 72, 76, 86, 92, 96, and 102. Ten years later
only eight of these same men were still listed at the same address.
Thus in 1907 all twelve registered voters at 66 Franklin Street had
moved; so had the nine at 68 Illinois Street and the ten at 70
Indiana Street. By 1900 northern Italians who first settled along
these streets in the 1870's and 1880's were abandoning the old
area of settlement to "Southerners." The outward appearance of
an Italian colony remained after the turn of the century, but both
the composition and the character of the district underwent a
complete change. Members of the leading northern families—
Arado, Cuneo, Cella, Garibaldi, Lagorio, Fontana, and others—
now lived elsewhere, many on the Far North Side. By 1915, Dr.
Antonio Lagorio, for example, lived at 417 Roscoe; Dr. Frank
Lagorio at 516 Aldine Avenue; millionaire fruit importer and commission merchant Frank Cuneo, President of Garibaldi and Cuneo,
at 4849 Sheridan Road; Andrew Cuneo, also a wealthy commission
merchant as senior partner in the firm of Cuneo Brothers, at 1364

North State Parkway. These and other northern Italians returned
to the old neighborhood only to attend religious services at Assumption Church, which they continued to support lavishly.[42]

While precinct lists indicate registered residents living on "Italian" streets from year to year, city directories make it possible to
trace the movement of individuals over the passage of time.[43]
Scores of unskilled laborers appeared in directories each year, only
to disappear suddenly; whether they moved to other cities or returned to their home village is impossible to determine. Some
"Southerners," like Luciano Correre (84 Milton Avenue), Paul
Criola (395 South Clinton), and John Orlando (116 Ewing Street),
remained in Chicago, living at the same address and working as
laborers throughout the years from the turn of the century until
after World War I. While these men could serve to illustrate the
traditional stereotype of immobile "Southerners" in Chicago, a
significant number of Italians simply did not fit the same mold.
Fred Campagna, a laborer living at 4063 Princeton Avenue in
1900, worked as a watchman by 1915 and lived at 5839 South
Morgan Street; Frank De Rosa, in 1901 a laborer living at 111
Ewing Street, by 1915 had become a foreman with a home at 828
South Bishop Street; Frank Rago, in 1900 a laborer living at 115
West Polk Street, was a stonecutter in 1915 residing at 8025
Parnell Avenue. To be sure, such economic achievements seemed
modest compared to the "rags-to-riches" American dream; but to
a "Southern" peasant they proved the validity of that dream.

Occupational mobility appears to have taken place largely within
the working class, with movement occurring from unskilled to
semiskilled or skilled labor, or occasionally to supervisory positions. Careers in medicine and law, which exerted a powerful
attraction for members of the "American" generation of Italians
(those born or raised in the United States), were virtually closed
to immigrants who arrived in the United States as adults. Even
with a minimum of formal schooling, however, immigrant youths
who indicated a willingness to work long and hard (particularly
if their willingness included tenacity and perhaps a touch of ruthlessness) found it possible to realize economic achievement in a

number of areas. Even an unskilled laborer could become a labor
agent (or padrone), a contractor, an immigrant banker, a labor
union official, or a wholesale or retail merchant. Politics and crime
also offered attractive opportunities to some ambitious newcomers.
Many Italians decided to seek fame and fortune in one or both of
these lines, and some were highly successful. James Colosimo, for
example, exhibited ambition, cunning, and ruthlessness. He also
had the good luck to come to the attention of First Ward political
bosses "Hinky Dink" Kenna and "Bathhouse John" Coughlin, who
greatly aided the newcomer from Calabria in his advancement
from laborer (in 1897) living at 416 Clark Street, to saloonkeeper
(1905) with a home at 2002 Armour Avenue, to restaurant owner
and crime "syndicate" boss (1915) residing at 3156 Vernon Avenue.

In addition to economic mobility, geographical mobility comprised another significant difference between the "Southern" experience in Italy and urban America. In a Sicilian or southern
Italian village, residents lived and died in the same houses in which
they were born. In Chicago, on the other hand, newcomers could
move frequently without arousing suspicion of authorities or comment of neighbors—Louis D. Blasi, for example, lived at 418 Clark
Street in 1899 for a few months, then moved within the year to
111 Sholto Street. Some "Southerners" moved frequently, but from
one street to another in the same general district; Costantino
Cataldo, for example, lived at 397 South Jefferson Street in 1900,
at 129 West Polk Street in 1905, and at 1015 Aberdeen Street in
1915, all residences within seven blocks of each other in the expanding Near West Side Italian colony. Others shifted from one
section of the city to another; often these moves took them to
neighborhoods containing sizable groups of Italians. Thus between
1900 and 1915, Antonio Magliano went from 126 Pacific Avenue
(in the lower Loop) to 6715 South Hermitage Avenue, Angelo
De Leo from 129 West Polk Street to 1350 West Ohio Street, and
Pasquale Schiavone from 155 West Taylor Street to 2638 West
Superior Street—the last two moves from the Near West to the
West Town community areas. Louis Costa, on the other hand, who
in 1895 lived at 187 Grand Avenue and moved several times during

the following years, settled at 5455 South State Street in 1915, in a neighborhood containing few other Italians. Oscar Durante, editor of *L'Italia,* moved frequently and—with his Scottish-American wife—eventually settled in a non-Italian community. In 1890 Durante lived at 333 Wabash Avenue, five years later at 45 Sixteenth Street, at the turn of the century at 2458 Wabash, in 1905 at 5323 Jackson Boulevard, in 1910 at 5824 Prairie Avenue, and by 1915 at 5628 Indiana Avenue, where he remained until his death some thirty years later. While upwardly mobile "Southerners" like Durante could leave the Italian quarter and settle in American neighborhoods in the years before World War I, a significant movement did not begin to take place until the 1920's, when members of the group moved not only into middle-class areas in Chicago's periphery, but into North Shore suburbs as well.

## IV

In summary, an undeniable and essential fact of Italian location in Chicago, at least to 1920 and even beyond, was that no set, rigid, and unchanging Italian colony existed. Italian areas of settlement expanded and shifted their location over the passage of years. In addition, individual "Southerners," no less than immigrants from northern provinces, exhibited a high degree of residential mobility. Movement of both colony and individuals generally proceeded outward from Chicago's core area toward the periphery, but Italian settlements did exist in outer areas of the city. These "outer" neighborhoods dated no later than the settlement of many inner urban communities, such as the Gault Court-Milton Street colony. The Italian experience in Chicago bears out the contention of Edith Abbott, that the "rather popular" ideas of city growth portraying "different population groups lying in a series of concentric circles around the business district . . . seem to be purely theoretical and not realistic." [44]

Contemporary descriptions usually exaggerated the size of Italian colonies and imparted to them a cohesiveness and unity they did not possess. Americans in general viewed colonies of the foreign born as permanent and unchanging in size, inhabitants, and location. Incoming masses of newcomers masked extensive amounts of individual mobility.

While some "Southerners" remained permanently in the colony and even on the same block, the majority quickly moved from the original place of residence in Chicago, and they moved frequently thereafter. Whether they remained unskilled laborers or became skilled workers, supervisory personnel in private or public employment, businessmen, or professionals, "Southerners" desired and sought better housing and neighborhoods.

For "Southerners" of the immigrant generation, movement in the years before 1920 generally was from one working-class neighborhood to another, but typically from one located in an undesirable slum area to a more pleasant and less congested environment. In the decades after 1900, improved and expanded mass transportation facilities (surface streetcars and elevated electric lines), accompanied by a decline in transit fares, made it possible for laborers no less than members of the middle class to live beyond walking distance from work.[45] Transportation mobility through public means was important, because for "Southerners," economic advancement took place largely within the laboring class during the decades of large-scale Italian immigration. Some individuals realized significant financial success, but economic advancement for the group at large came in the years after World War I.

# 3

## Economic Activity: The Padrone Era and After

As Chicago grew, expanding economic opportunities worked like a powerful magnet that attracted newcomers as well as native Americans. Critics of a later day, basing their arguments on the ostensibly scientific findings of the United States Immigration Commission (the Dillingham Commission), conveyed the impression that the motives of the newer immigrant elements were somehow less noble than those of the older elements from northern and western Europe. Reflecting the attitude of the age, one University of Chicago graduate student in sociology observed in 1914 that "the aim of the Italian seems to be to make money." Thus Americans assumed that Italians and other "new" groups journeyed to the United States for financial reasons. This assumption contained a valid, but incomplete, idea. It omitted the fact that economic factors also motivated the movement overseas of earlier arrivals from northern Europe. The generally unskilled work that later became associated with the capabilities and training of Italians, Poles and eastern European Jews, was previously the province of Germans, Irishmen, and Swedes.[1]

Immigrants from northern and western Europe, and especially those from Ireland and Germany, supplied common labor needed

in railroad and utilities construction and repair, factory work, and
building public and private structures. A change in the source of
unskilled labor (reflecting the shift in the source of immigration
in general) began to take place in the 1880's, and by the following
decade "Southerners" had replaced Irish workmen in railroad and
other types of construction jobs.

Contemporary literature stressed "Southern" employment as unskilled construction workers. This emphasis stemmed in part from
the (justly deserved) notoriety surrounding the padrone—or labor
boss—system. Overriding attention paid to the boss system had
the unfortunate result of obscuring the fact that during the heyday of the padrone, as well as in the period after his decline,
"Southerners" engaged in a wide range of economic activities.

## II

When they arrived in Chicago, "Southerners" generally understood
little about the English language. They also lacked contacts with
potential American employers, and knew nothing concerning American labor practices. To compensate for these deficiencies they
looked for an intermediary—someone who spoke both languages,
understood old-world traditions and new-world business operations, and could get in touch with American employers who needed
unskilled workers. This intermediary was the padrone, or labor
boss.

Some form of boss system seemed to be typical of non-English-
speaking immigrant elements newly arrived in industrial America
in the decades after 1880. Bossism existed among Italians, Greeks,
Austrians, Turks, Poles, Bulgarians, Macedonians, and others. It
was the method by which these groups overcame three immediate
problems: language difficulties, financial exigencies, and differences
in labor practices. It formed part of the price required of the newcomer because of his strangeness. Dr. Egisto Rossi of the Italian
Immigration Bureau defined bossism as "the forced tribute which
the newly arrived pays to those who are already acquainted with
the ways and language of the country." In a number of respects,

however, the Italian experience displayed unique characteristics, particularly in the tremendous extent and power attributed to it by Americans, which led in turn to the violent reactions it aroused in the native population. The factors responsible for its decline resulted, also, from a combination of atypical circumstances.[2]

Few Americans doubted that padroni operated among unskilled immigrant labor and especially among "Southerners" in the United States. Disagreement arose over the composition of the padrone group, its size, and when it operated. Available evidence suggests that a formal contract labor system did exist on a limited scale before the Foran Act in 1885 forbade it, and that this system involved women and children as well as adult males. After 1885 the padrone acted merely as a private labor agent, owning neither license nor office. Probably most padroni fulfilled only this function before, as well as after, the mid-1880's. For example, United States Bureau of Labor investigator John Koren discussed at great length the contract labor system among Italians. He noted that men "directly interested" in it denied its existence in the period before 1885. Recent findings of historian Charlotte Erickson agree. Contemporaries who argued that bosses directly induced immigration based their beliefs on information discovered neither by the labor investigator nor the historian. It is questionable that padroni should be credited with, or blamed for, chief responsibility for stimulating Italian immigration "to such an extent that the flow soon equalled the demand," as the United States Industrial Commission claimed in 1901.[3]

In the years after 1885, Americans concluded, erroneously, that Italian labor agents indulged in widespread violations of the Foran Act and that, as a result, a padrone system of vast proportions existed among "Southerners" in the United States. These assumptions emerged clearly in federal investigations conducted in the late 1880's and the 1890's that attempted to establish both the size of the system and the extent of contract labor law violations. Both the Ford Committee and the Immigration Commission of 1891–92, for example, "saw" evidence of extensive flouting of the Foran Act, but gave no proof to support their conviction. The Ford

Committee submitted statements of immigrants who testified that they had been imported into the United States under contract; the Immigration Commission, producing a long list of labor agents in Italy, made much of the fact that most Italian immigrants had their passages paid by inhabitants of the United States. The Ford Committee's findings proved only that some persons claimed that they had been hired under contract. Considerable confusion existed, however, among committee members (reflecting that of the general public) as to the nature of a work contract. Concerning "evidence" presented by an Italian ticket agent, for example, Legal Adviser Oates of the Committee felt obliged to inform Mr. Ford, "Mr. Chairman, I don't think I will put in that paper. It don't show any contract." [4]

Two problems arise from the findings of the investigations. First, did immigrants fully understand the questions that they had answered? The lack of competent translators proved to be a pressing difficulty not only for Congressional committees but also for courts of law in cases involving immigrants. Second, what proportion of the total immigrant group did investigating committees question? The Ford Committee's report provided insufficient facts to solve either problem. The Immigration Commission of 1891–92, in finding that the majority of Italian immigrants had their passages prepaid, undoubtedly discovered the truth, but failed to determine whether contractors or relatives bought the tickets. Probably in most cases, friends or family paid passage fares.[5]

The boss (usually of Italian birth or extraction, although some were Irish or American), met arriving immigrants at the docks in port cities and at railroad stations in other urban centers, and promised steady work at high wages. Some immigrants did not succumb to padrone promises at once. In Italian sections of any large city, however, stubborn newcomers met with padrone-promoted pressures and enticements intended to recruit their services for the boss. Many immigrants turned toward the boss rather than away from him because he offered opportunities to make ready money. A number of new arrivals, and particularly those who had no definite employment in sight, found the labor agent to be a

help and even a necessity. Indeed, after the system had fallen
into permanent decline, a hard core of workers remained in padrone employment.[6]

The boss knew individual employers, spoke English, and understood American labor practices. Therein lay his authority among
newcomers and his importance to American businessmen. Generally the labor agent negotiated directly with the contractor and
received from him or from representatives of a corporation a definite order for a specified number of men. In order to obtain employment through the padrone, immigrants paid him commissions
("bossatura") varying from one dollar to fifteen dollars per man,
the size of the fee depending on such factors as length of employment, amount of wages, and whether the men were to use padrone
facilities. Workers paid secretly and in advance; as an unlicensed
labor agent, the padrone found it expedient to carry on his activities with a minimum of outside attention.[7]

Bosses directed Italian immigrant laborers to all parts of the
United States and even into Canada to build railroads and work
at other construction jobs. Chicago became an important padrone
stronghold, partly because of the city's position as a railroad center
and partly because of its geographical location. Railroad and other
construction jobs tended to be seasonal, and Chicago served as a
clearing house for seasonal workers of the entire country as well
as the Middle West.[8]

Not all bosses deliberately made illegal profits, and not all set
out to cheat the laborer; but enough did so to give a bad name
to the entire group. Once in the hands of an unscrupulous labor
agent, workers suffered a number of devices designed to separate
them from their money. In some cases, for example, the padrone
charged first-class rates when the employer had provided free
transportation. On occasion a dishonest contractor or railroad official gave the laborers' wages directly to the boss, who then paid
what he wished, returned a portion to the official, and kept the
rest for himself. Some padroni collected fees and fares but did not
provide the promised work. Others sent laborers home after a few
days of work—frequently without giving reasons—and hired new

men in order to receive their commissions. In addition to the "bossatura," labor agents generally deducted weekly or monthly taxes during the entire period of work.[9]

Irregular employment resulting from seasonal activities gave bosses still another hold over workers. During the winter months almost the only construction jobs available existed in the South and West. Unemployed workers who remained in Chicago had no problems in obtaining food or lodgings, for padroni and Italian bankers owned and operated tenement houses where they encouraged "guests" to indulge in extravagances in order to place them more completely in debt. To tighten his grasp on the men, the boss would provide employment for a week, keep the men idle the next week, employ them again the following week, and so on, using scarcity of work as his excuse.[10]

The most serious and most numerous abuses took place in padrone camps. If, as often happened, the place of work was in the country, the boss generally boarded the men, sometimes having bought this privilege from the contractor. Even when the employer provided free housing for the men, the padrone collected rent money. Often the labor agent shipped workers to the camp earlier than necessary so that he could reap a larger profit. While at camp the laborers, who prepared their own meals, had to buy their provisions from the boss. Those who did not patronize padrone commissaries faced fines or dismissal. Foods provided by the boss tended to be, as a rule, inferior in quality and often unfit for eating. At a tidy profit for himself, the padrone stood ready to supply other items needed by the men, such as underwear, shoes, and overalls.[11]

Many descriptions of padrone camps still exist. One, by Domenick Ciolli, an American college student of Italian birth, showed the system in operation in Indiana. Hired as a common laborer, Ciolli received special privileges bescause of his education. Even so, he found living conditions to be execrable. Workers slept in windowless railroad cars; boards placed across boxes served as beds. Vermin covered the blankets while roaches and bed bugs "held undisputed sway of the beds and their immediate surroundings."

Ciolli noted a two-year layer of dirt everywhere. All doors remained closed at night, effectively shutting out fresh air. Workers received less protection from rain, which streamed through the porous roof and drenched clothing and bedding. The cars had never been repaired, for "they were too old to be used for carrying freight, and were only capable of being used as domiciles for human beings." One car had windows; it housed the padrone, the timekeeper (an American contemptuous of immigrants), and Ciolli.

The workers cooked for themselves on rusty, perforated tin boxes propped up by stones. An "undefinable" stench and heaps of rubbish on the ground made the outside little more bearable than indoors. Only at supper time did the men eat warm food. Breakfast consisted of a cup of coffee drunk at three or four in the morning while the men washed and dressed. Work began at five and continued without interruption until noon. Ciolli quoted the padrone's rule-of-thumb: "The beasts must not be given a rest. Otherwise they will step over me." Lunch consisted of cold sausage and bread for the younger men, and of bread only for older workers. Yet with coffee for breakfast and, at best, sausage and bread for lunch, these men worked ten hours daily, seven days a week, in all conditions of weather.[12]

The United States Bureau of Labor under the direction of Commissioner Carroll Wright studied the Italian element in Chicago. Published in 1897, the report showed, among other things, that "prices charged by padroni are frequently double those charged in Chicago markets for similar articles of food at the same quality." The average increase over Chicago prices was as follows:[13]

| Articles of Food | Percentage of Increase |
| --- | --- |
| Bread | 82.19 |
| Macaroni, per pound | 61.11 |
| Macaroni, box | 50.33 |
| Cheese | 46.02 |
| Tomatoes | 65.38 |
| Sausages | 72.40 |
| Bacon | 69.91 |
| Lard | 77.04 |

| Sugar | 44.58 |
| Coffee | 74.70 |
| Tea | 80.00 |
| Beans | 61.70 |
| All articles of food combined | 59.55 |

Significantly, an Italian-government study of padrone camp conditions compared camp foods with foods available in local villages in the Kingdom. Noting the limited, expensive, and inferior edibles supplied in labor camps, the Italian government admitted that "the feeding of the Italian manual laborer is more abundant, varied, and rich in the United States than in our native land. The immigrant, generally speaking, is not used to consuming in Italy the foods he acquires daily at the [padrone] commissary." [14]

A similarly complaisant attitude could not be taken toward working conditions. Construction labor regularly resulted in injury or death to the workers. An unusually sympathetic writer castigated with bitter sarcasm the callousness of the times in regard to immigrant disability and death:

> The slaughter of Italians in construction work near New York yesterday was simply awful. The men were torn and mangled and their blood was scattered all over the tracks, and there can be little doubt that the Erie road's bosses were responsible for the horrible affair; but the genial New York correspondents are of the opinion that it was caused by the "stupidity of the victims." Very stupid they must have been, for a fact, who could not escape two trains passing at the same time on tracks a few feet apart! Fortunately, the correspondents are able to state that a broken cow catcher and a splintered step were the injuries sustained by the company's valuable locomotive. And for this let us be truly grateful, as for other merciful favors.[15]

Immigrant lives also counted for little in labor camps, and many died in wrecks or construction accidents. Bosses paid scant attention to lost or missing workers unless they suspected that these men had returned to the city.[16]

Despite obviously undesirable characteristics, the labor boss performed a useful function: he brought together American capital and Italian immigrant labor. Most immigrants from the Kingdom

lacked education and money, but they offered strong arms, willingness to work, and ambition to earn as much money as possible.
Many who had no way of communicating with employers earnestly
desired manual labor. The padrone served them as well as the
employers, "who as a general rule would not themselves know how
to get Italian laborers in any numbers, and who would find it
impossible to proceed by picking up one man at a time." [17]

In addition to finding jobs, the boss provided workers with other
needed services. He collected wages, wrote letters, acted as banker,
supplied room and board, and handled dealings between workers
and employers. Unfortunately, too often he abused his trust. Yet
he could not be held solely responsible for the evils of the system.

According to United States Bureau of Labor investigator F. J.
Sheridan, American employers would "sell boarding privileges, ask
a bonus from the padrone for giving employment, refuse to pay
for overtime and the like." Railroad officials and contractors often
collaborated with the boss. In the 1890's, for example, padroni
deducted overcharges from payrolls without railroad interference.
Sheridan felt that "American employers have adopted padrone
methods, often on a large scale." [18] He might well have considered
whether Americans imitated padroni or whether labor bosses
adapted American practices to their own needs and circumstances.
When opportunities arose, American and Italian bosses alike took
full advantage of laborers.

The decade of the 1890's formed a "golden era" for the Italian
padrone. Of central importance, however, is the fact that Italian
immigration reached its peak in the fourteen years following the
turn of the century. It would seem that fortuitous opportunities
for unscrupulous labor agents would best present themselves at
this time, yet in 1911 the Dillingham Commission admitted that
the boss system could be found "only in a few isolated cases among
Italians." [19] What caused this rapid decline of bossism? No single
factor stands out, but several combined to bring about the waning
of the padrone system among Italians. These factors fell into two
general categories: actions originating outside the immigrant
group, and forces operating within it.

Writers in the American community—social workers and others concerned about the immigrant situation—favored the Italian colony as a whole while they deplored padrone evils and abuses. In articles and pamphlets, Americans agitated for action to break the power of labor bosses. Their writings appeared in such magazines as *Charities*, 1897–1905 (subsequently *Charities and the Commons*, 1905–9, and *Survey*, 1909–52), *Immigrant in America Review*, *American Journal of Sociology*, *Immigration*, *Forum*, and *Outlook*. Immigrant protective societies and leagues organized in New York and Chicago to attend to the interests of newcomers and their families, and to aid their adjustment to unfamiliar surroundings. Pressures from sources like these undoubtedly helped to pass legislation in New York State on April 27, 1904, and in Illinois on June 15, 1909, that sought to protect laborers from extortions and abuses practiced by many bosses.

The New York State law required that the boss who sent laborers out of the city in which he had hired them must file one copy of the work contract with the city mayor or the commissioner of licenses, and must give one copy to the workers. The contract had to contain the following information: "name and address of the employer; name and address of the employee; nature of the work to be performed, hours of labor, wages offered, destination of the persons employed, and terms of transportation." The Illinois law imposed slightly more stringent penalties for violations of its provisions than did the older New York statute. In Illinois the penalty was "not less than $50 or more than $200, or imprisonment . . . for a period of not more than one year, or both, at the discretion of the courts, in addition to revocation of such person's license." New York fines ran from $50 to $250, or imprisonment for one year, but made no provision for revoking licenses. These laws proved to be fairly effective in operation, particularly in New York. Even after the passing of the Illinois law, however, the Immigrants' Protective League complained of continued abuses.[20]

More rapid and beneficial results occurred from pressures applied to railroad and construction officials. Railroads began to terminate padrone services, replacing bosses with certified labor agents. This railroad action played a major part in the decline of the system in the years after 1900. In 1908 the Italian government's *Commissariato dell'Emigrazione* noted that until the railroads took action, "there was nothing to stop the padrone." To end abuses and satisfy public demands, companies placed railroad detectives dressed like workers along their lines in order to report actual conditions under which employees worked. Confronted with evidence of their wrongdoings, bosses received the alternatives of reform or dismissal. In addition, railroads encouraged nonpadrone agents to enter the field. In some cases, companies issued orders to foremen not to hire men through padroni.[21]

In contrast to actions of interested agencies and groups in the American community (almost all of which dated from the years after 1900), factors of a long-range nature operated within the immigrant colony. The large influx of Italians after 1890, partly stimulated by the work of earlier padroni, actually helped to reduce the need for the boss. As early as 1897 John Koren, writing in the United States Bureau of Labor *Bulletin,* found that the Italian immigrant had become more stable and settled, a condition indicated by the large numbers who came to the United States to join their immediate families or relations, and were "thus probably to a large extent put out of the reach of the padroni." This increased stability showed also in the growing numbers of newly arriving females. The following comparison of Italian and Greek adults in Chicago in 1904 reflects the fact that while Italian immigration after 1900 tended to be more permanent and settled, Greeks had just begun to enter the first, or padrone-oriented, stage:[22]

|  | MALES | FEMALES | TOTAL |
|---|---|---|---|
| Italians (born outside the U.S.) | 9,896 | 7,329 | 17,225 |
| Greeks (born outside the U.S.) | 1,751 | 258 | 2,009 |

The more stable nature of Italian newcomers, increased familiarity with American labor practices and the English language, and the resultant rise in economic status all helped to end the boss system among "Southerners." By the turn of the century, the Industrial Commission found that Italians worked not only at common labor on railroads and other construction and excavation jobs, but also at stone cutting, masonry, hod carrying and related occupations. Economic activities of "Southerners" had not, of course, been limited solely to padrone-controlled construction work even during the 1890's.[23]

In 1895–96 the United States Bureau of Labor conducted a study into "the social and economic condition of Italian families residing in the slum districts of Chicago." During the course of the survey, investigators obtained information from 6773 persons in 1348 families living in streets containing sizable Italian populations. Of the 1860 people who were asked whether they worked for a padrone, only 403, or 21.7 per cent, answered yes.[24]

A higher proportion of Italian workers in Chicago might have served under labor agents, but probably the total number never approached 50 per cent of the working force. Considering this point and the fact that the padrone system rapidly declined after 1900, the question arises whether bossism existed as extensively as Americans assumed. Nevertheless, the system continued to operate minimally among Italians after 1900. Ciolli's article about boss abuses in the Middle West appeared in 1917; and vestiges of the system remained in Chicago among older workers employed by railroads as late as the mid-1930's. Possibly these men felt unable to break loose from the clutches of the padrone; more likely they preferred the security of padrone employment.[25]

## III

Common laborers composed most of the newcomers from the "South." These men generally qualified only for unskilled labor in the United States. Many complained that lack of education prevented their attaining greater success in America, yet "Southerners" were notorious for inducing their children to leave school and find jobs. Contemporaries saw a shocking and serious problem in the tendency of many immigrants to put their children to work at the first opportunity. The reason, noted *L'Italia* in 1902, lay in the carry-over "on the part of Italian parents, especially those of the south of Italy, of an old country attitude." Although in time Italians complied with minimum requirements of compulsory education laws, they secured jobs for their children after school hours. American critics claimed that when Italian children reached the legal withdrawal age of fourteen, they were "to an alarmingly high degree withdrawn from school and put to work." [26]

Some parents preferred their children to attend parochial schools where they would receive religious training and learn to read and write Italian, a language not widely taught in public schools. Many of those immigrants who felt concern over the religious and language training of their children balked at paying the tuition required by private schools. As a result, in 1915 only 1937 children were enrolled in Italian-American parochial schools in Chicago, although more than 43,000 minors of Italian birth or extraction lived in the city. An Italian parent who believed that his children ought to contribute financially to the family's welfare would hardly look with favor on paying for the schooling acquired by his offspring, for this represented a double loss of money. Parochial schools were, however, often used by parents whose boys or girls were disciplinary problems. These children were withdrawn from public schools and sent to religious institutions in the hope that the Sisters would be more successful in controlling them.[27]

The problems of truancy and child labor involved more than a desire (spurred by necessity) to put all family members to work in order to survive the scramble for existence that characterized the slums. An additional factor, the cultural problem of adapting to new life patterns, resulted from movement from rural surroundings to an urban environment. An accommodation would have been necessary had the villagers migrated to a European city rather than across the Atlantic. In the United States, Americans of rural background as well as Italian and Slavic peasants experienced difficulty in adjusting to urban life.[28]

The conflict between immediate financial gain and long-range educational advantage was common to all newcomers who struggled to make the most of their new urban opportunities. Foreign-born children, including Italians, often left school at the first opportunity because of unpleasant classroom experiences. To a newly arrived immigrant child or a youngster whose family spoke English poorly or not at all, school could be a frightening world.[29]

Anthony Sorrentino, at present Delinquency Prevention Supervisor of the Illinois Youth Commission, suffered as a newcomer in school. Sorrentino arrived in Chicago's Near West Side Italian colony with his parents and older sister from Marsala, Sicily, at the age of six. In an unpublished autobiography he recalled his reaction to the public school in which he and his sister enrolled in 1919. "Most children from very poor homes, especially from immigrant families," he wrote, "are not adequately prepared for school—their first great experience outside the family." He, and others like him, lacked psychological preparation—"assurances, explanations, and introduction to some of the elementary tools of learning which children usually received from middle-class families." "Old world traits and foreign language" increased his difficulties, for although he attended school in an immigrant area, Sorrentino found that his "Italian lingo and Italian made clothes" set him apart from the other children, who ridiculed and derided him. "This feeling of being different, odd, and in the eyes of others, peculiar" contributed further to his growing feelings of inferiority and rejection. School itself increased his anxieties. The huge buildings, "the regimented appearance of the school atmosphere, the tall, rigid-looking teachers whose general countenance exhibited authority" combined to present an environment that was "strange and unfamiliar, and thus disturbing and disquieting."

Under such circumstances, work provided not only a source of income but also a means of gaining self-respect. His father's illness forced Sorrentino at the age of ten to work as a shoeshine boy. The four dollars a week that he earned contributed importantly to the family budget, especially after his father's death; even more valuable to the lad was the "sense of accomplishment at the end of the day" that the jingling coins in his pocket gave him. Many immigrant youngsters with experiences like Sorrentino's felt justified in absenting themselves from classes and in going to work at the first opportunity.[30]

In 1906 Gertrude Howe Britton, a Hull House resident, investigated violations of school attendance laws by Chicago's Italians and Slavs. Two faculty members of the University of Chicago School of Civics and Philanthropy, Edith Abbott and Sophonisba P. Breckinridge (both closely associated with Hull House), made a similar study, published in 1917. Both reports had as their objectives the passage of stricter and more comprehensive school attendance laws, and therefore both emphasized excessive violations. Chicago Public School Superintendent William L. Bodine expressed an opposite view in 1912. According to him, a "very small" number of immigrant children could be classed as truants and nonattenders. He believed that immigrant parents wanted "to have their children take advantage of our educational opportunities." [31]

State compulsory attendance laws required that children between the ages of fourteen and sixteen attend school or obtain a work certificate in order to hold a job. The Consumers' League of Illinois played a major role in forcing the state legislature to tighten procedures by which certificates were issued. Anna E. Nicholes of the League examined all work certificates granted in Chicago between July 1, 1903, and January 1, 1906. She found that foreign-born parents typically put their children to work at the first legally permitted opportunity; significantly, a larger number of American-born children of immigrants sought employment than did youngsters brought to this country. Native-born children, with their knowledge of the English language, found and kept jobs for which they could obtain work certificates—as office boys, clerks, errand boys, and the like. Foreign-born youth, on the other hand, with limited command of English, could qualify only for hard labor, for which they could not obtain certificates because of their age and growth levels. During the thirty months' period examined by Miss Nicholes, the state issued 30,643 certificates in Chicago.

Children of native American parents received 986; foreign-born children, 2841, and American-born children of foreign parents, 26,816.[32]

## Table 3

NATIONALITY OF WORKING CHILDREN IN CHICAGO,
JULY 1, 1903, TO JANUARY 1, 1906

| Country of Origin | American born of Foreign Parentage | Foreign born | Total |
|---|---|---|---|
| Germany | 8,404 | 553 | 8,957 |
| England | 3,761 | 200 | 3,961 |
| Bohemia | 3,608 | 323 | 3,931 |
| Ireland | 2,744 | 48 | 2,792 |
| Russia | 1,977 | 807 | 2,784 |
| Sweden | 2,304 | 161 | 2,465 |
| Italy | 800 | 345 | 1,145 |
| Poland | 1,025 | 110 | 1,135 |
| Holland | 620 | 98 | 718 |
| Norway | 598 | 63 | 661 |
| Denmark | 269 | 46 | 315 |
| France | 184 | 29 | 213 |
| Scotland | — | 43 | 43 |
| Greece | 28 | 12 | 40 |
| Turkey | 1 | 2 | 3 |
| Spain | 2 | — | 2 |

Source: Anna E. Nicholes, "From School to Work in Chicago. A Study of the Central Office that Grants Labor Certificates," *Charities and the Commons*, XVI (May 12, 1906), 232.

That Italians recognized the value of education showed in their attendance of adult education programs provided at settlement houses, the Young Men's Christian Association, and public schools. Italians followed Russians, Germans, and Poles in number of students making use of available facilities at Chicago's public evening elementary schools. (Jews were counted within nationality groups.)

For some newcomers, use of opportunities presented by adult-education classes reflected a delayed recognition of the values of

## Table 4

NATIONALITY OF STUDENTS IN CHICAGO EVENING ELEMENTARY
SCHOOLS, 1910–11

| Nationality | Foreign born | American born | Total |
| --- | --- | --- | --- |
| German | 1,736 | 880 | 2,616 |
| Russian | 2,265 | 235 | 2,500 |
| Polish | 1,845 | 514 | 2,359 |
| Italian | 1,675 | 235 | 1,910 |
| Bohemian | 1,236 | 331 | 1,567 |
| Swedish | 1,314 | 147 | 1,461 |
| Lithuanian | 640 | 52 | 692 |
| Austrian | 591 | 61 | 652 |
| Greek | 583 | 8 | 591 |
| Irish | 134 | 359 | 493 |
| Hungarian | 416 | 17 | 433 |
| Norwegian | 299 | 60 | 359 |
| Danish | 197 | 22 | 219 |
| Dutch | 197 | 21 | 218 |
| Others | 606 | 130 | 736 |

Source: City of Chicago, Board of Education, *Fifty-Seventh Annual Report of the Board of Education, for the Year Ending June 30, 1911* (Chicago, N.D.), 179.

education. Others compensated for the inadequate schooling forced upon them by economic necessity and other personal factors. Immigrants who arrived as uneducated adults found in American public schools a chance to make up for lack of training in their homeland. Chicago's Italian leaders considered public education to be a vital ingredient in the newcomers' adjustment process and took great pride in all educational interests and achievements of their compatriots and children. The Italian press lauded academic accomplishments of individual scholars. As early as March 23, 1889, *L'Italia* stated with satisfaction that evening schoolteachers spoke "with great enthusiasm of their Italian students because of their willingness to acknowledge that their education is very important to them." [33]

The high esteem given to education showed dramatically in the attitudes of newcomers who returned to Italy. Homeland Italians found concern over education and efforts to improve schools to be major distinguishing characteristics of those who had lived in the United States. In 1907 Protestant minister Antonio Mangano visited the "South" to determine the effects of emigration there. He wrote his observations and impressions in a series of articles for *Charities and the Commons*. In one, he described the impact of America on a small village, Toritto. "One good influence which America is exerting upon Italy can be seen plainly in . . . the awakening desire for an education." Earlier the illiteracy rate had reached perhaps 90 per cent. Few emigrants had been able to read or write. Of those who returned, however, many had learned "by dint of hard labor in night school," and their appreciation of learning meant that Toritto's schools became "filled with children." Through firsthand observation Edward A. Steiner also attempted to assess the impact of returned immigrants upon the homeland. He reported in 1909 that "public education in Italy has received an impetus directly traceable to the returned immigrant, who saw its value" in America. Former Hull House resident Victor Von Borosini wrote of returning Italians in 1912: "One lesson they all take home is the knowledge of how great a handicap is illiteracy in the struggle for existence." As a result "they favor strongly obligatory instruction for their children, and cooperate willingly to extend the system." [34]

For those who remained in the United States, increased interest in education made it possible for many to enter commercial, trade, or professional classes. Sociologist Robert Park noted in 1921 that along with immigrant community institutions, the public school ranked of vital importance in aiding the newcomer "to find his place and make his way in America." [35]


## IV

Italians in Chicago appeared to make little economic progress, at least in part because of a steady stream of new arrivals who settled in Italian quarters and started at the bottom of the economic pay scale. Many immigrants remained unskilled laborers through-out their lives and contributed to the city's economic growth through construction, maintenance, or factory work. Others became financially successful merchants, small manufacturers, professionals or businessmen, or qualified for jobs as skilled workmen. In 1919 a City Department of Welfare report observed, "The rapid rise of immigrant Italians in the business world of Chicago is one of the romances of our city commerce." [36]

Chicago Commons residents conducted a door-to-door survey in 1913–14 to determine both the type of business and industry existing in the Seventeenth Ward and the nationality of the owners. The investigation of ward business was not, however, complete, because it canvassed only those concerns located along "the principal business streets." In addition, the survey did not include saloons and taverns nor did it attempt to determine the number or nationality of professional men in the ward. Nevertheless, a breakdown of businesses by the nationality group of proprietors showed a significant number of Italians:

| | |
|---|---|
| Jewish | 221 |
| Italian | 161 |
| German | 124 |
| Polish | 114 |
| American | 67 |
| Norwegian, Danish, and Swedish | 50 |
| Others | 124 |

The 161 Italians included grocers, meat-market operators, barbers, shoemakers, bakers, blacksmiths, druggists, cigar-store owners, painters, fruit- and candy-store owners, coal and wood sellers, ice cream vendors, jewelers, tailors, realtors, and small factory owners.[37]

As early as 1895, Department of Labor investigators found "Southerners" employed as barbers, pavers, saloonkeepers, hod carriers, mosaic layers, shoemakers, fruit and vegetable peddlers, stonecutters, tailors, quarrymen, teamsters, and carpenters. This study, the most extensive and detailed examination made of Italian economic activities in Chicago, provided valuable information about financial conditions among slum dwellers, but those who succeeded in raising their economic and social status and who moved out of congested districts formed no part of it or of any other study. As a result, an incomplete picture of economic adjustment presented itself, even though without conscious intent. For example, Department of Labor investigators in the 1895–96 survey counted only six padroni; and not a single doctor, banker, or lawyer appeared in this or any published study of city Italians or in unpublished surveys like that conducted in the Seventeenth Ward in 1913–14.[38]

In the years before 1920, few Italians became wealthy by American standards. Those who accumulated money generally came of northern Italian families who had situated themselves in the city by the 1850's or 1860's and gradually acquired cash and land through legitimate business activities. Settled Italians quickly began to buy property. By 1900 numerous "Southerners" could be counted among the city's property owners. Generally their holdings were small—a single lot or portion of a lot—but some acquired several lots in various parts of the city. Earlier newcomers purchased extensive amounts of land and increased financial and property assets over the years. Frank Cuneo, for example, figured prominently as a real-estate developer. One of his many enterprises —the erection of a block of store buildings at Wilson Avenue and Sheridan Road in 1910—resulted in the formation of the Wilson Avenue business district, among the most successful on the city's North Side. Whether through legal or illegal means, "Southerners" attained more modest levels of financial achievement in the years before 1920 than did their northern compatriots. Prohibition rather than real estate provided opportunities for them, and especially for their children, to reach millionaire status.[39]

"Southerners" began to move into public employment soon after they arrived. City and related work included street cleaning, building and maintenance of public transportation and sewage systems, road building, and other patronage jobs. Private industry as well as public employment provided patronage opportunities for Chicago politicians. Reformer John Palmer Gavit, a Chicago Commons resident who gained intimate knowledge of local politics as head of the Seventeenth Ward Civic Federation's Municipal Committee, described the situation. "Not only the petty employments in saloons and even brothels have been at the disposal of the local dealers," he noted, but also "places for unskilled labor with street-railroad corporations and other public utilities needing the franchises and privileges in the public streets, have been utilized as the coincurrent of local political traffic." [40]

Such employment generally offered to unskilled laborers relatively steady income and job security, while to ethnic groups it gave convincing proof of the benefits of local politics. By the mid-1890's at least 126 Italians had jobs as street sweepers, while others worked as sewer diggers, asphalt helpers, road graders, lamp lighters (and, after the introduction of electricity, electric-light repairmen), garbage collectors, playground laborers, street repairmen, park laborers, and street or elevated-railroad employees. All of these positions were city jobs or private employment awarded to political worthies. After 1900 Italians moved into public employment in ever-increasing numbers even though city work (from 1895) came under Civil Service Commission control. In the years after the turn of the century hundreds of Italians found civil service jobs as laborers or supervisory personnel in the bureaus or departments of streets, playgrounds, electricity, parks, and engineering, and in the board of education.[41]

Italians joined the fire department at least as early as 1905, and the police force recruited three Italians before the turn of the century. In 1905 Joseph B. Casagrande began his career as a city fireman, and in the years prior to 1920, nine other Italians entered the force, including Joseph G. Raggio (1907), Frank J. Cafferata (1908) and Anthony Tossi (1910). An additional fourteen Italians joined between 1920 and 1930. Early Italian police officers included Charles P. Arado, appointed to the department in 1884; Peter Raggio (1887); and Edward E. Martini (1891). Between 1901 and 1920, another 27 entered the police department, seven of them by 1910. Italian policemen included Julian Bernacchi, appointed in

1906, and promoted to sergeant in 1921, lieutenant in 1924, and
captain in 1939; William Borelli, police surgeon from 1912 until
his retirement in 1943; Anthony Gentile, member of the force in
1911, promoted to sergeant eight years later and lieutenant in 1937;
Paul Riccio, new to the department in 1908, a sergeant in 1923
and lieutenant the following year; and Philip Parodi, a patrolman
from 1908 to 1921, sergeant until 1924, and then lieutenant. During
the transitional decade of the 1920's another 52 Italians joined the
force, including Ralph Catanese, born of Italian parents in São
Paulo, Brazil, who rose from patrolman in 1924 to sergeant in 1938,
lieutenant in 1946, and captain ten years later; Anthony De Grazio,
appointed in 1922, promoted to sergeant in 1933 and lieutenant in
1938; and Salvatore Corsi, born in London, England, who became
a policeman in 1929, and sergeant four years later.[42]

Italians worked as public-school employees, not only as maintenance personnel, but also as teachers. Over the years the number
of teachers slowly increased:[43]

| Year | Italian Male Teachers | Italian Female Teachers | Total |
|------|-----------------------|--------------------------|-------|
| 1898–99 | 1 | 10 | 11 |
| 1902–03 | 2 | 13 | 15 |
| 1909–10 | 2 | 14 | 16 |
| 1914–15 | 4 | 24 | 28 |
| 1920–21 | 9 | 33 | 42 |

Italians taught in all parts of the city, in high school and elementary
classrooms and in American as well as Italian districts. They
worked at Jenner, Dante, Jackson, and Jones Schools, which had
large Italian enrollments; and at Copernicus, Greeley, Motley, and
Yale schools, which, before 1921, had few Italian students, if any.[44]

The United States Immigration Commission greatly under-
counted the number of Italian teachers not only in Chicago (where
it recognized three), but in other cities as well. In New York City,
for example, the Commission noted 51 teaching Italians. The actual
numbers in 1905 and 1915 were:[45]

| Year | Italian Male Teachers | Italian Female Teachers | Total |
|------|------------------------|--------------------------|-------|
| 1905 | 39 | 164 | 203 |
| 1915 | 73 | 334 | 407 |

Significantly, women formed a large proportion of Italian instructors. While some of these women came from northern Italian backgrounds, probably most came from "Southern" families, especially after 1915. The stereotype of Italian womanhood chained to a job at home or in a factory must be modified to include the small but steadily increasing numbers who went into teaching and other middle-class occupations such as architecture. Some became successful in the business world. Chicago Department of Public Welfare investigator Frank O. Beck described one Italian immigrant woman who employed "a hundred or more people" and did business with "the largest and most successful business houses of the city." Another had "accumulated a quarter million dollars by a business" that she had "developed from its very beginnings" and that provided jobs for several hundred men and women.[46]

Most Italian working women, however, engaged in unskilled or semiskilled factory labor, generally as garment makers. Some found employment in candy, paper, or tobacco factories. Others worked at home making artificial flowers, knitting lace, or picking and cracking nuts. Whether at home or in a factory, they usually worked long hours under sweatshop conditions for low pay. They did not always accept these conditions without complaint.[47]

Alice Henry, former editor of the National Women's Trade Union League journal, *Life and Labor*, stated in 1915 that Italian women had begun to join labor unions. She based her conclusion at least in part on their active participation in the Hart Schaffner and Marx strike. Miss Henry pointed out that Italian girls seemed to be less active in unionizing than eastern European Jews, but she believed them to be more amenable to organization than Slavic women. "All expectations to the contrary," American girls proved to be the most resistant to unionizing, for "in the sewing-trades, and in some other trades, such as candymaking," they "accepted conditions, and allowed matters to drift from bad to worse." [48]

Italian men moved into organized labor somewhat earlier than the women. During the first years of immigration and before Italians learned American labor practices, they often acted as strikebreakers, to the annoyance of at least one writer, Neapolitan-born Oscar Durante, owner and editor of *L'Italia*. For fifty years he strove to help immigrants adjust to American standards, admonishing laborers that they had no right to accept "jobs made vacant by a strike of their fellow workers." [49]

After the turn of the century, new arrivals from the "South" continued to serve as scabs. In 1912 the conservative *L'Italia* enjoined Italians "for the sake of the Italian name and race, . . . not to be blind instruments in the hands of the enemies" of labor. Immigrants acted, in this case, as strikebreakers for the trunk and valise manufacturers. Three years later *La Parola dei Socialisti* voiced its disappointment over the presence of Italian scabs in the cigar makers' strike. Through these and similar activities, Italians gained a reputation which they did not fully deserve. As early as the 1880's and 1890's, Italians joined existing unions or organized new ones in the stone, garment, and building industries in the eastern section of the United States. In the following years they continued their union interests and activities there and in other parts of the country.[50]

When they had resided for a time in America, Italians from the "South" as well as those from the northern regions of the Kingdom joined their fellow workers (foreign born and American) in supporting the rights of labor. In Chicago, Italians helped organize unions or establish locals for various groups, among them garment workers, bakers, mosaic workers, sewer and tunnel laborers, pressmen, macaroni workers, cigar makers, hod carriers and building laborers, and barbers. Individual Italians joined unions of bricklayers and masons, carpenters, typographical workers, and other organizations composed predominantly of native Americans or of northern and western European immigrants.[51]

In addition to supplying rank-and-file support, Italians could be found as leaders of union locals in the city and even of the parent national organization. Joseph D'Andrea, for example, became vice-president of the International Hod Carriers' and Building Laborers' Union of America (now the International Hod Carriers', Building and Common Laborers' Union of America); Anzuino D. Marimpi-etri, one of the founders of the Amalgamated Clothing Workers of America, served as vice-president of that union.

The hod carriers' and building laborers' International organized in 1903 as a member union of the American Federation of Labor. Local 286 formed the same year in Chicago under Joseph D'An-drea's leadership. In addition to his work with the hod carriers' union, D'Andrea also acted as business agent of the Sewer and Tunnel Workers' Union and in 1910 stood as a candidate for the State Senate from Chicago. This bid for political office failed at least partly because the Italian-language press as well as the city newspapers revealed during the course of the campaign that "in 1902 D'Andrea killed a lame boot-black named Antonio Mezza, for which he narrowly missed serving a term in Joliet by pleading self-defense." This, along with strong hints of corruption in his labor-union activities and, perhaps more important, the presence of vigorous opposition during the campaign and election, marked the end of his political life. He continued, however, to function as a powerful force among Italians in Chicago's organized labor. His career reached its height in 1911 when he became third vice-president of the hod carriers' International.[52]

Early issues of the hod carriers' and building laborers' union publication, *The Official Journal,* appeared in Italian and German as well as English, reflecting the major language groups repre-sented among original members. Domenico D'Alessandro of Boston became its general president in 1908 and directed the organization during its early difficult years until his death in 1926, when Chicagoan Joseph V. Moreschi (like D'Alessandro, an Italian im-migrant) was elected president. Joseph D'Andrea, who, along with D'Alessandro helped to found the International, directed union activities in Chicago as well as serving as third vice-president of the parent organization from 1911 to 1914, when he was killed in

a Chicago labor dispute. Union control in Chicago then passed
into the hands of Joseph's brother, Anthony D'Andrea (who also
served as business agent of the Sewer and Tunnel Miners' Union)
until 1921, when he was murdered. Other Italians who emerged
as leaders in the International during the union's early years included N. R. Soletto, third vice-president (1909–11); A. Amodeo,
sixth vice-president (1909–11); Vincent De Falco, fifth vice-president (1911–38); and Alfonso D'Andrea (no relation to Joseph and
Anthony), third vice-president (1914–18).[53]

The union made extensive use of Italian field organizers to establish new Italian locals. In 1907 "for the benefit of the various Italian
locals" in the union, the Executive Board under the direction of
incoming president D'Alessandro provided for the employment at
the International office of an Italian "to correspond with the said
Locals in order to have no misunderstandings." Italians grew so
numerous and influential in the International that in 1909 the Sixth
General Convention passed a resolution requiring all motions to
"be put in English and Italian languages so that all delegates
present will understand them." Two years later when the union
met in convention at Scranton, Pennsylvania, Italians played a
dominant role. In addition to the general president, two vice-
presidents and the International's general organizer (Joseph Lucci),
Italians took part in a high proportion of all the International's
committees. At this conclave Chicago's Joseph D'Andrea occupied
positions on the Credentials Committee and the Committee on
Laws, and was unanimously elected third vice-president of the
International.[54]

Italians presented a unified front with other immigrant groups
in organizational and strike activities, as evidenced most clearly in
the Hart Schaffner and Marx strike (also called, more accurately,
the Chicago Garment Workers' Strike) of 1910. A principal reason
for the strike existed in the intolerable working conditions in
Chicago's clothing firms, including Hart Schaffner and Marx, L. B.
Kuppenheimer, L. Abt & Sons, and M. Born & Co. Workers also
bitterly resented the absolute and often tyrannical power wielded
by the foremen, and a system of fines by which loss of spools,

## Table 5

ETHNIC ORIGIN OF INTERNATIONAL HOD CARRIERS' AND
BUILDING LABORERS' UNION COMMITTEE MEMBERS,
SEVENTH GENERAL CONVENTION, SEPTEMBER 11 TO 14, 1911

| Committee | Total Committee Membership | Italians | Non-Italians |
|---|---|---|---|
| Credentials | 52 | 28 | 24 |
| Rules | 3 | 1 | 2 |
| President's Report | 3 | 2 | 1 |
| Secretary Treasurer's Report | 3 | 1 | 2 |
| Executive Council's Report | 3 | 2 | 1 |
| Resolutions | 5 | 3 | 2 |
| Organization | 5 | 3 | 2 |
| Laws | 5 | 4 | 1 |
| Grievances | 5 | 2 | 3 |
| Beneficiary Claims | 5 | 3 | 2 |
| Total | 89 | 49 | 40 |

Source: International Hod Carriers' and Building Laborers' Union of America, *Seventh General Convention, Held at Scranton, Pennsylvania, September 11 to 14, 1911, Report of Proceedings* (N.P., N.D.), 3–5.

bobbins, and needles, failure to punch the time clock, and worker carelessness on the job resulted in reduction of weekly wages. The immediate cause of the strike came from an industry-wide systematic reduction in the wages for piece work.[55]

Strike activities began on September 29 at Hart Schaffner and Marx Shop 21 (a pants shop) when a group of female employees, led by a Sicilian girl, left their jobs to protest a quarter-of-a-cent wage cut. The uprising spread rapidly, and within three weeks most of the firm's 7500 employees had joined the original group. Soon the greater part of the city's clothing workers (Jews, Italians, Poles, Bohemians, Lithuanians, and others—a total of nine nationalities, virtually all foreign born) had united in support of the work stoppage. A. D. Marimpietri described the hectic but exhilarating early days of the strike. "In sixteen halls in various parts of the city, the tailors met every day from early morning until late at night, listening to speakers and discussing among themselves the numerous complaints that had brought them together. In some of the halls the workers met in national or language groups: the Poles, the Bohemians, the Lithuanians, the Italians, the Jews. Such separate meetings were necessary," noted Marimpietri, because most of the workers "did not understand the English language." Those who did speak English "met by branches of the trade: cutters, coat makers, vest makers, pants makers." At the height of the strike an estimated 35,000 garment workers had stopped working. They rapidly won wide public sympathy as well as financial and moral support from the Chicago Federation of Labor, the United Garment Workers (A.F.L.), the Women's Trade Union League, and various socialist and anarchist groups, all of which attempted to influence the direction of the strike.[56]

The fifty firms affected by the strike retaliated with economic pressures, threatening employees with loss of jobs if they remained on strike and transferring work to shops in other cities. Local shops remained in operation, although far below peak capacity, with scab labor. While some Italians scabbed, the great majority supported the strike. During the course of the industrial struggle as many as 8000 Italians (almost all of them from the "South") joined their fellow workers in the union cause—a significant accomplishment considering their reputation as strikebreakers.[57]

Italians marched in picket lines, fought police and strikebreakers, and contributed money to the general welfare of union members. During the course of the strike they suffered severe beatings at the hands of city police officers and company-hired strikebreakers, and they replied in kind. Thus police arrested Joseph Franco and accused him of killing a nonunion driver working for one of the strike-bound tailoring houses. Police also accused Magdalena Debona of shooting a police officer. Workers contributed as much as they could afford to the strike fund but individual offerings were small. At a meeting held at Hull House's Bowen Hall in early December of 1910, for example, the Italian Socialist Women collected twenty dollars.[58]

Two committees coordinated and directed overall strike activities. One, the Strikers' Executive Board, functioned under the control of the United Garment Workers. The other, the Joint Conference Committee, received more publicity and enjoyed greater prestige because of its inclusion of representatives of the Chicago Federation of Labor, the Women's Trade Union League, the United Garment Workers, and the strikers themselves. Rivalry developed between the two committees in their struggle for public attention and control of the workers. Disagreements culminated in a declaration by the Strikers' Executive Board that the strike had officially ended. This statement, issued February 2, 1911, immediately elicited a bitter denunciation from the Joint Conference Committee through its president, John Fitzpatrick, who was also president of the Chicago Federation of Labor. The strike had lasted more than four months and cost the lives of two laborers. It had not failed, however, because an agreement reached with Hart Schaffner and Marx on January 14, 1911, provided for the creation of an arbitration board that included workers as well as employers. This agreement opened the door for additional concessions benefiting workers in following years.[59]

The strike of 1910–11 also furthered a sense of unity and a feeling of solidarity among union members. Each ethnic group, of course, considered its support to be the most dedicated, its contributions the most extensive and its sufferings the most intense. Effective leadership prevented ethnic rivalries from becoming a serious problem. Immigrant workers cooperated in large part because of efforts of organizers including, among Italians, Clara Massilotti (leader of the Italian girl garment strikers), Andrea Marotta (organizer of male workers), and a group of young radical leaders. Prominent among the radicals were Sidney Hillman and Italian-born Marimpietri (from Aquila in the "South"), who was also president of Coat Makers Local 39 and president of the Hart Schaffner and Marx Employees Joint Board.[60]

The new leaders soon rebelled against the United Garment Workers' Union and in 1914, in New York, formed a militant new organization, the Amalgamated Clothing Workers, with Hillman president and Marimpietri a vice-president. The new union pushed strike activities in Chicago. A protracted work stoppage in 1915 resulted in the union's recognition by Kuppenheimer, Meyer, and a number of small independent concerns. Workers gained also a 48-hour week, wage increases, paid vacations, and arbitration of labor-management disputes. Pressures exerted upon the city's clothing firms finally resulted in complete organization of the Chicago clothing market by 1919.[61]

The creation of an Italian local, the work of Italian organizers (among them William Rocco, Emilio Grandinetti, and Andrew Greco), and the encouragement of foreign-language periodicals gained and held Italian support. In addition to socialist and anarchist papers, elements of the bourgeois press sustained the union in its strike activities. In the 1915 work stoppage, for example, *L'Italia* appealed to Italian tailors to support the Amalgamated union and its Chicago strike. The paper even reported speeches made by socialist leaders Giuseppe Bertelli and Emilio Grandinetti. (Under the leadership of Luigi Antonini, Salvatore Ninfo, who became a vice-president in the International, and A. Baffa, Italians also entered the International Ladies' Garment Workers' Union and formed ethnic locals in New York City. Although a Polish local affiliated itself with the union's Chicago Joint Board, no strictly Italian locals of the I.L.G.W.U. existed in that city.)[62]

Socialists attempted to attract immigrant workers and organize them into radical groups. In the Hart Schaffner and Marx strike, for example, the *Chicago Daily Socialist* first recognized the developing work stoppage. Socialists then quickly entered the field, offering moral support and limited amounts of money in efforts to win the allegiance of strikers. Throughout the strike, however, control remained in the hands of moderate unionists. A number of socialist periodicals, among them *International Socialist Review* and *Solidarity*, condemned the *Chicago Daily Socialist* for its continued and unswerving support of "bourgeois unionism" and the January agreement with Hart Schaffner and Marx. In turn, the *Chicago Daily Socialist* reported with derision an effort by "a few Italians, led by old country syndicalists" who "attempted to cause a turmoil to prevent a vote" on the offer submitted by Hart Schaffner and Marx to the strikers (January 14, 1911). The paper reported with approbation that "others who believed in doing business in an orderly way" prevented syndicalists from realizing their objectives, for in a final vote two thirds of the strikers present approved the agreement. When the United Garment Workers of America Chicago district leaders brought a premature conclusion to the strike on February 2, 1911, their action received initial condemnation not from the socialist press, but from John Fitzpatrick and the Joint Conference Committee.[63]

In addition to its limited appeal to "Southern" garment workers, socialism won some support from northern Italians (mostly Tuscans) employed at the McCormick Works and at the Malleable Iron Company (called "Il Malabo" by Tuscans). Despite the miserable working and living conditions under which many newcomers existed, socialism enjoyed only a meager success among them. Membership in the Italian Socialist Federation reached one thousand by 1914, nine years after its founding, but never rose above that amount.[64]

Internal strains and stresses, caused by geographical, ideological, ethnic, and social-class divisions and conflicts, along with disputes with the more radical Industrial Workers of the World (or I.W.W.) over methods and objectives, prevented unified, coordinated actions. Thus in the Hart Schaffner and Marx strike, the I.W.W. made a strong effort in January, 1911, "to capture the strikers," in the words of the *Chicago Daily Socialist*. The paper's satisfaction over the I.W.W.'s failure no doubt kindled further antagonisms.[65]

Unyielding socialist opposition to the Italian war effort as well as to American entry in 1917 alienated many workers and brought down on the party the wrath of the American government and its agencies, particularly that of the Attorney General and the Post Office. Labor shortages during the war years benefited immigrant wage earners and made them less dependent on unionists and socialists for help in finding and keeping jobs with decent wages. In the postwar period, ideological quarrels continued to weaken radical activities, culminating in a split, with the left wing departing to help form the American Communist Party.[66]

To attract "Southerners," socialists and organized labor alike had to overcome immigrant indifference, inertia, and ignorance of the values and usefulness of organizing. While a number of northern Italian immigrants had previously experienced limited exposure to institutional activities (trade unions, mutual benefit groups, cultivators' associations, consumers' cooperatives, rural credit funds, and producers' cooperatives), and to the values and functions of strikes, these organizations and activities did not exist in the world of the Italian "South." In spite of their background, which emphasized individual effort rather than cooperative action, "Southerners" involved themselves extensively and significantly in Chicago's labor organizations. The absence of transplanted old-world traditions in the area of group action meant that the middle-class character of the labor movement in the United States determined in large part the character of activities in Chicago. This character, in turn, profoundly influenced the course taken by socialism in Chicago. Following the "Chicago tradition," an active socialist could be a hard-working trade unionist and a sincere social democrat at the same time.[67]

As they moved into organized labor, "Southerners" tended to be influenced by economic factors and grievances rather than philosophical considerations or intellectual panaceas. Thus the key factor in organization became (as historian Edwin Fenton pointed out) "bargaining power"—that is, some assurance that a union would achieve its stated objectives; an assurance that socialists could seldom guarantee. Where such prospects existed, Italian immigrants organized rapidly and effectively.[68]


## V

Thus, "Southerners" migrated to Chicago, as had Germans, Irishmen, and northern Italians before them, because they found there great economic opportunities. The Italian padrone system served useful purposes in helping to direct the flow of immigration from southern Italy into the United States, and in taking an intermediary role between Italian laborers and American contractors.

When contractors and immigrants no longer required padroni, the system faded away. Italian immigrants assimilated in spite of the boss, a point stressed in contemporary literature. Critics failed to note that Italians who worked for labor agents totaled a minority of the city's Italian laborers.

American emphasis on the boss system obscured four points. As "Southerners" adjusted to urban ideas, values, and methods, they grew to recognize the importance of education. In addition, they began to climb the economic scale. Although this trend did not make itself apparent for several years after their arrival in Chicago, the process began soon after settlement in the city, as was evident in the early entrance of Italians into business, the professions, and skilled and semiskilled employment. Third, at an early date newcomers began to take an active part in politics and to enter public employment. Finally, after 1900 Italians came to realize the benefits of organized labor and to join labor unions, while at the same time they rejected socialism and syndicalism. Thus by 1920—whether through legitimate business activities, criminal actions, or politics— Chicago's Italians had made substantial headway in an effective economic adjustment to urban America.

# 4

# Ethnic Group Politics

In the early 1890's, Italian traveler Giuseppe Giacosa visited the United States, including Chicago. He quickly recognized that "in America, he who does not vote does not 'get by.'" Oscar Durante, owner and editor of Chicago's *L'Italia,* constantly urged newcomers toward the realization that economic advancement came after naturalization and participation in politics rather than before. "It is generally easier to find a job when one is a citizen," he insisted, and enjoined all Italians "who wish to make their homes and raise their children in the United States" to become American citizens "as soon as possible, and the sooner the better." [1]

Durante indicated that newcomers could win respect from the native community by gaining a voice in the conduct of government through citizenship and political action. "Everyone is urged to become a citizen, because Italians will then have more power than they now have," he wrote, pointing to the Irishmen, Germans, and West Coast Italians. "In part because many have become American citizens," he noted, Italians living in Pacific coast states were "esteemed and respected" and their votes carried "a certain weight in the scales of public affairs." [2]

Politics served two important functions for Chicago's Italians.

First, it provided an invaluable source of income for many area residents. Through political connections businessmen successfully evaded bothersome city and state ordinances. Political advertisements offered sizable revenues to newspaper publishers. Patronage contributed substantially to the economic well-being of laborers in the colony, since the machine lavished political appointments, especially just before an election.

"Southerners" benefited from patronage jobs very early in the group's large-scale migration to Chicago. By January, 1894, they formed a sizable proportion of city employees, to the extent that the city hired Pasquale Villela as a full-time interpreter for Italian workers. One early Italian politician bitterly complained that "Southerners" got "the dollar-and-a-half-a-day 'jobs' of sweeping the streets" while Irish aldermen gave "the four-dollar-a-day 'jobs' of sitting in an office to Irishmen." Politicians supplied worthies with jobs not only as public employees, but also with private concerns holding city franchises or contracts, such as street railway companies and garbage collectors. In return for various favors granted, ward bosses expected recipients, along with relatives and friends, to support the machine and its candidates on election day.[3]

The second function of politics related to power and prestige. Even in Italian and other "new" immigrant wards, city politicians generally came from Irish backgrounds and found that they needed a contact man or intermediary between themselves and the ethnic masses. Thus the machine felt it expedient to employ as go-betweens men who spoke the language of the community and who knew customs, prejudices, and the best means of molding opinions and winning votes. Often these intermediaries first caught the boss's attention by organizing a segment of the colony, perhaps a benefit society or a group of fellow workers, and leading them to the polls to vote. Such leaders became small cogs in the ward machine; but they held power within the ethnic district because their recommendations meant patronage jobs for friends and lack of employment for enemies. For ambitious men, control of votes in the immigrant quarter could be turned to personal advantage,

either to obtain more important positions within the machine, or
to establish a competing organization. Winning elective office became a means of gaining esteem within the ward as well as a way
to win American recognition of Italian influence.

Heavy concentrations of Italians existed in only a few wards
located in the core area of Chicago. Italians were massed in
sufficient numbers to form most of the voters in some precincts in
the First, Seventeenth, Nineteenth, Twentieth, and Twenty-third
wards (after 1910 the Twenty-third became the Twenty-second).
Only in the Nineteenth Ward did Italians exceed 80 per cent of a
precinct total. Even there this unusually high proportion occurred
in but four or five precincts and only after 1910, when Italians
made up more than one half of the ward's total voting population.
In no other city ward did Italians constitute a majority of registered
voters.

Italian population and registered-voter concentration often coincided, but not invariably. In 1898, for example, Italians living
in Precinct Eighteen of Ward Nineteen made up 77 per cent of the
total population and 80 per cent of the total registered voters; in
Precinct Fifteen of Ward One they comprised only 26 per cent of
the total population and 58 per cent of the precinct voters. In the
Nineteenth Ward's Precinct Eighteen, therefore, four of every ten
Italians registered to vote; in the First Ward's Precinct Fifteen, fully
nine tenths of the Italian residents appeared on official registration
lists. The principal reason for this significant difference stemmed
from the composition of the two areas. The Nineteenth Ward precinct contained a large proportion of women and children, while
Precinct Fifteen of the First Ward was composed almost entirely of
adult males (nearly all foreign born) engaged in city employment,
generally as street sweepers.[4]

In sharp contrast to Precinct Fifteen of the First Ward, where
226 Italians lived (in a total population of 885), the Twenty-third
Ward's Precinct Twenty-five had 1975 residents, 64 per cent (or
1267) Italian. In this precinct, which formed the heart of Chicago's
oldest Italian colony, fewer than one immigrant in ten registered,
so that the "Italian vote" equaled 37 per cent of the total registered

vote of 252. Precinct Twenty-five contained a sizable number of women and children, and most of its inhabitants came from northern Italy, unlike the high voter registration precincts found elsewhere in the city (and especially in the First and Nineteenth Wards) where high proportions of "Southerners" lived. Italian precincts discussed in this chapter, therefore, are those which—through personal examination of precinct maps and voting lists—the author found to have a heavy concentration of Italian registered voters in the year and election under consideration.

Every ten years or so (1876, 1890, 1900, 1910, 1912, 1923) the city council redrew ward lines, while precinct lines changed more often. In central city wards, precinct lines shifted frequently as political bosses maneuvered to keep various ethnic groups under control. Techniques and objectives varied from election to election and from ward to ward. Sometimes bosses separated members of nationality groups by dividing them among several precincts; on other occasions they "packed" precincts with as many members of the group as possible. The number of precincts also fluctuated. Thus the Nineteenth Ward had 29 precincts in 1896; the following year voters were redistributed among 33 precincts, although ward lines remained the same. It is important to note that not only did precinct and ward lines shift over the years, but also the composition of the voting group itself altered drastically. The turnover of registered voters in Italian precincts formed an extensive and continuous movement.[5]

Newspaper editors and other middle-class Italians, like their counterparts in the wider community, seemed unable to recognize or accept the realities of core-area and ethnic group politics in Chicago. Reflecting their orientation, they viewed politics as a struggle between good and evil, and this outlook formed a basic factor in their lack of achievement in the political arena. To inner-city immigrants, politics represented a means of obtaining jobs or neighborhood facilities (like bathhouses). Machine politicians recognized these expectations and adjusted their actions accordingly.

In his nearly forty years as boss of Chicago's Nineteenth Ward, John Powers (known to his Italian constituents as Johnny De Pow

and Gianni Pauli) proved himself a practitioner par excellence
of all political expedients. The major concern of Powers and other
core-area bosses consisted of retaining political power by winning
elections in center-city wards, where the ethnic composition was
undergoing rapid and extensive changes from Irish, German, and
Scandinavian residents to Italian, eastern European Jewish, and
Slavic groups. Methods that seemed corrupt to reform-minded
residents eased achievement of the boss's goal. Political corruption
proved to be a general urban problem; politics is based, and
politicians exist, on "service." Bargains, compromises, connections,
patronage, and favors were and are essential ingredients of practical politics. In themselves they are not necessarily corrupt, but
they are easily misused. Ward politicians found jobs and did
favors for constituents, obtained franchises for companies, and
reimbursed themselves at public expense (so-called "boodle").
Politicians also made widespread use of wholesale issue and sale
of fraudulent naturalization certificates, often trouping newly arrived immigrants before compliant judges. This situation was not
unique to Chicago. "It was common knowledge that these frauds
were prevalent wherever there were large numbers of foreign-
born people and that both of the great political parties vied with
each other in exhausting ingenuity to devise methods for the exploitation of the alien population. Which party excelled in the
business depended almost entirely upon which was dominant in
any particular community." In addition, through means of criminal
elements in their wards, bosses used intimidation, violence, and
trickery to prevent the rise of rivals from new ethnic groups who
might threaten their own positions.[6]

## II

To social worker and reformer Jane Addams of Hull House, John
Powers represented the forces of evil and corruption that prevented essential reforms. In an effort to remove this cancer from
the ward, Miss Addams battled the Irish boss in three highly

publicized aldermanic campaigns in the 1890's. Italian leaders saw Powers as an insurmountable obstacle barring the election of Italian candidates and making impossible control of a ward that contained the largest Italian group in the city. It appears that Powers' hold over the ward could have been broken in the years prior to his retirement in 1927 had reform elements and the Italian community worked together to effect his defeat.[7]

Powers owned and operated a grocery store after serving an apprenticeship as a grocery clerk. Later, consciously aiming toward a career in politics, he went into the saloon business, although he himself never drank, and opened a gambling establishment, although he did not gamble. He acquired a saloon at 243 South Canal Street and with Alderman (until 1890) "Billy" O'Brien became associate owner of another at 170 East Madison Street. In 1888, when he was forty-two years old, Powers won his first election as Alderman for the Nineteenth Ward, then heavily Irish in composition. In the City Council he became a disciple of Alderman "Billy" Whalen of the First Ward and after that master boodler's accidental death in 1890, Powers established himself as Whalen's successor. In the following years the Nineteenth Ward politician emerged (according to the Municipal Voters' League) as the "recognized leader of [the] worst element in the Council" —the so-called "Gray Wolves."

Powers reveled in the title "Prince of Boodlers" and worked diligently to retain it along with the monetary benefits that derived from his activities in winning Council support for a succession of boodling schemes. Among the measures Powers personally introduced and championed (and for which the companies concerned rewarded him financially) were the granting of franchises to the North Chicago Electric Railway, Union Elevated Railway, Chicago Economic Fuel Gas, Chicago and Jefferson Urban Transit, West Chicago Street Railway, Ogden Gas, Chicago General Electric, and Union Consolidated Elevated. Traction "czar" Charles Tyson Yerkes provided the economic drive behind the Prince of Boodlers in most of these ventures. Powers' influence came from his position in the Council and the county Democratic organization. In the

City Council he headed the Finance Committee and was a member of several other committees, including Judiciary, State Legislature and Rule, Buildings and City Hall, and Water. He controlled county Democrats until after the turn of the century through his position as chairman of the Cook County Democratic Committee.[8]

Powers' base of support lay in the Nineteenth Ward, where he resided, attended church, and operated a saloon. Jane Addams, who challenged his control over the ward, found that he remained in power because he provided services that residents needed but could obtain nowhere else; in addition, by the community's rating system, Powers stood as a respected and friendly man. "The successful candidate must be a good man according to the standards of his constituents," Miss Addams discovered. "He must not attempt to hold up a morality beyond them, nor must he attempt to reform or change the standard. If he believes what they believe, and does what they are all cherishing a secret ambition to do, he will dazzle them with his success and win their confidence." Such a man will also win their votes.[9]

More practical aspects of the Alderman's control related to the favors he performed for voters and potential voters. "An Italian laborer," decided Miss Addams after her unsuccessful campaigns against Powers, "wants a 'job' more than anything else, and quite simply votes for the man who promises him one." Powers used his prominence in city politics and his influence with businessmen to procure employment for his constituents. Grace Abbott, director of the Immigrants' Protective League, indicated an example of the boss's method of obtaining jobs for ward residents, and their resultant sense of responsibility to him. In a book published in 1917 Miss Abbott quoted from a letter written by John Powers for an Italian resident of the Nineteenth Ward: " 'This is a neighbor and a friend of mine. Please give him work.' " She lamented that "long after the man has passed from the group of laborers who are dependent upon casual and irregular work and has become the prosperous owner of a grocery store, he will remember his 'neighbor and friend' and be glad to do for him any small favor that he can." The "favor," of course, was a vote for Powers or some member of his machine on election day "and in his gratitude the Italian will in all probability vote against his own and the city's interest." [10]

At one time Powers boasted that his ward had 2600 people of various nationalities on the public payroll. This total included day laborers, but each felt indebted to the man who had provided the work. The number reflected approximately one third of the entire voting strength of the ward in 1898, a rather considerable nucleus on which to build a voting majority. Of the 50,000 residents of the ward, only about 9000 were registered to vote. Because of the high degree of residential mobility in ethnic colonies as well as the difficulties involved in maintaining control over voters who felt under no obligation to the machine, politicians made little effort to register all qualified precinct residents. They concentrated on those who appeared to be amenable to voting the "right" way. This element included politically ambitious inhabitants, local merchants and businessmen (who benefited from political favor in being permitted to ignore or bypass restrictive ordinances), and patronage jobholders.[11]

Besides jobs, Powers provided numerous other services and favors for his constituents. He furnished bond for ward residents charged with crimes; obtained exemptions from city ordinances for community businessmen; distributed turkeys at Christmas; gave presents at weddings and christenings; sponsored ward dances, parades and picnics; supported church bazaars and other functions staged by local churches; and attended funerals—indeed, it was said that he made an appearance at every wake in his ward. He became so adept in his use of funerals for political purposes that he won another nickname, "The Mourner." By arranging for funeral services for the poorest of his constituents he gained admiration and respect for saving "his" people from "that awful horror of burial by the county." In exchange for his many services, Powers asked from his followers (in the words of Miss Addams) "a sense of loyalty, a standing-by the man who is good to you, who understands you, and who gets you out of trouble." The

Prince of Boodlers knew the value of publicity and saw to it that his virtues received widespread attention. An official party publication, *Illinois Democracy*, praised Powers' character in 1899 and proclaimed the boss's concern for his constituents. "His generosity is proverbial. The poor of his Ward have in him not only an official representative, but a personal friend." [12]

The publication failed to note that Powers did not effectively preside over all aspects of ward residents' welfare. He had no aversion to encouraging force and fraud during elections, and used pliable Italian candidates in order to divide opposition within the colony. He also utilized promises of political office to buy his opposition. Hull House investigators found public schools badly overcrowded, with 3000 more school children in the ward than seats available for them. Dirt, garbage, and other refuse filled streets and alleys, making a serious health hazard for inhabitants. The area badly needed parks and bathhouses. Hull House women realized the community's desperate plight and determined to improve the situation, in the obvious absence of Boss Powers' intention of doing so. They quickly found themselves blocked from taking effective action by the boss, who benefited from keeping things as they were. When reformers compared notes, they discovered that similar situations existed in other core areas of the city.[13]

In 1896 a reform group, the Municipal Voters' League, formed to combat John Powers and his fellow Gray Wolves and to defeat them at the polls. According to the League's *Minute Book* the organization intended to promote the "nomination and election of aggressively honest and capable men to public office, to investigate and publish for the information of voters, the records of candidates for office, to secure the separation of the municipal business of Chicago and Cook County from national politics, and to aid in the strict enforcement of the civil service laws." In the following years the League managed to restrict severely, although not to eliminate, opportunities for boodling through its introduction of expert administrators and better administrative techniques,

including accounting methods, into Chicago's city government.
By publicizing corrupt practices the League played an important
role in the election of more honest aldermen. The surviving Gray
Wolves, however, consisted of the most powerful bosses, among
them "Hinky Dink" Kenna and "Bathhouse John" Coughlin of the
First Ward, and Powers of the Nineteenth.[14]

Other reform elements within the ward sought to curb or destroy
the power of the Prince of Boodlers. In 1895, the year before the
founding of the Municipal Voters' League, Jane Addams and her
Hull House workers embarked upon the first of three attempts
to challenge Powers' control. The Hull House Men's Club selected
a member, Frank Lawler, to run as an Independent against the
incumbent alderman, a Powers follower (Powers' aldermanic seat
came up for election the following year). Two other candidates
also sought the position. Lawler won the election by more than
200 votes over his nearest rival. According to Miss Addams, his
victory came about solely because Powers "was apparently only
amused at our 'Sunday School' effort and did little to oppose" Hull
House. In any case, once Lawler took office he quickly succumbed
to Powers' inducements. Reformers realized that reform would not
come about with the defeat of Powers' henchmen; they had to
overcome the boss himself.[15]

An effort the following year to outpoll Powers "encountered the
most determined and skillful opposition" and ended in failure
when he retained his aldermanic seat, winning over reformer-rival
William J. Gleeson by a vote of 4064 to 2703. Gleeson won in five
precincts and Powers in 24, including the ward's only heavily
Italian precincts, the Eleventh (66 per cent Italian) and Thirteenth
(64 per cent). Although Powers received a large vote in both
Italian precincts, his opponent did also. In fact, precincts Eleven
and Thirteen awarded Gleeson the largest vote totals that he obtained in the election: 182 (to Powers' 205) in the Eleventh, and
197 (to 230) in the Thirteenth. Even though Johnny De Pow
carried both precincts, it was clear that large numbers of Italians
felt free to vote for an attractive rival. Miss Addams determined

to continue the struggle and prepared for the grand confrontation
to take place two years later, in 1898, when Powers would seek
reelection.[16]

In 1898 a number of new organizations joined Hull House in
opposition to the Prince of Boodlers. These organizations had
been created to mobilize the various ethnic groups in the ward
(twenty different nationalities) against Johnny De Pow. Italian-
language newspapers and Italian reform elements united in support of Simeon S. Armstrong, chosen by Miss Addams and her
forces to oppose the boss.[17]

*L'Italia* vigorously opposed Powers and called upon all "good"
Italians to repudiate him. Durante's campaign began with the
January twenty-second issue and continued until the election
(April 5), constantly emphasizing the politician's broken promises
and insults to Italian residents of the ward. The first article demanded to know the location of the "beautiful school" promised
by Powers to his constituents. Along with emotional appeals to
ethnic pride went demands that Powers and his fellow boodlers
be replaced by reformers in order to inject ideas and methods of
good government into ward and city affairs. Sarcastically, Durante
described the Nineteenth Ward machine's techniques as "a fine
school for the younger generation. What commendable examples
of citizenship are presented to our sons by these 'grand gentle-
men.'" A week later, January 29, he called upon Italians to elect
an honest candidate. Nationality, he advised, "is not important, it
is enough that he be an honorable man who will protect the interests of the laboring man." *L'Italia* felt that Armstrong, an Irish
Catholic, qualified for the Italian vote.

On February 9 and in subsequent issues the paper printed
Powers' boast: "*I can buy the Italian vote with a glass of beer
and a compliment.*" On March 12 *L'Italia* quoted Powers again:
"It is known that two years ago I bought the Italian vote for fifty
cents each, well this year I will buy it for twenty-five cents each."
The last issue before the election appeared on April 2 and reprinted both "base insults against the Italians" as well as calling

upon "all Italian voters! Republicans! Democrats! Independents!" to cooperate in ousting Powers by voting for Armstrong.

A new paper joined *L'Italia*'s efforts to mobilize the Italian vote against Johnny De Pow. *La Tribuna Italiana* (later renamed *La Tribuna Italiana Transatlantica*) was launched as a campaign organ for the sole purpose of weakening Powers' hold over the ward's Italian voters. Italian-born publisher and editor Alessandro Mastro-Valerio resided at Hull House and fervently supported Jane Addams and the cause of urban reform. In reporting the birth of the new journal the *Chicago Tribune* expressed the hope that "the alderman will find his following among the Italians limited to those who have been favored with positions in the distribution of patronage." Election results showed that this hope had some promise of eventual fulfillment, although the ward boss won over Armstrong by a vote of 5411 to 2227. Powers lost only one of 33 precincts, the Seventeenth, which contained the highest concentration of Italian voters in the entire ward. In this precinct, Italians (by birth or parentage) accounted for 85 per cent of the registered voters, or 438 out of a total of 513. Armstrong received 154 of the 281 votes cast in the precinct, and Powers the other 127. Significantly, in only four precincts besides the Seventeenth did Armstrong receive 100 votes or more, and three had heavy Italian concentrations: the Sixteenth, which gave him 123 votes; the Eighteenth, 116 votes; the Nineteenth, 104 votes; while the other, which gave the reform candidate 100 votes, contained Hull House (this was the Twentieth Precinct).[18]

In the words of Oscar Durante, the election of 1898 equaled a declaration of war against Gianni Pauli on the part of Nineteenth Ward Italians. More than any other ethnic group they resisted Powers' blandishments and supported Jane Addams and her reform candidate as well as the appeals of Italian-language newspapers. Beginning in 1898 and continuing to 1925, *La Tribuna Italiana Transatlantica, L'Italia, La Parola dei Socialisti,* and other Italian-language journals of Chicago worked to bring about Powers' defeat. Unfortunately for the political hopes of the Italian element and the cause of reform within the ward, contemporaries, including Miss Addams, did not recognize this trend.[19]

After her disheartening failure to dethrone Powers, Jane Addams faced a decision as to her future course of political activity. Fellow Hull House reformer Florence Kelley maintained that the settlement group "entered the campaign in 1896 and 1898 to make its protest on behalf of municipal honesty; and from that task it cannot turn back." From the point of view of the ward's Italian voters

### Table 6

ITALIAN POPULATION AND REGISTERED VOTERS IN FIVE
NINETEENTH-WARD PRECINCTS, 1898

| | Population[a] | | | Registered Voters[b] | | |
|---|---|---|---|---|---|---|
| Precinct | Total Population | Italian Population | Percentage of Italians | Total | Italian Voters | Percentage of Italians |
| 16 | 1889 | 1156 | 61 | 490 | 356 | 73 |
| 17 | 1863 | 1464 | 78 | 513 | 438 | 85 |
| 18 | 1580 | 1212 | 77 | 609 | 486 | 80 |
| 19 | 1860 | 909 | 48 | 374 | 170 | 45 |
| 20 | 1776 | 441 | 25 | 432 | 70 | 16 |

[a] "School Census of 1898," City of Chicago, Board of Education, *Proceedings, July 13, 1898, to June 28, 1899* (Chicago, 1899), 188.
[b] City of Chicago, Board of Election Commissioners, *Official Precinct Voter Registration Lists*, April 1898.
(For the location of these precincts, see p. 32, Map 5.)

(who increased rapidly in numbers over the years—before 1920 they constituted a majority) Hull House should have followed Florence Kelley's line of reasoning. Miss Addams, however, decided after the 1898 debacle that John Powers had correctly proclaimed, "I am what my people like, and neither Hull House nor all the reformers in town can turn them against me." In the following years she turned away from the sordid and vicious arena of ward politics to seek her objectives at city and state levels, and eventually at the national level (during the presidential election of 1912). The Prince of Boodlers remained indisputably in control of the Nineteenth Ward.[20]

## III

With his dominance over the ward assured, Powers decided in 1904 to move on to bigger and better things, perhaps to become a force in state affairs. He ran for, and won, a seat in the State Senate from the Seventeenth Senatorial District, which included the Nineteenth Ward. He served there only until 1905, when he returned to reclaim his seat in City Council. Powers had discovered as a first-term legislator that he lacked the influence, prestige, and authority that he had enjoyed as a long-time member of City Hall. Furthermore, in Springfield, the state capital, he lived far from his base of support and sources of patronage. He realized quickly that he must remain in the ward within touch of the electorate, because the area was in a state of flux with the composition of the population changing rapidly. In addition, his ward "overseer," Alderman Patrick Morris, was (in the words of the Municipal Voters' League) "a stupid, incompetent understudy." [21]

Indicative of the depths of ineptitude to which the once-powerful ward machine had sunk was the fact that Powers won election to the City Council in 1905 with a minority of the total votes cast. Only a division of the majority vote among four other candidates permitted his victory:

| Name | Political Party | Total Votes |
|------|----------------|-------------|
| John Powers | Democratic | 3657 |
| Simon O'Donnell | Independent | 3238 |
| Julius C. Bressler | Republican | 1110 |
| Morris Kaplan | Socialist | 440 |
| John McMurray | Prohibitionist | 36 |

Powers won more than his old seat in the Council; he triumphed over reform elements, whose premature retirement from the struggle allowed the weakened Democratic machine to creak to victory. Once again in control, Johnny De Pow quickly revitalized his organization. James Bowler, a shrewd and able politician in his

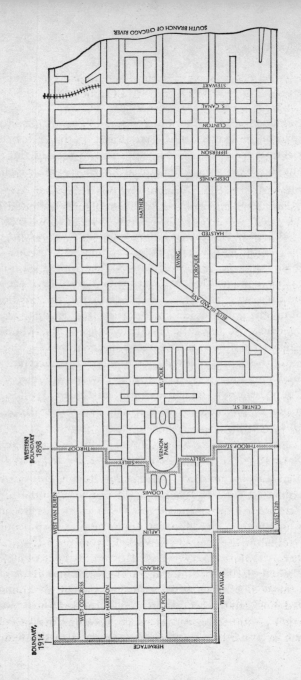

8. Nineteenth Ward Boundaries in 1898 and 1914

Based on Ward Maps prepared by the Board of Election Commissioners of the City of Chicago for the years indicated.

own right, emerged as Powers' second-in-command and, in 1906, joined the Prince of Boodlers in the City Council.[22]

During the period between 1888, when Powers won his first aldermanic election, and 1925, when he ran for that office for the last time, the ward's ethnic composition altered radically. In 1898, when Miss Addams last opposed the ward boss, for example, Irish residents made up the largest ethnic group, first and second generations numbering 15,842. Germans comprised another 6417 residents, Russians 4698, and Poles 2087 (these figures included large numbers of Jews, not counted separately). Italians, who formed the largest single group in the ward in later years, totaled 7722 in 1898. By 1914 first- and second-generation Italian residents exceeded 27,000; the Russian community reached almost 14,000; Greeks, who had totaled only 476 in 1898, numbered 1881. By 1914 only 2973 Irishmen and 1542 Germans remained in the ward. The ward's total population actually increased during the decades between 1898 and 1914 (from 52,166 to 59,224), but only because the geographical area of the Nineteenth increased by nearly one third. Despite this expansion in territory, the ranks of the older elements dwindled as successful Germans and Irishmen moved from the ward toward peripheral regions of the city and even into the suburbs. Adjusting members of newer immigrant groups followed their predecessors at the first opportunity.[23]

Ever a shrewd and practical politician, Powers adjusted his techniques to the ward's changing composition. From outward manifestations of contempt and disdain for Italians, he moved to a friendly show of concern for the plight of poor "Southern" residents and an appearance of readiness, even eagerness, to accept politically aspiring Italians into his organization. As the number of Italian voters in the ward increased, Powers used them as replacements for Irish precinct workers. He and his lieutenant James Bowler watched alertly for forceful, ruthless and ambitious young men who might otherwise provide the nucleus of an opposition to the ward boss; the organization quickly added these men to lower echelon positions. Important posts, including the key offices of alderman and ward committeeman, remained in the hands of

Powers or fellow Irishmen. Ethnic antagonisms inevitably developed. Community leaders and the Italian press fanned group resentments by demanding Italian political control over the ward and the defeat of Powers and his Irish henchmen, particularly Bowler.

In its attacks the Italian press combined resentment over presumed and real insults toward Italians, demands for the election of Italians to political office, dissatisfaction with ward services, and middle-class concern over the corrupt nature of Powers' rule. Thus on May 25, 1901, *L'Italia* reported a meeting of concerned residents who bitterly protested the "indecent manner with which, under the 'reign' of Johnny Powers, the streets of that ward have been maintained." Community businessmen saw the "broken up and dirty" streets as a particularly serious problem that retarded "the commercial, industrial, and economic growth of the ward." Durante added the personal observation that the Alderman "pretends to represent and protect the interests of the citizens of the Nineteenth Ward, but in reality he does not."

*La Tribuna Italiana Transatlantica* noted on February 18, 1905, that "the ill-famed Senator, Gianni Pauli, a local Irish politician, and boss of the Nineteenth Ward, has asked to be elected alderman of the said ward, because he does not find any substantial profit in being a senator." His reason, the paper maintained, was that "this year the City of Chicago must give the franchise to the Street Car Company and Mr. Gianni Pauli likes to have his hands in the pockets of the company." The journal described as "disgraceful" the creation of a political club among Italians of the ward to whip up support for Powers' candidacy. In a statement that clearly presented the paper's middle-class orientation, *La Tribuna* characterized Powers as "corrupted and without any semblance of civic education"—an argument with little meaning for job-hungry and uneducated laborers. An additional statement, "Pauli is an insulter of our people," probably had greater impact among many Italian residents of the ward.

Despite the tremendous advantages that Powers enjoyed through his business contacts, his connections with city, county, and state

political leaders, his lavish use of patronage, and his readiness
to use force when necessary, Italians in his ward not only opposed
the Prince of Boodlers in 1898 but continued in the years thereafter to challenge his control over the Nineteenth Ward. By the
time Italians began to realize the potential strength their increasing
numbers offered them, Powers' position had become almost in-
vulnerable, particularly in the absence of a well-known and widely
respected local reform leader after Jane Addams left the field. In
this situation an effective challenge could come only from a man
as adept as Powers in techniques of Chicago-style politics; a man
as cynical, vicious, corrupt, pragmatic, and well connected with
criminal elements in the ward. Such a man existed, and contested
ward control with Johnny De Pow in a long and bitter duel.

Unfrocked priest, red-light district luminary, and convicted
counterfeiter in the years prior to 1910, Anthony D'Andrea in
the following decade headed the Italian revolt against the Irish
ward bosses. He steadily built a solid base of support through his
positions as business agent for the Sewer and Tunnel Miners'
Union, president of the Hod Carriers' and Laborers' local organization, and president of the *Unione Siciliana.* These labor unions
and the *Unione,* the largest and most influential Italian fraternal
group in the city, provided D'Andrea a ready nucleus of voting
strength when he began to test Powers' control over the ward.[24]

In the 1915 Democratic Party mayoralty primary differences
between the two powerful and self-willed men first came into
public view. Powers supported Carter H. Harrison while D'Andrea
backed Robert M. Sweitzer for the party nomination. D'Andrea's
man carried the Nineteenth Ward. Lavish use (or misuse) of
patronage papered over the difficulties between the Irish and
Italian bosses. In the following years the Prince of Boodlers appeared to be as strong and unbeatable as ever. Powers recognized,
however, that the ever-increasing Italian vote showed definite signs
of slipping out of his grasp, and that the situation called for drastic
and unprecedented action. In exchange for D'Andrea's support of
James Bowler's candidacy in the February 24, 1920, aldermanic
election, Powers offered his rival a political plum—the position

of Democratic Ward Committeeman, which Powers had held for years. This move equaled an open admission of D'Andrea's strength, because the prime source of patronage in the ward resided with the Committeeman. D'Andrea ran unopposed for the office in the April 13 primary and received a total of 966 votes. On June 16, 1920, only two months after the election, the Supreme Court of Illinois declared the results void and the 1919 Primary Law (under which the election had been held) invalid. D'Andrea, of course, lost his position and prestige, and Powers regained his old post. (The Republican ward leader, Christopher Mamer, also remained Republican Ward Committeeman, although "Diamond Joe" Esposito won the April 13 election by a vote of 1410 to 900.) The political truce no longer existed and D'Andrea moved immediately to challenge Powers personally in the aldermanic election—to be a nonpartisan contest—on February 22, 1921. Evidently both sides concluded that the election was crucial and acted on the assumption that the battle would be violent, with no quarter asked and none given.[25]

By 1921 the Italian vote predominated in the Nineteenth Ward, and an Italian candidate stood for office who had mastered the practical and none-too-subtle method of mobilizing and directing that vote. The Irish politicians in control of the Democratic ward machine recognized these two facts and felt justifiably worried. During the campaign, Italian residents received a barrage of literature from the Nineteenth Ward Non-Partisan Organization (actually part of the D'Andrea machine) headed by Dr. Gaetano Ronga and other leaders of the Italian colony. One letter, dated February 1, 1921, emphasized the incumbent alderman's inability to provide for basic needs. It pointed to the ward's inferior streetcar service, lack of street lights, unsanitary housing conditions, inadequate schools, and nonexistent playground equipment and facilities. The missive also decried Powers' relationships with criminals and his activities designed to thwart justice by providing bail for accused men. Furthermore, declared the letter, Alderman Powers no longer resided in the ward at 1284 Macalister Place, although he used this as his voting address, but in the Third

Ward at 4500 South Michigan Avenue. The letter claimed that Powers' wife had registered to vote using the Michigan Avenue address.[26]

James Bowler, fellow alderman with Powers from the Nineteenth Ward, used equally effective weapons in the propaganda war. He issued a statement, which the *Chicago Daily News* printed on February 10, 1921, revealing his concern over D'Andrea's willingness to employ force. In this statement Bowler claimed that D'Andrea's men could threaten Powers' supporters in Italian and that police and poll watchers from the Municipal Voters' League would be unable to understand them. The Board of Election Commissioners promptly forbade the use of foreign languages at polling places. It is ironic that Powers and Bowler, who in earlier years had despised reformers, found their presence highly beneficial at polling stations in 1921.

Propaganda skirmishes formed only one aspect—the least violent and destructive—of the campaign. Both sides resorted to bombing as a technique of political "persuasion." On February 11 more than 300 people attended a rally in support of D'Andrea at 854 Blue Island Avenue. A bomb exploded in the hall and injured 17 persons, five severely. The two principals reacted predictably. On February 12, the *Chicago Daily News* quoted D'Andrea's comment that the bombing was "the work of political enemies." Alderman Powers "inclined to the opinion that the explosion was caused by the enemies of D'Andrea in the labor world." Significantly, every home in the Nineteenth Ward received a letter from Powers on the same day that city papers carried the story of the Blue Island bombing. Powers' letter bitterly assailed D'Andrea for the bombing of Powers' Macalister Place home on September 18, 1920.[27]

Chief of Police Charles Fitzmorris dismissed the bombings as "politics." Bombing had indeed become a commonplace method of handling problems in Chicago. The *Daily News* quoted State's Attorney Robert E. Crowe's bitter complaint that "everybody in Chicago seems to be settling private business by means of bombs —labor interests, race trouble agitators and political factions."

Crowe demanded that the death penalty be enacted against those involved in bombings, the *Herald and Examiner* reported, for "there is no more vicious criminal than the man who would bomb a home where women and children are asleep, a public meeting or a factory." He vowed, according to the *Tribune*, that "these outrages must be and are going to be stopped." [28]

On February 14 both the *Tribune* and the *Daily News* gave special editorial attention to D'Andrea's reaction toward bombing incidents; the Italian had stated that bombings were "all in the game" of labor union activities but denounced "with some indignation" the use of bombs in politics. The *Tribune* feared for Chicago's future. "The man, the gang, or the organization which sanctions or adopts bombing as a method of obtaining results in ordinary activities cannot expect to be able to restrict the uses of such methods to one line of business." The *Daily News* even more vehemently condemned D'Andrea's unconcern: "Evidently some of the ward leaders are disposed to treat the matter lightly, drawing as they do fine distinctions between bombing a private residence—whether there are women and children in it or not—and attacking a crowded hall during the progress of a political or labor meeting. The people of Chicago do not share the notion that 'reasonable' bomb throwing is 'part of the game' to be forgotten with other trivial incidents of ward politics." D'Andrea's comment had been politically unwise, and doubtless cost him votes; it was certainly not calculated to win the votes of female residents of Ward Nineteen (who received the franchise in 1913). [29]

In a front-page article titled "Hurl Bomb No. 3 in 19th Ward," on February 18 (four days before the election), the *Tribune* reported another incident in the Powers-D'Andrea conflict. This time the bomb exploded at 1028 Newberry Avenue, home of Joe Spica, President of the Sewer and Tunnel Miners' Union, for which D'Andrea worked as business agent. Spica's son-in-law, a political lieutenant for D'Andrea, lived in the same house. The *Tribune*'s reaction appeared the next day and blended black humor with anxiety over the future course of ward politics in Chicago. "If the system [of bombing] continues to grow in popularity we may expect ward leaders to be chosen for the amount of TNT they can inject into a campaign and precinct captains to be selected for their accuracy in throwing hand grenades."

Because of enmity among rival candidates, ward residents had lived with the fear of violent death long before the 1921 campaign began. According to State's Attorney Crowe, "A reign of terror is said to have existed in the Nineteenth Ward for more than a year and political leaders have had to be on their guard because of threats against their lives. Part of the trouble has been due to feuds among the Italians, who are in the majority." Feuds among Italians, of course, raged between those who supported the Powers machine and those who backed their fellow Italian. The Nineteenth Ward, as a result, turned into an armed camp. Citizens of the community, caught between competing warlords, existed in a state of terror and hysteria. Mayor Thompson responded to the furor by ordering more police officers into the ward, but efforts to reassure residents had no measurable success, since violence and intimidation increased as the 1921 campaign progressed. Hecklers and unruly mobs disrupted Alderman Powers at every campaign speech. His fear of bodily injury became so great that police guarded his home and person day and night. Opponents threatened and slugged his workers. D'Andrea received similar threats and faced equally hostile crowds; his supporters suffered physical abuse, and his political headquarters were bombed.[30]

The Nineteenth Ward's political chaos led the Municipal Voters' League to conclude that neither candidate deserved support from reformers, since both seemed equally unfit to hold responsible office. The League described Powers as "still a leader of the discredited element in the council," while D'Andrea "was convicted in 1902 of counterfeiting . . . and was pardoned by President Roosevelt." In contrast to the *Tribune*, which printed the League's recommendations without comment, the *Daily News* made clear its own choices as well as those of the League. The paper supported the Prince of Boodlers in the Nineteenth Ward, but in urging residents to vote for Powers, the *Daily News* pointed out his unsavory record and emphasized that it favored him only as a

slightly lesser evil. "In spite of the highly unsatisfactory service of
John Powers during his many years in the city council," the paper
editorialized on February 19, "the present shocking conditions in
Nineteenth Ward politics seem to demand that law-abiding voters
support him in an effort to prevent the ward from suffering the
shame of worse representation." [31]

In opposing D'Andrea on those terms the *Daily News* implied
that he and his supporters bore the major responsibility for the
campaign's violence and destruction. Other city newspapers, among
them the *Chicago Herald and Examiner* and the *Chicago Evening
Journal*, refrained from endorsing either candidate. Except for a
paid advertisement that appeared on February 20 in *L'Italia* and
a general summary of the various city elections in *La Tribuna
Italiana Transatlantica* on February 26, the Italian-language press
also chose to ignore the Powers-D'Andrea struggle.

February 22, election day, marked the sordid culmination of a
bloody and vicious campaign. In a vain effort to avoid trouble the
Board of Election Commissioners assigned extra poll watchers and
delayed providing ballots to the ward's polling stations until election morning. In spite of all precautions, political workers on both
sides in this "nonpartisan election" suffered abuse, while accusa-
tions of vote fraud spewed from both headquarters. Despite, or
because of, bombings, threats, and kidnappings, John Powers triumphed by the narrow margin of 381 votes over the most tenacious
and troublesome rival of his political career. D'Andrea, according
to *La Tribuna Italiana Transatlantica*, claimed to be the innocent
victim of violence and voting irregularities. Beyond any doubt
both candidates indulged in "voting irregularities," but a careful
examination of voting returns indicates that foul play did not cause
the Italian's defeat. In the final analysis, D'Andrea's tarnished
background as an unfrocked priest and an immoral and corrupt
man provided Powers with the opportunity (which he exploited to
the fullest extent) of posing as a humble, God-fearing, church-
going family man. This characterization tipped the balance in favor
of the Irish boodler over his Italian rival. Significantly, the recently
enfranchised women's vote decided the outcome. Powers barely

carried the male vote in the ward—2781 to D'Andrea's 2657, a plurality of only 124. The female vote could have compensated for this deficit, since 2123 women cast ballots. Powers carried this group by nearly four to three, or 1203 to 946, a plurality of 257. Two other candidates also received votes: Ellis Dubustein, one male vote; James Hamacker, two male votes.[32]

Ironically, the only candidate who seriously threatened Powers' control over the ward failed because he could be pictured as even more corrupt and disreputable than Johnny De Pow himself. One is tempted to speculate on the possible outcome in any of the aldermanic elections after 1910 (when the Italian vote clearly formed a major factor in the ward) and especially in 1921, if Jane Addams and other reform elements centered in Hull House had persisted in opposing Powers—perhaps by emulating Graham Taylor and his Chicago Commons supporters in the Seventeenth Ward.

As in the Nineteenth Ward, the first reform candidate elected alderman through Taylor's efforts quickly came under the control of boodling elements in the City Council. The ward machine attempted to steal the election from James Walsh, the Chicago Commons candidate, in the second confrontation, that of 1897. Instead of abandoning the struggle, Taylor and his forces fought back. As a result of their agitating, police arrested a judge and two clerks of the election for attempting to alter the vote from one of the precincts in order to cause Walsh's defeat. The three men were brought to trial and convicted, and the forces of reform seemed well on their way to establishing control over the ward.[33]

While Taylor did not face a leader of the power and cunning of The Mourner, he did have to overcome, in his own words, "an Irish boss and his organization [which] dominated politics" in the ward. He also had to convince a variety of ethnic groups, including Norwegians, Swedes, Poles, eastern European Jews, Germans, Irishmen, and Italians to suppress group antagonisms and join together in support of candidates who were not of their own background—for example, in 1901 a Polish lawyer, John F. Smulski, in 1902 an Irish tanner, William E. Dever (who later became superior court judge, appellate court judge and eventually mayor), and in

1903 Lewis D. Sitts, a German. Taylor, himself a shrewd political realist, attracted a group of aggressive, intelligent, and dedicated young reformers, among them John Palmer Gavit, Allen T. Burns, James Mullenbach and Raymond Robins, who provided powerful aid in reform politicking within the ward. Consequently, Italian voters in the Seventeenth Ward, according to Graham Romeyn Taylor, by 1906 were refusing "to be delivered in the customary way, but went upon record for independence, as the Scandinavians have before them during the past successes of the Community Club." This Community Club formed the Chicago Commons equivalent of the Hull House Mens' Club.[34]

While she faced a more securely entrenched rival than did the Seventeenth Ward reformers, Miss Addams after 1910 (and perhaps as early as 1905) might have realized considerable success against Powers and Bowler had she concentrated upon a single ethnic group—the Italians—and exploited the antagonisms, rivalries, and suspicions that existed between them and the Irishmen who controlled ward politics. It is also possible that Miss Addams, her supporters, and the hopes of reform might simply have suffered greater defeats at the hands of the Powers forces, repeating the events of 1896 and 1898. From the standpoint of ward residents and the cause of local and city-wide civic reform, possible gains would have made the effort worthwhile. In their "struggle for self-determination" Nineteenth Ward Italians fought to displace the Irish leader who had first come to power during the heyday of the preceding wave of immigrants. Because of the absence of reform candidates or backers with city-wide prestige and support, in the words of John Landesco of the Illinois Crime Commission, "only a D'Andrea, willing to use force without stint or limit, could rise to leadership in the situation against the use of fraud, the connivance and protection of politics, and the highly developed qualities of 'ward heeler' leadership which John Powers possessed along with the availability of protected, armed partisans." After the 1921 contest, Irish bosses arranged for the political dismemberment of the Italian community, thus preventing any consolidated effort of Italians and reform elements against Powers or the machine.[35]

## IV

Prior to 1920 only a handful of Chicago's Italians succeeded in gaining elective office, and generally these men came of northern Italian background. Two of them, Stephen P. Revere and Frank F. Gazzolo, served as the city's only Italian aldermen before the twenties. Revere, elected from the Tenth Ward in 1885, became the first member of his ethnic group in the City Council. In his bid for reelection in 1887 he lost (in a four-man race) to J. N. Mulvihill by a vote of 647 to 571. In 1895 Revere returned to the City Council for another two-year term as alderman from the Seventeenth Ward (redistricting in 1890 changed ward numbers as well as ward lines). Gazzolo, a druggist by trade, won his terms as alderman from the Eleventh Ward in 1892, 1894, and 1896, and from the Eighteenth Ward in 1913 (the city again underwent redistricting in 1900, 1910 and 1912).[36]

Both Revere and Gazzolo ran as regular machine candidates who worked closely with ward and city political bosses, opposed reform and reformers, and were opposed by them. Thus when Revere ran for reelection in 1897 the Municipal Voters' League reviewed his term in office and concluded that "the interests of the public demand his defeat." The League observed that upon entering the City Council in 1895, Revere "immediately" aligned himself with the boodling element and supported the passage of franchises that were not in the best interests of the city. Among these were the Calumet and Blue Island, Clark Street Trolley, Central Electric, and the North Chicago Electric and Trolley ordinances. Graham Taylor and the Seventeenth Ward Civic Federation joined Revere's opposition, and entered a member of the Federation, James Walsh, in the electoral race. The initial declaration announced victory for Revere, but reformer protests of voting irregularities brought an investigation that verified claims of voting fraud. The corrected vote count gave Walsh 1629 to Revere's 1484 (he ran as the Republican candidate), 1112 for Democrat Nicholas Maggio, and 144 for Arvid Okerlund, Independent Republican.[37]

At the time of this election, Italians did not form a numerically large part of the Seventeenth Ward's voting power. Indeed, the registered "Italian vote" consisted of 600 names. Of this total, however, 400 held patronage jobs, and the Irish Republican ward boss boasted to Graham Taylor that this bloc of city employes "held the balance of power between the parties in the ward, and voted as he told them or lost their jobs." Contrary to the boss's expectations, Taylor not only mobilized "good citizens" but also effectively split the Italian bloc. He persuaded enough Italians of the necessity for reform to overturn the corrupt ward machine.[38]

The Seventeenth Ward's largest concentration of Italian voters in 1897 massed in the Eleventh Precinct, bounded by Ohio Street on the north, Austin Avenue on the south, Union Street on the east, and Green Street on the west. This precinct held a total of 489 registered voters, 125 of them Italian; the other 364 consisted mainly of Irishmen and Scandinavians. Italians in other precincts registered in smaller numbers. The next largest group lived in the Fifth Precinct, with 89 Italians in a total of 450 registered voters; the Second had 79 Italians of 307 voters; the Third, 78 of 404; the Tenth, 56 of 367; and the Fourteenth, 71 of 302. Other precincts had considerably smaller numbers of Italians, and many had none at all.[39]

In his 1895 victory and in the strong showing he made in the 1897 loss, Revere attracted not only Italian voters but members of other ethnic groups as well. That he possessed this ability showed even in the defeat he suffered when he attempted to return to the City Council in 1912. The Democratic Party, Graham Taylor, and Chicago Commons supported incumbent Stanley S. Walkowiak, who also enjoyed general popularity among Slavic voters in the ward. Walkowiak won reelection with a total of 2953 to Revere's 1753 (two other candidates received 340 votes). In this election Revere gained his largest total vote in the precinct with the greatest Italian concentration, which was also the only precinct that year in which Italians comprised as much as half the registered vote. In this precinct, the Twenty-fourth, which was 64 per cent Italian, Revere received 153 votes to 36 for Walkowiak. In the Thirteenth

Precinct, however, where the Democratic Party candidate polled
his second-lowest total (48 votes) and Revere his fifth largest,
Italians made up only 46 of 203 voters, with most residents in the
area being of Slavic background. Revere also carried the Twelfth
Precinct, which held an even heavier Slavic concentration, by a
vote of 120 to 75. He won in precincts that were dominated by
Irishmen and Scandinavians (with a scattering of Slavs but no
Italians), such as the Fourteenth, Twentieth, and Twenty-seventh.
Revere and Walkowiak had faced each other in a special election
on April 4, 1911, to fill an aldermanic vacancy from the Seventeenth Ward. This election formed a prelude to the 1912 campaign
for a full two-year term. The two contests paralleled each other
not only in candidates but also in vote returns from the ward as
a whole and from individual precincts.[40]

Machine support and ability to appeal to non-Italian voters held
even more importance for the career of Frank Gazzolo. In 1892,
when Democratic Party candidate Gazzolo won his first aldermanic
election, the Eleventh Ward had a total of 8457 voters, 15 of them
Italians. The Municipal Voters' League opposed Gazzolo when he
came up for reelection in 1898, accusing him, like Revere, of joining corrupt elements in the City Council. The Republican Party
candidate, who received League endorsement, won the election.
Gazzolo returned to the City Council several years later with
broad-based support in the ward (at this time the Eighteenth).[41]

A major problem for most Italian candidates was the inability
of the Italian group alone to ensure electoral success. Italian voters
generally heeded the advice of their press and other community
leaders and cast their votes for fellow Italians, regardless of party
affiliation. In order to gain electoral office, however, candidates
found it necessary to attract voters of other ethnic groups. Some
office seekers in addition to Revere and Gazzolo did achieve this
objective, most for only one term in office. Italians who won elected
seats were: Frank J. Brignadello (1892–98), William Navigato
(1906–08), Anthony Trimarco (1907–09), and Thomas Froley
(1918–20), all to the State House of Representatives (Charles
Coia, Democrat, first became a Representative in 1918 and con-

tinued in that office into the 1920's); Dr. Camillo Volini (1898–
1900), County Commissioner; Bernard P. Barasa, first elected to
fill a vacancy as Associate Judge of the Municipal Court in 1916
and reelected for a full term in 1918. Unsuccessful Italian candidates numbered far more. During the period between 1896 and
1920 at least 24 sought aldermanic positions, 14 ran for the office
of County Commissioner, 7 for State Senator, 21 stood as candidates for the State House of Representatives, 8 aspired to municipal
court judgeships, 1 ran for the office of Lieutenant Governor and
1 for State's Attorney. In a single year, 1914, eighteen Italians
sought political offices ranging from Alderman to County Commissioner to State Senator, but not one won an election. Italian candidates, it should be noted, bid for election as Democrats, Republicans, Socialists, Independents, and Progressives. Like the "Italian
vote" at this time, Italian candidates had no ties to a particular
party.[42]

The size of the group, the number of registered voters, some
degree of voter apathy, and the lack of capable local leadership
formed vitally important realities that determined the success of
Italian candidates. Those who relied on appeals to ethnic consciousness (as many candidates did) found their efforts ending in
failure. Ambitions and wishes could not change the fact that the
Italian population never came close to forming the largest of
Chicago's immigrant groups. While the Italian element in the city
increased from 74,943 in 1910 (a figure that included 45,169 foreign
born and 29,774 native born of foreign parentage) to 124,457
(59,775 first generation and 64,682 second generation) ten years
later, Chicago's Italians formed only 6.4 per cent of the total white
population by 1920. They still ranked behind Poles, Germans, Jews,
Swedes, and Irishmen, in numbers.[43]

A further restriction on Italian voting influence was the small
proportion of immigrants who became American citizens. Of 22,668
foreign-born Italian males of voting age in 1910, only 6408, or 28.3
per cent, were naturalized. Ten years later the totals rose dramatically to 35.5 per cent, or 11,097 of the eligible Italian males, and
34.7 per cent, or 7059, Italian females of voting age who became

citizens. Yet only Poles, Greeks, Lithuanians, and Yugoslavs had lower naturalization percentages; and even with a lower percentage of naturalization (34.5), Polish-Americans outnumbered Italian-Americans 43,840 to 18,138. The low naturalization figures among southern and eastern Europeans resulted from the short span of time since their arrival in the United States and their unfamiliarity with the economic, social and political advantages accruing from citizenship.[44]

When Italians became citizens and registered to vote they tended to cast their ballots in national rather than local elections. Italian precinct votes characteristically totaled lower in ward-level elections than in mayoral and other city contests. National elections showed high voter participation. The most notable exception to this tendency, the 1921 Powers-D'Andrea donnybrook, generated such interest that more voters turned out in Nineteenth Ward Italian precincts than did for the 1919 mayoral campaign (between William Hale Thompson and Robert M. Sweitzer) or the Harding-Cox presidential contest. Aside from this event, ethnic voters, whose main political interests lay in economic issues, indicated by their vote totals that they believed financial and monetary policies reached at the national level had a more profound effect on their lives than local decisions. As early as 1905, Oscar Durante complained that "Italian laborers, . . . while they became agitated and excited when faced with a Presidential election, remain later indifferent when the elections concern the municipality." Ironically, *L'Italia* and other Italian-language newspapers reinforced this tendency by emphasizing famous persons, like Woodrow Wilson, and national issues, such as the tariff.[45]

Because ethnic leaders felt the tariff formed a vital ingredient promoting or retarding individual prosperity, they stressed its importance and encouraged newcomers to register their opinions of tariff legislation at the ballot box. *L'Italia* strongly supported the protective tariff in the belief that by aiding business the tariff also helped labor; *La Tribuna Italiana Transatlantica* and *Il Progresso Italo-Americano* (New York) opposed the tariff because they considered it to be disadvantageous to labor. When tariff controversies arose, colonial journals focused on them and related their influence to all areas of immigrant life.[46] As important as the tariff question loomed in Italian-American papers, the presidential elections of 1912 and 1920 stirred "Southerners" to a feverish pitch unequaled by any other national issue.

Italian-Americans opposed Woodrow Wilson largely because of the anti-Italian comments in Volume V of his *History of the American People*. Wilson saw immigrants from the southern part of the peninsula as men with "neither skill nor energy nor any initiative of quick intelligence." Furthermore, "the Chinese were more to be desired, as workmen if not as citizens, than most of the coarse crew that came crowding in every year at the eastern ports." The Italian-American press furiously lashed back. Durante fumed, "Wilson has classed the Italians as lower than the Chinese? Very well, let him go to the Chinese for votes." An examination of precinct statistics indicates that Italian voters shared this sense of outrage, for in 1912 they favored either the Republican candidate and incumbent President William Howard Taft, or the Progressive Party standard-bearer and former President, Theodore Roosevelt. Of the four major candidates only Socialist Eugene V. Debs received fewer Italian votes than Democrat Wilson. In the city as a whole, Roosevelt outpolled Wilson, his closest rival, by 24,183 votes (144,392 to 120,209); Taft received 67,859; and Debs 49,959 votes.[47]

Italians continued to oppose Wilson in following years, and in 1920 Democrat James M. Cox felt the full effect of Italian-American reaction to President Wilson's actions at the Paris Peace Conference. Cox received virtually no attention as the press attacked Wilson for real and imagined insults against Italy, Gabriele D'Annunzio, and Italian immigrants in the United States. Wilson prevented Italy "from getting what is rightfully hers," complained *La Tribuna Italiana Transatlantica* on August 21, 1920. The paper contrasted the President's position with that of the Republicans, who, it reported, had ardently championed Italian claims.[48] Until the Wilson Presidency *La Tribuna Italiana Transatlantica* had opposed the Republican Party on all counts. Italian voters overwhelmingly chose Harding over Cox and Debs, as returns from representative Italian precincts show.

Unfortunately for their voting prestige, and in spite of almost unprecedented press unity, Italians could not claim that they had swung the vote or caused the final results, because Harding won a resounding victory in the city and nation. In Chicago, Harding outpolled Cox by a vote of 549,243 to 182,252, while Debs received 46,776 votes and three minor candidates together garnered 6730.[49]

## Table 7

CHICAGO'S ITALIAN VOTE (IN SELECTED PRECINCTS)
FOR PRESIDENT, NOVEMBER 2, 1920

| Ward | Precinct | Total Registered Voters | Registered Italian Voters | Percentage of Italian Voters | Total Votes cast for | | |
| | | | | | Cox | Harding | Debs |
|---|---|---|---|---|---|---|---|
| 17 | 14 | 303 | 216 | 71 | 64 | 191 | 4 |
| 17 | 15 | 430 | 329 | 77 | 58 | 309 | 12 |
| 19 | 3 | 300 | 275 | 90 | 78 | 121 | 0 |
| 19 | 13 | 225 | 181 | 80 | 53 | 118 | 10 |
| 19 | 16 | 287 | 242 | 84 | 65 | 150 | 11 |
| 20 | 1 | 313 | 242 | 77 | 101 | 148 | 17 |
| 22 | 26 | 360 | 210 | 58 | 23 | 291 | 3 |

Sources: Voter registration figures from City of Chicago, Board of Election Commissioners, *Official Precinct Voter Registration Lists* for Presidential Election, 1920 (Oct. 1920). Vote statistics from City of Chicago, Board of Election Commissioners, MS of Official Election Returns (Nov. 2, 1920).

While national campaigns sparkled with the glamour and excitement often lacking in municipal affairs, local politics undeniably yielded the more immediate results, perhaps the most important ones to immigrants. Political bosses and interest groups within the immigrant colony (among them city employees, saloonkeepers, gambling-hall operators, rag pickers, and peddlers) realized this fact and made full use of the vote in their own interests. Saloonkeepers, for example, took "an active part in all political campaigns, contributing money and doing personal work if necessary in the interests of the ward politician." In exchange for their services, saloons operated "quite undisturbed by the authorities" and remained open after closing hours, served minors, functioned as places of prostitution, and doubled as "resort and place of retreat for the worst elements of the Italian colonies," observed an anti-crime organization, the White Hand Society, in 1908.[50]

The city's Italians lacked an able, dynamic, and reform-minded leader in the mold of Fiorello LaGuardia, who could weld together the Italian element and also attract voters from outside the community. In the words of Luigi Carnovale, who worked as a reporter for *La Tribuna Italiana Transatlantica* shortly after the turn of the century, early political leaders were "a sorry lot" with "neither learning, manners, patriotic sentiment, nor human dignity." Even worse, although Carnovale omitted mentioning it, these Italian leaders had great difficulty in winning elections.[51]

This unhappy situation became acutely unbearable in 1919 when LaGuardia was elected President of the Board of Aldermen of New York City, the most important elective position that any Italian had gained in a major American city. This achievement made Chicago's Italians both proud and envious. Bernard P. Barasa, the first Italian elected to the Municipal Court (1916) and like LaGuardia a Republican, became a rallying point for the press and others in the colony eager for an honorable leader able to guide them to electoral victory. *La Tribuna Italiana Transatlantica* lauded Barasa as "the man of the moment of Chicago politics," a perfect candidate for mayor, "Chicago's LaGuardia." [52]

With his usual exuberance, *La Tribuna*'s incurably romantic publisher-editor Alessandro Mastro-Valerio analyzed Barasa's current and potential status in city politics. Despite Mastro-Valerio's grand predictions, in 1919 Barasa held no real power in Chicago and he did not acquire any during the following years. The Michigan-born Barasa indeed became a prominent figure within the Italian community, admired and respected by "Southerners" as much for his fortune in being born of northern Italian parentage (his family came from Genoa) as for his reputation as an able judge. Although he ran as a candidate in the primaries for state's attorney in 1920 and for mayor in 1923 (losing both times), he never developed into "the leading Italian in politics in Chicago," an inaccurate tribute applied by Italian-American author Giovanni E. Schiavo in 1928.[53]

The distinction of wielding dominant political influence in Chicago belonged to James Colosimo in the years prior to his death in 1920, then to John Torrio until his retirement in 1925, when Alphonse Capone took control of the political organization as well as the crime syndicate forged by his predecessors. These three men, while they never held or sought elective office, became, in succession, the most powerful and influential Italians in city politics. Through them and others like them, Italians made their most significant impact in local politics both before 1920 and after the formative era had ended.

Rather than existing as an experience unique to Italians, political-criminal activities actually conformed to a Chicago pattern which was also an urban American tradition, and which antedated large-scale Italian immigration. Chicago's reputation for nurturing an intimate connection between politics and crime dates back at least as far as the early 1870's. Southern and eastern European immigrant groups quickly adjusted to this "urban tradition." [54]

*"Political power in a democracy,"* John Landesco emphasized, *"rests upon friendship."* Successful politicians fully appreciated this axiom. Criminals also recognized reality and utilized this knowledge to their advantage. As a result, said Chicago Crime Commission Director Virgil W. Peterson (referring to the years after 1870), "the underworld, composed chiefly of gamblers, saloon-keepers, and vice resort operators, . . . constituted the most powerful political force in the city. The balance of power rested in their hands." [55]

James Colosimo became the first Italian to take full advantage of this crime-politics connection. In the First Ward, "Big Jim's" base of operations, stood Chicago's most notorious saloons, gambling halls, and houses of prostitution. The political bosses of the ward, "Hinky Dink" Kenna and "Bathhouse John" Coughlin, the "Lords of the Levee," reigned over an ethnically mixed domain inhabited by more than 25 nationalities. In 1898 the ward population totaled 28,305, of which Italians numbered only 1379; of these, 1239 were foreign born and 140 American born. Neither at this time nor at any other thereafter did the Italian element approach a majority of residents or of registered voters in the levee ward.[56]

Nevertheless, through a combination of shrewdness and violence, Colosimo emerged after 1900 as a consolidating force within the Italian minority. He welded newcomers from the Kingdom of Italy into a highly effective voting bloc that exerted an influence in the ward far beyond its numerical importance. "Big Jim" excelled in the use of politically oriented social and athletic clubs, lavish amounts of patronage, threats and force to deliver the "Italian vote" on election day. A violent and destructive political confrontation between Irish and Italian leaders—like that between Powers and D'Andrea in the Nineteenth Ward—did not occur in the First Ward. Unlike his counterpart in the Nineteenth Ward, Colosimo remained in the background as Irish politicians retained control of elective offices. In exchange, "Big Jim" gained absolute freedom from police and other officials for his criminal operations in the ward. A similar situation, but on a considerably smaller scale, existed in other core-area Italian districts.[57]

The Italian press and other middle-class members of the community took some notice of political corruption, but in a minor way, compared with the extensive attention devoted to national issues and candidates. The "better elements" in the Italian group either did not recognize or did not wish to acknowledge the political function fulfilled by Colosimo and others of his type. Their lack of perception in this area is significant, for corruption and crime formed the means by which Chicago's Italians made their presence felt in city politics in the years prior to 1920. During the decade of the 'twenties, Italians won numerous positions in both elective and appointive offices through the influence of criminal elements.

## V

By 1920 Italians had effectively adjusted to politics in the various parts of the city where they lived. In the First, Nineteenth, and Twenty-third wards, where corruption and violence formed accepted and integral elements of political life, Italians bought and sold votes, intimidated and indulged voters and candidates (as suited the occasion), and practiced other fine points of local politics. The Powers-D'Andrea struggle of 1921 capped years of bitter frustrations and a succession of humiliating failures for Italian office seekers; the years ahead seemed to offer little hope for improvement. Italian ward leader Anthony D'Andrea died of wounds from a sawed-off shotgun on May 11, 1921—a brutal show of force from opponents and a warning to ambitious D'Andrea followers. Reapportionment provided what appeared to be an even more effective way of silencing vote-seeking Italians. Under legislation passed by the City Council in 1921, to go into effect in 1923, Chicago's wards increased from 35 to 50 and existing ward boundaries changed. In the process, Boss Powers managed to have the huge West Side Italian colony, which provided a majority of votes in the old Nineteenth Ward, carved up and distributed as groups of minority residents in four new wards: the Twentieth, Twenty-fifth, Twenty-sixth, and Twenty-seventh. Despite such treatment, Italians from the West Side won election to the City Council before the end of the decade. Their successes came, however, not through reform programs and activities but by tried and true machine methods. During this period Al Capone, a Republican, forged for Italians a rich and powerful voice not only in the political life of the (Democratic) First Ward, but also in the (Republican) Twentieth Ward and even in the municipal government of William Hale Thompson.[59]

Italians in the Seventeenth Ward showed that local politics could be conducted in an entirely different manner. Before Graham Taylor guided Chicago Commons in its long-term campaign against

bossism and corruption, political methods and morals resembled
those in other core areas. As elsewhere, Italian residents cooperated
fully for practical reasons—jobs, personal safety, money. At that
time and place, dishonesty and corruption offered rewards; reform
politics did not. Through the patient, persistent and practical
activities of Taylor and the Seventeenth Ward Community Club,
Italians began to understand the advantages of an honest local
government. More important, these advantages were clearly within
reach. By 1906, with reformers solidly entrenched, those Italians
"who had hitherto voted as they were bidden by the party bosses
who herded them to the polls," for the first time "broke rank and
cast their own independent ballots when they got inside the booth."
In the following years, as the Chicago Commons' Warden's Report
for 1920 pointed out, Italians joined northern European residents
of the ward in supporting reform politicians.[60]

# 5

## Italians and Crime:
## The Formative Years

Americans reacted to crime among Italian newcomers with a frenzy of emotion aroused by no other immigrant activity. Official reports, books, pamphlets, magazine articles, and newspaper stories criticized and analyzed, lamented and decried "Southern" criminalty which, in the period to the 'twenties, invariably meant the Black Hand or Mafia. Some writers argued that Italians naturally possessed criminal inclinations, others blamed slum conditions in American cities, and still others denied the existence of lawbreaking organizations in the United States patterned after the Sicilian Mafia or the Neapolitan Camorra.

Contemporaries emphasized such problems as possible operating procedures of the Black Hand among Italians in America, whether Italian crime represented a reaction to new-world conditions or a carry-over of old-world traditions, and whether Italian criminals worked from centralized headquarters or as independent groups and individuals. Preoccupation with these and similar aspects obscured factors of deeper significance. First, the groundwork of Italian dominance of Chicago's crime after 1920 was laid in the years prior to national prohibition legislation. In addition, Italian lawbreaking in the era before 1920 involved a wide variety of operations, many of them with no Black Hand connections. In those years also—a time of mass immigration from the Italian Kingdom—crime served an important (although not necessarily desirable) function as one method of group adjustment to a new environment. Finally, two separate and relatively distinct levels of criminal activity involving Italians developed during the formative period of Italian crime in Chicago, one entirely within the immigrant quarter and affecting only its residents. The other took place as Italians began to move into "big time" crime, which operated within the larger society. Before January 16, 1920, most "Southern" crime took place only within the colony. Prohibition encouraged many to move into organized crime, which, in Chicago, they eventually came to dominate.

## II

Like many others, John Chetwood, Arthur Train, and the United States Immigration Commission believed Italians to be inherently criminal. Chetwood, an ardent restrictionist, insisted that "the Mafia and other Sicilian assassins have been uprooted by the authorities and driven out of their native country" to the United States. He saw a critical need for enacting new and more stringent immigration legislation.

Train, at one time an assistant District Attorney of New York County, believed that a distinct dichotomy existed within the Italian character. Northerners, "*molto simpatico* to the American character," displayed many "national traits . . . singularly like our own" and resembled Americans in being "honest, thrifty, industrious, law-abiding, and good-natured." On the other hand, "Southerners" exhibited "fewer of these good qualities" and were "apt to be ignorant, lazy, destitute, and superstitious." In addition, "a considerable percentage, especially of those from the cities, are criminal."

The United States Immigration Commission claimed that "certain kinds of criminality are inherent in the Italian race." Immigrants carried these antisocial tendencies to the United States and thus infected the mainstream of American life. The Commission went so far as to state that "crime had greatly diminished in many communities [in the "South"] because most of the criminals had gone to America." [1]

Other American observers took issue with this emphasis on hereditary factors. Isaac Hourwich disputed the Immigration Commission's conclusions, and insisted that "this criminality theory is significant in so far only as it betrays the bias of the commission against the immigrant." He maintained that claims of greater criminality on the part of Italians or members of other "new" immigrant groups were invalid as well as ridiculous. Examination of census returns convinced Hourwich that "an increase in immigration goes parallel with an increase of business prosperity and decrease in crime," for "during the latest ten year period, 1900–1909, the wave of criminality rose when immigration was at its lowest ebb, while the high-tide of immigration was contemporaneous with a decrease in crime."

According to former New York State prison official Samuel J. Barrows, "A careful examination of police reports, secured from every city in this country, where nationalities are distinguished in the records of arrests, does not justify the assumption that the criminal tendencies of the Italians exceed the average of the foreign born or of the native population." Barrows believed that most concern over Italian criminality stemmed from the more sensational character of Italian crime, which could easily be inflated into popular stories. "Hence they are expanded in print under headlines that catch the eye and make an impress out of proportion to their comparative number."

Congressman William S. Bennet of New York, a member of the United States Immigration Commission, disagreed with the Commission's general conclusions when he reported, "Italy does not impose its criminals upon us." Rather, he said, conditions encountered by immigrants in urban America caused crime among Italians in the United States. To Arthur H. Warner, writing in *Survey*, "the idea that Black Handers are bred exclusively in Italy to slip into this country through lax immigration precautions is a myth fostered by police officers anxious to shift responsibility." Warner further affirmed that the Black Hand did not consist of "crafty and experienced criminals whose ways are too deep to fathom," for "what is called the Black Hand is not . . . a single united band, but many scattered ones which would as lief prey on each other as on anybody else." The editors of *Cosmopolitan* agreed: "There is no central organization. There are no blood-sealed oaths. There is no international organization. The Black Hand is the generic name of innumerable small groups of criminals operating under its flag to blackmail and murder." If a central organization had existed, the editors conjectured, "its suppression would be less difficult. As it is the police have to deal with individuals." [2]

Views expressed by Italian leaders in Chicago and other cities also tended to concentrate on the Black Hand and to show a wide variance in opinions and beliefs concerning its existence and character. According to Gaetano D'Amato, former president of the United Italian Societies in New York City, the Black Hand in the United States was "a myth, in so far as the phrase conveys the impression that an organization of Italian criminals exists in America, or that the Camorra or the Mafia has become naturalized here." Tomasso Sassone, also of New York, declared that Italian crime in the United States flourished as "a transplanted product. To this class crime is not a makeshift, but a trade and a cult." [3]

In Chicago, Consul Guido Sabetta maintained inflexibly, "There is no such thing as a 'black hand' organization." Stephen Malato, legal counsel for an anticrime society and for many years a close observer of Chicago's lawbreakers, concluded that no "formal, large society" of outlaws existed; the Black Hand consisted of small "groups of criminals" out for money. One of Chicago's vice lords, James Colosimo, employed Rocco De Stefano to clear up any misunderstandings that arose between him and the law. Lawyer De Stefano held the opinion that a strongly organized, highly efficient Black Hand operated among Italians and indulged in extortion as well as other crimes. [4]

Some writers suspected that American and Italian-language newspapers exaggerated Italian criminal activity out of proportion to its significance. As early as 1891, *L'Italia* charged that other colonial papers devoted too much attention to crime in the community and not enough to more favorable aspects of immigrant life. In 1925 the monthly magazine *Vita Nuova* renewed the complaint, charging that American newspapers had tried to "outdo each other to pin anything detrimental on the Italian race." The magazine did not exempt Italian-language papers from its indictment: "We . . . would like to suggest to the Italo-American press that it should desist from printing stories of misdeeds and, rather, concentrate on publishing articles relating to the doings of the many Italians who are truly honoring their race and adopted country." [5]

Socialist papers complained bitterly that crime seemed to lead to success in an Italian neighborhood, for the outstanding man there was too often a criminal—a swindler, thief, or murderer. "Still he is respected, esteemed, elected president of a society; he sponsors banquets and patriotic celebrations, and is supported by misinformed Americans for public office." [6] Most nonsocialist colonial journals disagreed with this outlook and fully subscribed to the position taken by Consul Sabetta. Like him, they declared that accounts of Italian criminality were unfounded, inaccurate, and distorted; at the same time they took great pains to report each Black Hand crime to their readers, thus benefiting from the sensational aspects of the organization while denying its existence. An article that appeared in *L'Italia* following a murder in Tilden Street in early October, 1892, summarized the attitude of most Italian-language newspapers.

> [The murder was one which] the American newspapers as usual are loudly proclaiming . . . as committed by the Mafia, since they have been told by an Italian barber and an Italian storekeeper that it really exists in Chicago. To give the lie to these two clowns who have so little consideration for the reputation of the Italian colony in Chicago, we have called in representatives of the leading Chicago newspapers for a group interview on the subject of the Mafia.
>
> This was Mr. Durante's reply to the Mafia question in Chicago. "This fable of the Mafia is an unreasonable stupidity, an im-

becility pure and simple. Every small quarrel between Italians
gives rise to the cry of the 'Mafia.' This organization does not
now and never did exist.

"Several of my reporters have been at the scene of the crime
and through them, I have definitely established the fact that
the shooting occurred because of women and that they were
more than intoxicated.

"If this had occurred between members of other nationalities
it would not have aroused the present furor. We Italians are
becoming fed up with this continued chatter of the existence of
a Mafia society.

                              •   •   •

"To make a long story short, the Mafia exists neither in Chicago nor in Italy." [7]

*L'Italia* felt compelled to issue this denial of the Mafia on ac-
count of the intensive public attention focused on that Sicilian
organization following a series of events that began two years
earlier, in New Orleans.

## III

On October 15, 1890, New Orleans Superintendent of Police David
Hennessy was murdered. City residents assumed Sicilians to be
responsible, for Hennessy had been engaged in a crackdown on
crime in the Italian colony. In a city-wide atmosphere of near
hysteria, the police arrested hundreds of Italians for the crime
and brought nine to trial. To the consternation of the American
community, the jury found six defendants "not guilty" and could
reach no verdict on the other three. Rumors of bribery and intimidation of witnesses filled New Orleans; public officials and city
newspapers demanded that "the failure of justice" be remedied.
With widespread local support, a mob raged to the parish prison,
dragged from it eleven Italian prisoners and lynched them.

The incident quickly grew into a national crisis and an international affair. Italy demanded punishment of the lynch mob and
financial compensation for the victims' families. For a short time
in 1891, war between Italy and the United States appeared to be a
distinct possibility. President Harrison eased the situation some-

what when he spoke of the New Orleans Affair in his annual mes-
sage to Congress (on December 9, 1891) as "a most deplorable
and discreditable incident, an offense against law and humanity."
Relations between the two countries improved in the following
months, and the breach healed rapidly after Harrison offered an
indemnity payment.[8]

Chicago's Italian leaders sympathized with the New Orleans
Italian community and subscribed money to pay for the defense
of the nine accused men. They emphasized the need for group
solidarity and cooperation and tended to view the New Orleans
Affair as part of a general pattern of anti-Italian attitudes on the
part of Irish policemen and English-language newspapers in New
Orleans, Chicago, and other American cities. Applauding the Italian government's involvement on behalf of the families of the
eleven murdered men, they strongly supported the mother country
in its diplomatic exchanges with the United States. They were
shocked by Italy's acceptance of the American government's offer
to pay what *L'Italia* described on March 19, 1892, as "a small
indemnity" without recognizing or suitably condemning American
responsibility in the Affair.

Prior to 1890, crime in Chicago's Italian community consisted
of illegal activities in employment, child labor, crimes of passion
growing out of alcoholic indulgence or presumed insults to female
family members, and vendettas from the old country. Outlaws
within the community had not organized, and the city's newspapers made little use of the term "Mafia" in connection with
Chicago's Italians. The New Orleans Affair marked a complete
turning point.

To their horror, Italians in Chicago found themselves objects of
open fear and contempt during the course of the Affair. "Mafia"
began to appear frequently in Chicago's newspapers, and many
tabloids proclaimed the criminal inclinations of all Italians, doubtless as an outgrowth of the popular assumption that the Mafia had
effected Hennessy's murder. Americans concluded that the Mafia
flourished wherever "Southerners" lived. This belief strongly affected Chicagoans, for by 1891–92 the city contained a sizable

and rapidly growing Italian community composed largely of
"Southerners." Italian leaders reacted, for personal reasons (in
order to gain American acceptance) as well as through ethnic
pride, by denying the existence of the Mafia in Chicago. Some, like
Durante of *L'Italia,* insisted that it did not exist even in Italy.[9]

In order to make clear to Americans that old-world criminal
patterns and groups did not carry over into immigrant colony
crime, shortly after the turn of the century Italian-language newspapers began to use the term "Black Hand" to identify crimes
within the immigrant community. "Black Hand" became favored
by both American and immigrant newspapers in the first two
decades of the twentieth century. From 1904, for example, "Black
Hand" supplanted "Mafia" as the preferred term for crimes committed by Italians against each other, at least so far as *L'Italia*
was concerned, and the replacement remained in use until the
1920's.[10]

Whichever name they used to publicize Italian crimes, foreign-
language journals at first denied the existence of organized gangs.
In an article printed on August 27, 1904, Durante repeated in
*L'Italia* the belief he had stated in 1892: "The 'Black Hand' does
not exist, the crimes must be treated singly as individual events
which do not have any relation with organized groups." As time
passed, the immigrant press attributed an increasing number of
crimes to the Black Hand. Even *L'Italia* credited a quantity of
blackmailings, bombings, and murders to the secret society: "Black
Hand in Chicago. Blackmail Letter for $300" (July 14, 1906);
"Italians on Trial. 32 Italians Accused as Members of the Black
Hand" (April 27, 1907); "Once Again the Black Hand" (June 5,
1909).

In 1910 *L'Italia* reported the capture of Black Hand leaders:
"Chicago police are elated over the arrest of four Italians accused
of being leaders of the so-called Black Hand organization of
Chicago." As in earlier cases, however, crimes continued even
after gang leaders had been caught and their criminal societies
smashed.[11]

Oscar Durante admitted in February, 1911, that "if we continue at the present rate, the Italian colony of Chicago will soon take the lead over that of New York, in the matter of bombings, murder and blackmail." The number of criminal activities in the Italian colony did, in fact, increase as the community grew in population, although few contemporaries recognized the relationship between crime and population growth. The editor blamed Italian-Americans for the fear-ridden situation, for "when they are questioned by the police they become as dumb as fish and answer with the usual shrug of the shoulders"; as a result the criminal element could flourish "until its effect is felt from one end of the city to the other." Displaying his middle-class orientation, he complained that these conditions worked "to the detriment of the better class Italians." [12]

Although in April, 1910, *L'Italia* congratulated the police on their fight against the Black Hand—"This arrest is proof that the forces of law and order in our city are always on the alert"—one year later Durante held local officials responsible for the Black Hand's existence. "There have been 34 murders in the past two years, and not one of these murders has been solved by the police. This lack of capacity shown by the police gives criminals the courage to strike again. The police must cooperate with us to clear up this situation." Mastro-Valerio and other community spokesmen agreed that corrupt, incompetent police encouraged or permitted widespread criminal activity in the Italian colony. Many Americans reached the same conclusion. The Black Hand, they argued, could not possibly function without police complicity or inability. The Massachusetts Commission on Immigration, for example, identified police corruption, "which takes the form of protection of criminals," as the factor primarily responsible for Black Hand successes in cities outside Massachusetts, including Chicago.[13]

Fear and concern pervaded the Italian district because of the Black Hand's notoriety. Editor Mastro-Valerio warned in *La Tribuna Italiana Transatlantica* of the all-encompassing menace of the secret society: "Yesterday this one, today that one, tomorrow it may strike even you." Durante felt compelled to publicize the seriousness of the Black Hand problem, which he had for so long denied: "Day after day, week after week, more and more crimes are being committed, the perpetrators of which are invariably Italians . . . ." Admitting that almost every crime involved the name of the Black Hand, he described a typical method of acquiring money. Blackhanders simply demanded cash "from innocent people who work for a living." If the gangsters received nothing, they murdered their victim; should they spare his life, they bombed his home. "Naturally, these frequent crimes give a bad impression of the Italian colony to other nationalities. . . . Italians! We must do something to prevent these crimes." [14]

As more and more "Southerners" flocked to Chicago, they became an increasingly tempting source of money, more readily intimidated by threats because of the reputation of the Mafia in Sicily. After the publicity surrounding the New Orleans Affair, American papers quickly labeled all lawbreaking in the immigrant community as Mafia crimes. The successes or failures of gangs in Chicago's Italian neighborhoods, however, depended less on old-world techniques and personnel than on local conditions and opportunities. [15]

## IV

In 1907 and 1908 leaders of the Italian colony cooperated with leaders of the press in a concerted effort to combat and eliminate Black Hand crimes. On November 11, 1907, they organized the White Hand Society, largely through the efforts of Italian consul Guido Sabetta. The *Unione Siciliana* played a leading role in the formation and operation of the White Hand, a significant fact in the light of that society's involvement with criminals in the 1920's and the last years of the preceding decade. The *Unione*'s unfortunate entanglement with criminals in later years should not detract from its sincere concern in 1907 and 1908 over the unfavorable image that Black Hand activities presented of "Southerners" and especially Sicilians, and its efforts to eradicate crime within the immigrant area.

Chicago's Italian-language newspapers, particularly *L'Italia* and *La Tribuna Italiana Transatlantica*, fully supported the new organization, as did the Italian ambassador in Washington and the Italian Minister of Foreign Affairs in Rome. The organizers felt that a glorious era had begun with their "war without truce, war without quarter." Bubbling enthusiasm filled early meetings held to plan action against the enemy.[16]

By the end of November the idea of the White Hand had spread to other cities and the founders conceived the notion of organizing a White Hand "in all the cities which contain large Italian colonies, which suspect the existence of mafiosi or camorristi in their midst." The eventual goal, "the day in which the Italian colonies, free of the festering evil of the Black Hand, will become models among the foreigners," unintentionally publicized the problem of crime among Italians in the United States. Ironically, many of the leaders who formulated this goal had minimized the seriousness of Italian crime or publicly denied the existence of the Black Hand. Some continued to deny its existence while supporting White Hand activities against it.[17]

The White Hand was legally incorporated in December, 1907. Joyously, the members announced that at last Chicago's *cafoni*, or ignorant "Southern" peasants, too often the victims of Black Hand hoodlums, had "a protector in the White Hand." As stated in the Society's constitution, the White Hand intended "to paralyze and eradicate individual and organized crime which exists in the midst of the Italian colony, forcing it to submit to threats and violence," to eliminate a pervasive atmosphere of "mystery and terror," and to "present to the American public the truth concerning Italy and the Italians, frequently misrepresented by incorrect reports." [18]

In January, 1908, the White Hand called for closer cooperation with various Italian societies in the city and a program to educate *cafoni* (in Chicago and other cities) as to their duties and obligations. The Society also announced its first tangible success, claiming that it had driven ten of Chicago's most dangerous criminals—Italians—out of the city. By February the Society listed additional successes in Chicago and similar achievements in other American cities. *L'Italia* jubilantly announced, "Black Hand in Hot Water. The Arrest of One of the Heads Places the Black Hand in the Hands of the Police." The White Hand's attorney, Stephen Malato, played a major role in this capture.[19]

Never again did the White Hand achieve such glory, although it remained in existence for a number of years. It soon became a dead letter, failing in large part because of inadequate financial support. White Hand leaders lamented as early as 1908 that "so wealthy a colony as that of Chicago should have given such niggardly support to a movement intended to . . . purge it" of the Black Hand menace. The seemingly widespread "Southern" trait of indifference led to this financial distress. Reluctantly, the Society's leaders admitted that they could not gain, much less hold, the support of immigrant-area residents, the American public, or the police. The Society maintained that newcomers believed it planned to use the money collected from impoverished workers "to defend the lives and wealth of the prominent men of the colony." Among upwardly mobile members of the community the conviction had grown that by admitting the gravity of the problem of crime among Italians, the White Hand had "thrown suspicion and discredit upon the Italian name." [20]

More fundamental to rank-and-file immigrants, however, was their sense of self-preservation, which, rather than apathy or desire to protect their Italian good name, determined their behavior. "Southerners" knew that crime pervaded their communities; they knew also that authorities could or would do little to terminate it. They believed the White Hand to be powerless in the face of official corruption or tolerance of corruption, and they had no desire to involve themselves with it.[21]

While this situation existed in Chicago, it did not necessarily operate elsewhere. Domestic factors at work in individual cities strongly influenced and determined the course taken by Black Hand gangs. The Illinois Crime Commission noted that "in some American cities where the law is effectual, the 'black handers' have ceased to operate." According to John Landesco of the Illinois Crime Survey, who observed conditions in Chicago and Milwaukee for a number of years, the Black Hand in Milwaukee had a much shorter life and "Southerners" adjusted to their new surroundings with a minimal amount of crime and dealings in corrupt politics. John S. Kendall stated that in New Orleans the Sicilian immigrants "under the leadership of the better element of their own nationality, . . . set their faces against the activities of such organizations," with the result that after 1907 the Black Hand disappeared in that city.[22]

The adjustment of Italians in Boston and elsewhere in Massachusetts contrasted even more sharply with the Chicago experience. In a study published in 1902, social worker Robert A. Woods maintained that few murders committed by Italians in the North End of Boston could be attributed to premeditation, for in the majority of cases impulse and passion formed the motivating forces. Furthermore, no murder had been traced "directly or indirectly" to the Mafia. Twelve years later the Massachusetts Commission on Immigration reported that "so-called 'Black Hand' crimes are practically unknown in Massachusetts," although Italians committed criminal violations. As a "very large proportion" of the immigrants came from the "South," the Commission considered the absence of Black Hand crime to be proof that "local American conditions are responsible for those criminal organizations elsewhere." [23]

Even more striking in indicating the impact of local conditions upon crime were differences between Italian colonies in the United States and those in Latin America, specifically Brazil and Argentina, the countries of major Italian immigration. Radicalism rather than crime in the Chicago style constituted the most serious social problem involving Italian immigrants in South America. Argentinians, for example, viewed socialism and anarchism among Italians as grave difficulties, in contrast to the more limited appeal that these doctrines exerted upon "Southerners" in the United States.[24]

While southern Italians committed violent crimes in Latin America, neither Brazil nor Argentina exhibited any indication of the Black Hand or any equivalent of Anthony D'Andrea or Al Capone.

The principal reason for this difference was that in the United States, and Chicago in particular, "social and political conditions are so favorable" to the rise and spread of crime for profit.[25]

Many Chicago policemen worked illegally and in close harmony with criminals and politicians. Models of success in the city's immigrant neighborhoods often turned out to be (as Chicago's few but vociferous socialists claimed and the White Hand Society found to its distress) corrupt politicians and lawbreakers who operated under the protection of the guardians of the law. They displayed all the outward signs of economic achievement: expensive clothes and cars, quantities of ready money, food and drink of excellent quality. They also commanded attention, often respect, from the American community and Italian-language newspapers. Socialists blamed the Italian-language press, "with few exceptions," for permitting itself to be "the main lever for the elevation of these rascals" and "an accessory to all the disgraceful things befalling our colonies." [26]

Socialists might well have had Anthony D'Andrea in mind, for he exhibited characteristics decried by the socialist press as typical of colony leaders. He (and, during the 1920's, other presidents of the *Unione Siciliana*) commonly associated with criminal friends and businessmen, involved himself in gangland activities and rivalries, and held a criminal record. Before his death, D'Andrea had been not only president of the *Unione*, but also labor-union president and candidate for political office. He and those like him gained leadership of the *Unione* and other societies through their own personal power and connections. They aspired to such offices because of the prestige and influence that accompanied these positions, including some measure of political power through control of members' votes on election days. On the other hand, members of societies willingly or knowingly elevated men of questionable reputation to positions of authority, possibly through ethnic pride, hope of reward, or fear of injury.[27]

Many Chicagoans, however, abhorred poverty more than crime. Dishonesty, bribery, and misuse of power simply provided ready methods for overcoming lack of money. Native-born as well as immigrant residents of the city held this view, as concerned Chicagoan Samuel Paynter Wilson observed in 1910. Conditions in Chicago favored many types of lawbreaking, and Black Hand groups flourished in the city for a number of years.[28]

Chicago attracted professional Italian crooks, generally from Sicily, because of opportunities available to extort money from fellow "Southerners," unimpeded by police and under the magic name, "Black Hand." In the Illinois Crime Survey John Landesco reported the results of a study of more than 300 crimes attributed to the Black Hand. He found that these crimes were "limited almost entirely to the Sicilian neighborhoods" of Chicago. Writing in 1909, Arthur Woods, Deputy Police Commissioner of New York City, reported a similar situation. New York police discovered that "in almost every case" Black Hand crimes were committed by men who had been involved in criminal activities in Italy and who had immigrated to New York in order to continue "fattening off the main body of their fellow-countrymen." At this period, such criminals were not, however, members of a tightly organized, highly centralized structure. "The Black Hand is not a cohesive, comprehensive society, working with mysterious signs and passwords," maintained Woods. "Given a number of Italians with money, and two or three ex-convicts, you have all the elements necessary for a first-rate Black Hand campaign." Landesco reached a similar conclusion concerning the Black Hand in Chicago and further insisted, "It is the purest banality to excuse the nefarious, bloody practices and wide-spread tribute paid by the victims, by the historical explanation that blackmail and the conspiracy of silence are old-world traits transplanted." Rather, the Black Hand's success in Chicago grew out of local conditions that "have favored the rise, spread and persistence of extortion by violence" even among groups "which did not import the pattern" from the old world.[29]

Black Hand activities in Chicago virtually disappeared in the 1920's. At least three factors caused this decline. First, the supply of simple, pliable victims dwindled soon after the termination of immigration in the years after 1914. Action by federal authorities formed a second factor; enforcement of laws prohibiting use of the mails to defraud forced personal delivery of threatening Black Hand notes, potentially a dangerous activity because of possibilities of being recognized.[30]

While the preceding two factors limited opportunities for criminals in the ethnic colony, a vast new city-wide field of endeavor had presented itself because of new federal laws prohibiting the manufacture and sale of alcoholic beverages. American drinking tastes and capacities did not adjust to the new regulations, and enterprising young men found themselves in a position to reap immense profits. Many American robbers, murderers, blackmailers, burglars, and thieves left their former fields of labor for the more lucrative work offered through Prohibition—for which their former professions had provided good training. It is likely that many well-qualified Blackhanders also forsook the less-profitable extortion rackets of the Italian quarter in order to join the liquor-traffic scramble. Thus immigration restriction along with Prohibition marked the end of the Black Hand era and introduced many who had been involved in crime within Italian areas into the mainstream of American gangsterdom.[31]

## V

Black Hand activities—mainly extortion and terrorism—received most publicity inside and outside the immigrant colony, but many other types of neighborhood crimes existed. Over the years Chicago's Italian-language newspapers described a wide range of wrongdoings not limited to the Black Hand, including padrone (or labor agent) abuses and the illegalities of immigrant bankers.

Labor agents prospered in Chicago because of the city's prominence as a transportation center. While they fulfilled a vital function for newly arrived immigrants as well as for American businessmen, padroni generally cheated and shortchanged their less-knowledgeable, more-gullible compatriots until effective safeguards frustrated or hampered their efforts.

Immigrant bankers flourished in every part of the country where newcomers from southern and eastern Europe had gathered in any considerable numbers. The principal financial transaction of these bankers consisted of receiving deposits and sending money abroad. Most also served as steamship ticket agents, and often conducted some other business as well. Hence some "banks" could be found in grocery stores, saloons, or other natural gathering places. Investigators of the Immigrants' Protective League visited 55 Chicago bankers of Italian birth or extraction in the spring of 1912. Of these, 35 also functioned as steamship-ticket agents, 15 were labor agents, 11 operated grocery stores, 4 managed drugstores, 2 owned saloons, 1 a barber shop and 1 a real-estate office.[32]

The typical banker had little experience in business methods, ran his office with a minimal accumulation of capital, and for the most part worked freely outside legal controls. Immigrant bankers were not, for example, restricted as to the kinds of investments they could make with money deposited (restrictions that applied to state and national banks). As a result, speculative ventures of private bankers often ended in disaster, particularly for immigrant depositors; since they had no adequate legal safeguards, they lost their savings. Immigrants who transmitted money to Italy provided bankers with lush opportunities to defraud, either by using the money for investment purposes with the intention of sending some of it overseas when investments paid off, or else by accepting the money and keeping it. Because of the conditions under which they operated, many immigrant bankers went out of business, some through inefficient business methods, others because they absconded with customers' savings.[33]

One of Chicago's Italian bankers, Francesco Gugliemi, left town with $10,000 in customers' funds. When his departure was discovered, L'Italia reported in 1912, "a crowd of defrauded Italians gathered menacingly in front of the bank," where they found a squad of police stationed "to prevent any violent action." Gugliemi's bank had been in operation only a short time, during which the owner had successfully gained the confidence and trust of neighborhood Italians "who without hesitation placed their savings in his hands." Their trust and money reposed in the wrong place, for when Gugliemi absented himself he took all the cash in his care with the exception of sixty-five cents, which he left—undoubtedly through oversight—in the bank's vault. Another banker, Michele Camo, operated a grocery store at 737 West Taylor Street that doubled as his banking office. In June, 1911, Camo fled Chicago with nearly $10,000 of his bank's deposits. Several months later he returned without the money, assumed the name of Michele Postorici and took residence at 943 West Taylor, only two blocks from his former business. Two Italian officers (Paul Riccio and Michael De Vito) discovered and arrested the thief, but depositors never recovered their savings.[34]

The last two decades of the nineteenth century provided Italian bankers with almost unlimited opportunities for exploiting their customers. Conditions for depositors improved somewhat after the turn of the century. By the Italian Emigration Law of 1901 the Bank of Naples became designated as the financial institution entrusted with transmission of savings from all parts of the world, including the United States. The Bank of Naples, therefore, exerted a strong influence in forcing immigrant bankers to improve services for their clients, modify rates of exchange, and lower charges for transmission of money.[35]

In addition, after 1900 various states that contained large immigrant populations enacted legislation intended to control immigrant banking operations. Massachusetts, New York, New Jersey, Pennsylvania, and Ohio passed such laws, which contained regulations far less stringent than those governing state and national banks. In Illinois, rural private American bankers effectively opposed rules that might have limited their own free and easy activities. The state legislature did not enact or enforce measures over private banking operations until the 1930's, following the failure of numerous American and immigrant banks. Consequently, Italians (and other immigrant bankers) continued to operate in Illinois with few restrictions throughout the period of large-scale immigration.[36]

Legislation on the books did not mean, of course, that police enforced the laws, that illegal activities ceased, or that the native community supported the new statutes. This situation in Chicago caused great confusion among immigrant residents, and showed clearly in the case of the efforts of Italian leaders to limit and control the occupation of rag picking in the late 1880's and the 1890's. On August 13, 1887, *L'Italia* proposed the formation of "an Italian association for the suppression of rag pickers and organ grinders" for the honor and good name of Italy and Italians in America; the journal supported the passage of the necessary legislation, continuing its attack to the extent that the *Chicago Herald* labeled it a "crusade."

The *Herald's* editorial on August 21, 1887, summarized American press reaction to *L'Italia's* efforts by describing the organ grinder as "a mendicant and a nuisance" who "ought not to be permitted to ply his beggary in the streets"; on the other hand, continued the editorial, "why assail the rag-picker?" He might be "humble and unpicturesque," but he was also "useful and honest," a respectable businessman and therefore "not to be classed with the man who chains a monkey to an organ and begs his way through life. Both may offend the aesthetic sense of the Italian editor. Neither is a thing of beauty, but the industry of one is as commendable as the mendicancy of the other is disreputable."

Despite the *Herald's* opinions, the city passed an ordinance in September, 1888, designed to limit and control beggars as well as rag pickers. Expected improvements did not take place. In 1894 Durante complained in *L'Italia* that Chicago's Italians viewed with "intense stupor and amazement" the failure to enforce laws and ordinances "while the people and the press loudly denounce these nuisances, which would be stamped out with the enforcement of said laws and ordinances." Italians, "instrumental in pushing through the City Council the ordinances against the filthy rag pickers and professional beggars," saw these laws enforced "for a week or a trifle over that" and then dropped because "the rag pickers were voters and consequently under the protection of their ward politicians." Durante concluded that Americans failed to support Italians even when the newcomers did their best to improve their district.[37]

In 1895 Mastro-Valerio reviewed the "crusade" against Italian rag pickers. Noting the passage of legislation forbidding rag pick-

ing, he reported that rag pickers "formed a sort of political association, and let the party in power [Democratic] understand that they
. . . would vote against that party at the next election if the interference of the police in their occupation was not stopped." Mastro-
Valerio charged that immediately "the police, by secret orders, let
the rag pickers alone." [38] During Prohibition also, Americans ignored existing legislation, patronized illegal bars ("speakeasies")
operated by Italians and others, and once again provided a confus-
ing example for immigrant newcomers.

Other businessmen in the immigrant quarter supplied needed
services and products, and lined their own pockets by overcharg-
ing or otherwise cheating compatriots. Among these were quack
doctors, shyster lawyers, and merchants who adulterated their
wares—storekeepers, for example, who mixed linseed with olive
oil and sold the mixture as pure Sicilian or Luccan oil. Italian-
language journals reported these and many other crimes, including
robbery, embezzlement, and misappropriation of funds; arson;
counterfeiting; election fraud; and a number of rackets and sharp
practices executed by peddlers, restaurant owners, labor agents,
bankers, and community businessmen, all contriving to relieve in-
experienced newcomers of their money. In addition, corruption
and violence often marked the organization and operation of
Italian locals and unions.[39]

Chicago's Italian colony youngsters sought economic mobility
through many channels, including crime. Children raised in "delinquency areas" could and did turn to work in legitimate lines and
found success in commercial, trade and professional occupations.
Nevertheless, illegal activities appeared to offer the quickest means
available for monetary gain. Many youngsters early realized that
in the highly competitive, rootless society in which they lived,
achievement, measured in financial terms, had high value while
the methods used to realize success received little attention or
condemnation.[40] Young Italian-Americans, Alberto Pecorini noted
in 1916, "furnished an alarmingly high percentage of young criminals." He maintained that all immigrant groups, from Irish and
German to Italian and eastern European Jewish, had passed

through the same experience. This juvenile lawbreaking stemmed in large part from the fact that criminal activity offered opportunities for quick and substantial monetary gain and therefore success. Without perhaps understanding the significance of his observation, Durante lamented that "today, not many crimes are committed to avenge the honor of wives, sisters or children as in the past; most of them are for money." [41]

Despite the wide range of immigrant illegalities, most "Southerns" led law-abiding lives. The bulk of arrests and convictions involving Italians in Chicago resulted from minor offenses (misdemeanors), particularly violations of city ordinances, rather than Black Hand crimes. In 1908, the last year in which the Department of Police *Annual Report* listed city ordinance violations separately from state misdemeanors, Italians committed a total of 1935 criminal offenses. Felonies accounted for 294 while the other 1641 offenses were misdemeanors, of which 1276 involved city ordinances.[42]

The Chicago City Council Committee on Crime, under the chairmanship of Alderman (and University of Chicago political science professor) Charles E. Merriam, presented in March, 1915, a comparison of arrest and conviction statistics for native-born (white and black) and foreign-born groups. The committee found a considerably greater percentage of arrests and convictions among native groups than their ratio of the population. Foreign-born elements, on the other hand, showed "almost uniformly" smaller percentages than their proportion of the population. Italians exhibited an excess of one tenth of one per cent in convictions (misdemeanors and felonies combined); the Committee remarked, "This is surely so small as to be negligible!" [43]

The professional criminal knew, or had ready access to lawyers who knew, the nuances of the law and how to avoid retribution for antisocial actions. He had money and connections with politicians as well as with corrupt policemen who would delay or circumvent efforts to bring him to justice. He also could arrange for bribery or intimidation of witnesses and victims so that they would remain silent. The average immigrant Italian, on the other hand,

## Table 8

NATIVITY OF MALE PERSONS ARRESTED AND CONVICTED
FOR FELONIES, 1913

| Nativity | Arrests | | Convictions | | Per Cent Distribution of Male Population of Chicago 21 Years and Over |
| | No. | Per Cent | No. | Per Cent | |
| --- | --- | --- | --- | --- | --- |
| *American:* | | | | | |
| White | 5,756 | 56.3 | 2,241 | 56.9 | 43.1 |
| Colored | 882 | 8.6 | 354 | 9.0 | 2.6 |
| *Foreign:* | | | | | |
| Austrian | 401 | 3.9 | 158 | 4.0 | 11.2 |
| English | 166 | 1.6 | 79 | 2.0 | 5.2 |
| French | 22 | .2 | 10 | .3 | .... |
| German | 815 | 8.0 | 366 | 9.3 | 12.6 |
| Greek | 139 | 1.4 | 29 | .7 | .6 |
| Dutch | 19 | .2 | 8 | .2 | .7 |
| Irish | 186 | 1.8 | 98 | 2.5 | 4.4 |
| Italian | 392 | 3.8 | 108 | 2.7 | 3.2 |
| Russian | 1,027 | 10.0 | 331 | 8.4 | 8.5 |
| Scandinavian | 214 | 2.1 | 93 | 2.4 | 6.7 |
| Other | 218 | 2.1 | 64 | 1.6 | 1.2 |
| Total Foreign | 3,599 | 35.1 | 1,344 | 34.1 | 54.3 |
| Total | 10,237 | 100.0 | 3,939 | 100.0 | 100.0 |

Source: Chicago City Council, *Report of the Committee on Crime* (Chicago, 1915), 56–57.

often faced arrest and severe punishment for violating laws and ordinances about which he, and most newcomers, knew nothing. If the immigrant spoke no English he labored under an additional disadvantage because most court interpreters lacked knowledge of court procedures, were unacquainted with the various dialects used by Italian residents of the city, and often had a limited familiarity with the English language. In some courts, police officers served as interpreters, in others court officials (usually clerks) translated, while in still others the officials simply "got along the

## Table 9

### NATIVITY OF MALE PERSONS ARRESTED AND CONVICTED FOR MISDEMEANORS, 1913

| Nativity | Arrests | | Convictions | | Per Cent Distribution of Male Population of Chicago 21 Years and Over |
|---|---|---|---|---|---|
| | No. | Per Cent | No. | Per Cent | |
| *American:* | | | | | |
| White | 50,999 | 58.5 | 23,656 | 59.6 | 43.1 |
| Colored | 4,741 | 5.4 | 2,179 | 5.5 | 2.6 |
| *Foreign:* | | | | | |
| Austrian | 3,282 | 3.8 | 1,492 | 3.8 | 11.2 |
| English | 1,240 | 1.4 | 537 | 1.3 | 5.2 |
| French | 181 | .2 | 90 | .2 | .... |
| German | 6,942 | 8.0 | 2,977 | 7.5 | 12.6 |
| Greek | 1,592 | 1.8 | 947 | 2.4 | .6 |
| Dutch | 209 | .3 | 115 | .3 | .7 |
| Irish | 2,354 | 2.7 | 901 | 2.3 | 4.4 |
| Italian | 2,972 | 3.4 | 1,333 | 3.4 | 3.2 |
| Russian | 7,519 | 8.6 | 3,314 | 8.3 | 8.5 |
| Scandinavian | 2,857 | 3.3 | 1,330 | 3.3 | 6.7 |
| Other | 2,268 | 2.6 | 819 | 2.1 | 1.2 |
| Total Foreign: | 31,416 | 36.1 | 13,855 | 34.9 | 54.3 |
| Total | 87,156 | 100.0 | 39,690 | 100.0 | 100.0 |

Source: Chicago City Council, *Report of the Committee on Crime* (Chicago, 1915), 57.

best they could" by picking a bystander who claimed to speak the language. Court decisions based on the work of such interpreters often showed little justice or impartiality.[44]

## VI

Within the immigrant colony, bankers and padroni, Blackhanders and other lawbreakers realized small but important profits by swindling or terrorizing compatriots. Another level of crime involved Italians. Organized crime, business operations reaping vast profits in and from the whole city, offered almost limitless opportunities for promotion within the hierarchy.

Chicago's organized crime originated in the 1870's with the activities of Michael Cassius McDonald. In the years before the Great Fire, gambling dens operated openly with police protection, some of them 24 hours a day. Joseph Medill, elected mayor in 1871 on a "Let's Rebuild Chicago" platform, openly fought gamblers, liquor interests, and the criminal elements of the city. McDonald retaliated by organizing the underworld for political action, and he and his forces succeeded in electing Harvey D. Colvin mayor in 1873.

Gambling interests suffered a temporary setback with the election of Monroe Heath in 1876, but they returned to power in 1879 and except for a brief eclipse during the mayoralty of John A. Roche (1887–89), McDonald controlled city politics until the mid-1890's. Recalling the McDonald era on August 18, 1907 (a few days after his death), the *Chicago Record-Herald* stated that "he never held office, but he ruled the city with an iron hand. He named the men who were to be candidates for election, he elected them, and after they were in office they were merely his puppets." Chicago historian Bessie Louise Pierce described him as "virtually the dictator of the City Hall." With his political power established following Carter Henry Harrison's mayoral success in 1879, "Mike" McDonald turned to organizing the city's first "syndicate," which centered on gambling. During his reign, McDonald, as political party boss and head of the "syndicate," forged the powerful and highly effective coalition of criminals, politicians, and compliant policemen that the Torrio-Capone organization utilized so successfully during the 1920's.[45]

Following the assassination of Mayor Harrison in October, 1893, McDonald's star began to fade, and a number of new independent organizations or "syndicates" formed. By 1907, when "Mike" died, various spheres of interest controlled gambling in Chicago. Mont Tennes gave orders on the North Side, James O'Leary on the South Side, and Alderman Johnny Rogers on the West Side. First

Ward political bosses "Hinky Dink" Kenna and "Bathhouse John" Coughlin, early patrons of "Diamond Jim" Colosimo, presided over gambling in the Loop.[46]

After years of gang warfare most of McDonald's former gambling empire centered in the hands of Mont Tennes, who ruled, in turn, until the 1920's when the Torrio-Capone group pushed him aside and seized control of gambling as well as other illegal activities in the Chicago area. Although the real entry of Italians into a big-time crime (and most of their successes therein) came after 1920—that is, during Prohibition—they did make a strong beginning under Colosimo in the first two decades of the twentieth century.

While still a youth, Colosimo left Calabria for the United States. His first employment in this country, and the work that took him to Chicago, was that of waterboy for a railroad section gang. Before the turn of the century Colosimo became a streetsweeper and established his residence in the First Ward at 416 South Clark Street. Rocco De Stefano, who later became "Big Jim's" lawyer, also lived in this tenement. Colosimo organized his fellow street sweepers (or "white wings") of the First Ward into a political bloc that he led as a unit to the polling station at election time in order to vote for candidates supported by the Democratic machine. This action quickly brought him to the attention of aldermen Kenna and Coughlin, who had dominated First Ward politics since 1893. They made "Big Jim" a precinct captain and he delivered the vote so successfully for his patrons that before his death he rivaled Kenna and Coughlin as a political power in the ward.[47]

In the meantime Colosimo and his wife, Victoria Moresco, acquired a string of brothels and saloons, as well as a legitimate business—a nationally known restaurant called "Colosimo's Cafe." (Socially prominent Chicagoans patronized it and dined among theater and opera personages, including George M. Cohan and Enrico Caruso.) By 1914, "Big Jim" and associates had built a "syndicate," the first one organized by Chicago Italians, based on vice operations and gambling. In that year State's Attorney Maclay Hoyne launched a grand jury investigation of vice in Chicago's First Ward and found the existence of three vice rings or "syndicates." The first and largest consisted of the Colosimo-Torrio outfit, headed by "Big Jim" and his chief lieutenant, Johnny Torrio.[48]

Colosimo brought his number two man to Chicago in 1909 to deal with Black Hand extortion threats, since Torrio had effectively arranged for the elimination of bothersome Blackhanders in New York. Within five years, his efficient and ruthless methods advanced Torrio to second-in-command and a power in his own right through his organizing of gambling in the city and some nearby suburbs. (At this time Torrio lived in the same building as "Big Jim," 101 West Twenty-first Street.) In 1919 Henry Barrett Chamberlain, Operating Director of the Chicago Crime Commission, described increasingly efficient "syndicate" crime: "Modern crime, like modern business, is tending toward centralization, organization, and commercialization. Ours is a business nation. Our criminals apply business methods. . . . The men and women of evil have formed trusts.[49]

When the National Prohibition Enforcement Act (The Volstead Act) went into effect on January 16, 1920, the Colosimo-Torrio organization expanded from prostitution and gambling into an even more lucrative business, the manufacture and distribution of liquor. Colosimo did not live long enough to reap the full financial harvest of his bootlegging ventures, for he was murdered on May 11, 1920.

Responsibility for his death was never determined. Some maintained that the murder formed the climax of a struggle for political control of the First Ward, with Kenna and Colosimo allied against Frank Brady, the ward's Republican leader, and Frank Chiaravalotti. The *Chicago Daily News* advanced this possibility the day after Colosimo's death. More people accepted the theory that the shooting grew out of Colosimo's affection for Miss Dale Winter, a hired singer in his restaurant. For love of Dale, "Big Jim" divorced Victoria. A big, crude, gross man with a passion for diamonds (which shone from his belt and suspender buckles, his shirt, vest, fingers, and even his garters), Colosimo won the affection of Miss Winter, described by contemporaries as a lovely girl, gentle and sweet, with a beautiful singing voice. According to this second theory, the first Mrs. Colosimo hired thugs to murder the man who had cast her aside for a younger woman. The fact that Victoria remarried only two weeks after the divorce and some three weeks before "Diamond Jim" married his Dale weakened this argument.[50]

Another popular theory held that John Torrio, tired of being the number two man, lusted for full control of the organization and took steps to achieve this end. After Colosimo's death, Torrio did indeed succeed to the "syndicate" throne, which he occupied until his retirement in 1925. In contrast to his rough and vulgar predecessor, Torrio was quiet, crafty, and businesslike; he shunned alcohol, tobacco, personal violence, and foul language. An able and effective leader, Torrio excelled as a master strategist and organizer and quickly built an empire that far exceeded Colosimo's in wealth, power, and influence. He received invaluable aid from his chief lieutenant, Alphonse Capone. Italian domination of Chicago's organized crime had made a strong beginning indeed.[51]

## VII

Several factors facilitated Italian successes in the highly competitive (and deadly) business of organized crime. Some related to old-world backgrounds and characteristics, others to conditions and opportunities in the host society. Mafia-expert Michele Pantaleone has presented a brilliant exposé of the Sicilian Mafia in a recent book, *The Mafia and Politics*. His comments on Sicilians in American crime, however, raise more questions than they answer. According to Pantaleone, men schooled in the Sicilian Mafia "founded and organized gangsterdom in America fifty years ago"— that is, in the decade following 1910. These criminals operated in "St. Louis, Chicago, Kansas City, Detroit, New Orleans, New Jersey [sic] and other cities." The list omits, significantly, Boston and Milwaukee. Also pointedly missing are—first—any indication that "organized gangsterdoms" existed in Chicago, New York and other cities long before 1910, and—second—the fact that when an Italian "syndicate" developed after 1910 in competition with organizations composed of members of other ethnic groups, it was not staffed solely by Sicilians or even entirely by Italians, any more than Irish, Jewish, or Polish criminal organizations contained only members of these groups. Thus many alleged *capo mafiosi* (leaders) of Chicago's Italian "syndicate" had no Sicilian ancestry, while others born in Sicily emigrated as children and grew to maturity in urban America. James Colosimo, for example, was born in mainland Italy (Calabria) and arrived in Chicago as a boy; John Torrio, a native of the province of Naples, immigrated (with his parents) at the age of two and grew up in Brooklyn; Al Capone was born in Brooklyn of Neapolitan parents; while Jake Gusick (or Jack Cusick), the "so-called brains of the Capone organization," was only one of many non-Italian members of the "American Mafia hierarchy." [52]

The ethnic cohesion and group loyalty exhibited by the Italian criminal element in its struggle to dominate Chicago's organized crime formed a more significant factor than the Sicilian origin of some gangsters. The "Southern" background of most of the city's Italians included a deep loyalty to clan traditions held to be sacred from "outside" interference. As some writers on Italian-American criminality have pointed out, these traditions and connections provided a ready-made nucleus for criminal gangs in the new world and ensured a fierce partisanship toward the group's laws and rituals rather than to "outside" rules and regulations. [53]

To a Southern Italian or Sicilian living in the Kingdom, however, the concept of *paese* (homeland) meant locality of origin, rather than the nation. Localism—due to the mountainous character of the country, which isolated communities—operated to the extent that even adjacent areas in Italy developed their own characteristics, customs, speech patterns, and loyalties. "There are Campanians, Abruzzians, Apulians, Calabrians, Lucanians (Lucania being another name for Basilicata), Sicilians and Sardinians, all differing greatly from each other, while inside each region are many varieties of type," as English historian Margaret Carlyle pointed out. "Not only is a Campanian, particularly a Neapolitan, as different from a Calabrian as a Norfolk man from a Cumbrian, but a peasant from one of the primitive agricultural towns of the

Ionian side of Calabria is a completely different type from the man who farms a tiny bit of good land on the Tyrrhenian coast." [54] This meaning of *paese* contrasted sharply with the situation in the United States, where Sicilians and mainlanders alike regarded themselves as Italians, and were so regarded by Americans.

In Chicago this expanded sense of loyalty and patriotism manifested itself in celebrations supporting the Italian Kingdom, membership in mutual-aid and fraternal societies based on regional or national groupings, and support of an "Italian" press and Italian Catholic parishes. In the new homeland, therefore, village loyalties grew into national loyalties and members of the ethnic group came to look upon non-Italians, rather than people from outside a particular village in Italy, as foreigners. "American" Italians, who established and operated Chicago's Italian "syndicate," excluded members of other ethnic groups until they had proved themselves to be worthy of acceptance. Since conditions in Chicago offered fertile ground for lawless activities, gangs composed predominantly of other ethnic groups—Irish, German, Scandinavian—operated openly and often under the protection of the law and elected officials long before "Southerners" arrived. This "favorable" situation could not be found in all urban areas to which "Southerners" migrated, with the significant result that second-generation Italians became prominently involved in criminal organizations in some cities and not in others. Undoubtedly many Sicilian Blackhanders moved into the "syndicate," but "American" Italians provided the leadership. Hence local conditions permitting or even encouraging lawlessness clearly occupied a place of basic importance in Italian successes within Chicago's organized crime. [55]

Chicago's early Italian settlement, largely composed of northern Italians, took little interest in, and avoided contact with, "Southerners." Most of the city's southern Italians, especially those from Sicily, arrived between 1900 and 1914. Children of "Southern" immigrants grew to maturity at a time when educational requirements were increasingly important when qualifying for jobs in public as well as in private employment. The fluid political, social, and financial patterns, which had aided (and in fact had speeded) the assimilation of Germans, Irishmen, Bohemians, Poles, Swedes, and Norwegians in the three decades following 1870, gradually grew more rigid and unyielding as earlier immigrant elements became entrenched. These early arrivals sought to establish barriers to prevent later ones (with other ethnic backgrounds) from challenging their positions.

If at all possible, ethnic group members tried to "look after their own" whether in politics, crime, organized labor, or the professions. Thus Anton J. Cermak, whether in his capacity as alderman, president of the Cook County Board of Commissioners, or mayor, made sure that his fellow Bohemians (Czechs) received patronage jobs and support when they tried for elective office. Early arriving northern Italians, however, did not consider "Southerners" to be "of their own." Lacking established patrons, southern Italians did not make their political presence in the city really felt until the 1920's when, under the leadership and guidance of John Torrio and Al Capone, they found politics and its urban handmaiden, crime, to offer an increasingly important source of money as well as a means of social mobility.[56]

## VIII

Chicago's Italians enjoyed great success in criminal activities, whether within immigrant areas through Black Hand and other extortion methods or by "syndicate" techniques in the larger, American environment. The Black Hand existed, but as a method of criminal action, a *modus operandi,* and not a formal organization. As the White Hand Society pointed out in 1908, many other Italian-community residents who did not consider themselves Blackhanders—among them bankers, interpreters, labor agents, and small businessmen—worked diligently to extort fellow immigrants. They employed more subtle and refined methods than did the Black Hand thugs, "but they too are means of exacting tribute from the sweat of the Italian working man, who pays because of his ignorance, and because of the absolute lack of any assistance and protection in a foreign land." [57]

Profits gained through Black Hand methods in the immigrant colony seemed small when compared with the lucrative returns won by "syndicate" gangsters from Prohibition law violations, gambling, prostitution, and drug peddling. Italians born or raised in Chicago quickly learned to adapt American business techniques to crime by organizing compatriots (and acceptable "outsiders"), centralizing the chain of command, and controlling and directing the flow of money. In this process of "Americanizing" Italian criminal activities, "American" Italians established the Italian "syndicate."

Crime even facilitated immigrant adjustment. The "syndicate" required the repression of lingering old-world prejudices against fellow members from other provinces or countries, because of the overriding importance of cooperation in the common quest for money, that symbol and substance of success. In the new urban home—cynical, cruel, vulgar, avaricious Chicago—Sicilians and Italians, northern as well as southern, joined together for mutual benefit and profit. Because of its function as a means of economic betterment and social mobility, crime occupied a place in the acculturation of Italians in the United States, along with immigrant-community institutions, education, the padrone system, and politics.

# 6

## Community Institutions and Assimilation

Italians who, in the Kingdom, never considered the possibility of cooperation or even of contact with co-nationals from other towns and provinces found themselves forced to deal with urban difficulties in the United States as members of groups. In the process, newcomers modified familiar institutions (like the Church), organized some that had scarcely touched their lives in Italy (such as the press and mutual-benefit societies), and established agencies that did not exist in the home country (like the immigrant bank). Thus while some immigrant institutions had counterparts in the old world, "Southerners" either came into contact with them for the first time in America or cast them in new molds.

Many Americans mistakenly assumed that ethnic districts and institutions reproduced homeland surroundings and perpetuated "isolated group life"; hence through "churches and schools, and in social, fraternal, and national organizations," immigrants could maintain "the speech, the ideals, and to some extent the manner of life of the mother country." Actually the colony represented an important step *away* from old-world patterns. Because the city prevented isolation, neither the community nor its institutions were fully Italian in character; nor were they American. They served an interim group, the immigrant generation with its old-world traditions and new-world surroundings. Constantine M. Panunzio, himself an immigrant, noted this fact when he described an Italian colony (in Boston) where he had resided as being "in no way a typical American community, [but] neither did it resemble Italy." [1]

Community institutions of all new immigrant groups in the United States more closely resembled each other and native-American counterparts than they did homeland organizations. Mutual-benefit and fraternal societies, for example, existed among Poles, Ukrainians, Lithuanians, and Jews, among others. Italian publishers used similar techniques and faced problems much the same as those of other foreign-language press groups. Non-Italians also depended upon services provided by immigrant bankers and padroni. "In America," sociologist Robert E. Park noted, "the peasant discards his [old-world] habits and acquires 'ideas.' In America, above all, the immigrant organizes. These organizations are the embodiment of his needs and his new ideas." [2]

Within the colony three institutions developed that sought principally to provide guidance and leadership for neighborhood residents. These were the benevolent societies, the Church, and the Italian-language press (the banker and padrone labor agent, who have been discussed elsewhere, concerned themselves entirely with financial profits and made no claims about contributing to group welfare or morale). Members of each institution believed their contributions to be the most significant and vital to the whole ethnic group. According to Italian-American journalist Luigi Carnovale, who worked for *La Tribuna Italiana Transatlantica* in Chicago and *La Gazzetta Illustrata* (a magazine) in St. Louis, the foreign-language press provided the immigrant with his best and truest friend in the new homeland. "In the colonial press, in short, the Italian immigrants have always found all that is indispensable—wise advice, moral and material assistance, true and ardent fraternal love—for their success and triumph in . . . America." [3]

## II

Chicago's first Italian-language newspaper, the short-lived *L'Unione Italiana,* began in 1867. Despite efforts in 1868 to inject new life along with a new name, *Il Messaggiere Italiano dell'Ouest,* the paper lasted only until 1872. Unfortunately for the prospects of this early attempt, the Italian settlement in Chicago at the time was too small to support a newspaper, and exhibited little group consciousness. After 1880 the Italian colony grew in size yearly as ever-increasing numbers of immigrants arrived. While the second generation quickly turned away from everything foreign— that is, Italian—the rapidly expanding numbers of first-generation immigrants made journalistic ventures directed toward Italians more attractive.[4]

During the period between 1886 and 1921, at least twenty Italian-language newspapers appeared in Chicago. Among the many varieties of these, the most popular and influential were *L'Italia* and *La Tribuna Italiana Transatlantica,* founded in 1886 and 1898 respectively. Small in circulation but influential in their particular fields, *La Parola dei Socialisti,* begun in 1908, and *Il Proletario,* dating from 1896, reported leftwing activities and viewpoints, while the Protestant journal, *La Fiaccola,* first appeared in 1898. Although published in New York, *Il Progresso Italo-Americano* enjoyed a wide readership among Chicago's Italians, especially during and after World War I, and wielded at least as much influence as any local paper. It should be noted that the Italian-language newspapers of Chicago also exercised influence beyond the boundaries of the city. *L'Italia* and *La Tribuna Italiana Transatlantica* reached subscribers throughout the country. While small in total circulation, socialist and anarchist papers went from Chicago as far east as New York, Massachusetts, and Vermont, and as far west as Iowa.[5]

Oscar Durante and Carlo Gentile founded *L'Italia* in 1886. Sixteen at the time, Naples-born Durante became sole owner and editor just four months later when he bought Gentile's share of the paper. From its first year in existence, *L'Italia* claimed a nationwide readership and carried news items and advertisements from communities throughout the Middle West, the Rocky Mountain area, and the East Coast. Even in 1886 *L'Italia* maintained an office, or at least an address, in New York as well as in Chicago. In 1888 Durante announced that Chicago had become the center of Italian-American journalism and *L'Italia* ranked "above all others, the most worthy and popular paper of its kind in the United States," for "after three years of indefatigable work we have succeeded in placing *L'Italia* in every Italian household in Chicago, and with nearly every family, from New York to California and Maine to the Gulf." The young newspaper was, Durante maintained, "a complete artistic-journalistic success." [6]

This early optimism increased in intensity when, in 1889, the paper's caption proclaimed that *L'Italia* possessed "the largest circulation of any Italian newspaper in the United States." Throughout the 1890's, the paper continued to call itself "the largest-selling Italian newspaper in the country," and cited figures from Rowell's *American Newspaper Directory* to substantiate its claim. In 1892 *L'Italia*'s circulation exceeded 17,500, although the paper had been in operation for only six years. Its closest rival, *Il Progresso Italo-Americano* of New York, claimed slightly more than 7500 subscribers. Other Italian-American journals in the United States reached circulations no higher than 4000. The "largest circulation" caption, first used by *L'Italia* in July 1889, continued until January 1, 1901, when it, along with earlier bubbling optimism, ended. [7]

After the turn of the century there could be no disputing the fact that New York contained the largest and most important Italian colony in the United States as well as the country's leading Italian-language newspaper, *Il Progresso Italo-Americano*. In 1915, when *L'Italia*'s circulation reached 30,000, *Il Progresso*'s jumped to more than 82,000. *L'Italia*'s subscribers grew to more than 38,000 in 1921, at which time *Il Progresso* reached 111,000 readers. *L'Italia* continued to be the largest-selling and most influential

Italian-language journal published in Chicago and remained, as a journalistic rival admitted, "a newspaper read from the Atlantic to the Pacific, from Canada to the Gulf of Mexico." [8]

Alessandro Mastro-Valerio and Giuseppe Ronga founded *La Tribuna Italiana* in 1898. In 1903 Mastro-Valerio, then sole owner, altered it to *La Tribuna Italiana Transatlantica*. Born in the Italian "South" and an early resident of Hull House, Mastro-Valerio started his newspaper as an organ of expression and communication for Italian inhabitants of the Nineteenth Ward. As time passed, the paper developed a city-wide interest in activities and problems of immigrants, although its primary concern throughout its existence remained with the happenings and welfare of the Near West Side Italian colony. It maintained, above all, a local, ward-level perspective; only secondarily did it show an interest in Italians of other American cities. This focus contrasted sharply with that of *L'Italia,* which claimed to be a journal for Italians throughout Chicago and the rest of the country.[9]

Mastro-Valerio displayed a great interest in the economic and social situation of Italian common laborers. Unlike Durante of *L'Italia,* he generally supported labor against capital, feeling that the latter abused the former. To Mastro-Valerio one obvious solution to problems faced by immigrants in urban industrial America lay in agricultural colonies, and *La Tribuna Italiana Transatlantica* reflected this idea. Mastro-Valerio lacked Durante's grasp of the importance of politics to economic and social advancement in the United States, yet in a regular column, *Della capitale,* his paper provided the most comprehensive coverage of national politics attempted by an Italian paper in Chicago. It paid special attention to antitrust activities, for example, which *L'Italia* generally ignored.

*La Tribuna Italiana Transatlantica* began as, and remained, a weekly paper unlike its major rival *L'Italia,* which in 1913 grew from a weekly publication, appearing on Saturday, to a tri-weekly (Tuesday, Thursday, Saturday). *La Tribuna's* circulation increased from 5500 in 1905, the first year for which figures are available, to 25,000 in 1908, and stayed at that level until 1921. Its editor's influence made *La Tribuna* into a more colorful and sensational journal than any of its major rivals. Although contemporaries regarded Mastro-Valerio as a well-educated man, his paper made free use of Italian-American jargon such as "storo" for store, "bosso" for boss, "ganga" for gang, "grosseria" for grocery store, and "sciarap" for a command to be silent. Poor typesetting and editing often resulted in peculiar English spellings, a problem not unique to this paper, for carelessness, sloppy proofreading, stylistic shortcomings, and use of Italian-American slang characterized all Italian-language periodicals. Mastro-Valerio made little effort to compete with *L'Italia* or *Il Progresso Italo-Americano* in factual reporting, but rather emphasized opinion, special features such as news from Washington, and Italian theater and opera.[10]

*La Parola dei Socialisti,* stated Egisto Clemente (editor of *La Parola del Popolo* and Socialist Party member for over fifty years), aimed to create and maintain worker solidarity and to protect workers' interests in the American environment, to give them news of the "Movement" in the United States, and to provide general news of Italy. The paper and the Party sought to help immigrants, to bring more of the good things of life to the workers, and to win these essentially economic objectives through political activities and use of the strike.[11]

First published in 1908, *La Parola dei Socialisti* consistently criticized and attacked Mastro-Valerio and his paper. Since both journals appealed to immigrants with leftwing leanings, *La Parola dei Socialisti* considered *La Tribuna Italiana Transatlantica* to be a dangerous rival. Its founder, Giuseppe Bertelli, had been called from Italy to Philadelphia in 1906 to assume direction of *Il Proletario,* the oldest leftwing Italian-language newspaper in the United States. A Social Democrat, Bertelli found that he could not work with the syndicalists who controlled and operated *Il Proletario.* He resigned and moved to Chicago, where he founded Italian socialist sections in the Nineteenth Ward (and others) and started his new, more moderate periodical.[12]

In the early years of *La Parola dei Socialisti*'s existence, Bertelli wrote almost all the articles with some help from G. Artoni and

Guido Podrecca. These first issues kept alive a bitter controversy by attacking the rival wing of the socialist movement and especially *Il Proletario,* through Bertelli's biting articles about syndicalism and syndicalists.[13]

While *La Parola dei Socialisti* was published in Chicago and printed considerable news about conditions and activities of Italians there, it did not limit its outlook to that city but concerned itself with Italians throughout the country and printed news of events in all parts of the United States. It maintained correspondents in each town in which Italians worked and in all coal-mining settlements.[14]

The two wings of the Italian-language press in the United States existed with few areas of common interest. Bourgeois periodicals devoted little attention to events of avid interest to the socialist press, such as the Russian Revolution of 1917. On the other hand, socialist papers took superficial notice of things emphasized in other periodicals, including events in Italy, the glories of the Kingdom, and American politics. Thus while socialist and anarchist publications strongly opposed patriotic (that is, pro-Italian) manifestations among Italian-Americans, the bourgeois press gloried in supposed diplomatic and military successes of Italy, including the Abyssinian venture in the 1890's and the Libyan War of 1911–12. Socialist journals emphasized the disastrous consequences of Italian foreign policies and lamented the waste of money that could be better used by the Italian government to educate its people.[15]

The outbreak of war in Europe in 1914 marked the beginning of socialism's decline among Italians in America, and the corresponding decline of the socialist press. *La Parola dei Socialisti* opposed the conflict from beginning to end, reflecting the attitude and policy of the Socialist Party. This position won little support from residents of Italian neighborhoods or from the American government. In order to evade wartime postal restrictions imposed by federal authorities on radical as well as German-American newspapers and magazines, the directors of *La Parola dei Socialisti* found it expedient to change the paper's name four times between 1916 and 1921—to *La Parola Proletaria* from 1916 to early in 1918, then to *La Fiaccola* (the same name as the Protestant journal); later the same year to *L'Avanti!* (*Avanti!* after March 1, 1919); and in 1921 to *La Parola del Popolo*. Problems of small circulation and inadequate financial resources always plagued the journal. Subscription figures fluctuated between 3500 and 5000 during the years from 1914 to 1921 (figures prior to 1914 are not available).[16]

Inevitably the paper relied upon appeals to subscribers and friends for funds to meet current expenses and expand services. Through a subscription, it managed to increase from four to eight pages in 1914, and the editors proudly announced on January 31, 1914, that as of that date more than $600 had been collected. A significant amount when compared with the usual immigrant area collection, this sum was nevertheless pitifully inadequate for operating a newspaper. Its wartime and postwar policies, moreover, magnified the journal's financial needs. Almost every issue of *Avanti!* from October to December in 1919, for example, contained frantic pleas to readers. The issue of January 8, 1921, begged for funds "for the continued existence of our *Avanti!*" The paper's name changed again in 1921 (to *La Parola del Popolo*), but financial and ideological difficulties continued without interruption.

Financial problems also threatened the existence of two other journals that appealed to limited audiences within the Italian community, the Industrial Workers of the World paper *Il Proletario* and the Protestant *La Fiaccola,* both published for a brief time in Chicago. *Il Proletario*'s offices operated in the city from 1918 to 1921, first as *La Difesa* (May to November, 1918) and then as *Il Nuovo Proletario* (November, 1918 to 1921). It existed solely to further the class struggle through violent and disruptive means, a sharp contrast with the socialist press, and viewed the I.W.W.-led textile workers' strike in 1912 at Lawrence, Massachusetts, as the first battle in the campaign to overthrow capitalism in America. It opposed the capitalistic system and World War I, supported the Bolshevik Revolution in a manner more complete and extreme than *La Parola*'s, and thus severely limited both potential readership and sources of income. As a result, *Il Proletario* led a precarious existence, harried by a constant struggle with financial problems. The paper attempted to solve its difficulties through subscriptions such as the one initiated on July 31, 1915: "For the life of *Il Proletario*," read the caption, and the following article pleaded for contributions to keep the paper solvent. This monetary campaign never ceased during following years as new financial emergencies aggravated the journal's plight.

The Methodist Book Concern founded *La Fiaccola* (not to be confused with the socialist paper of the same name) in 1898. This Protestant newspaper originated as "a weekly periodical for Italian immigrants devoted to the cause of religious, moral and civic reform." Although published in New York City, except for a few months in 1914, when it was printed in Chicago, it was directed to and intended for Italians throughout the country. *La Fiaccola* appeared in Italian with the exception of part of one page which featured articles in English. Whether in Italian or English, writings generally concentrated either on the progress of conversion among immigrants or on the evils of the papacy and the Catholic Church. The paper regularly ran two editorials, one in English and the other in Italian. Both vigorously upheld Italian nationalism and denounced Catholicism, and during and after World War I preached "one hundred per cent Americanism." Confidently the editors predicted that *La Fiaccola* would grow into "one of the most widely circulated Italian periodicals in America." The paper never reached its objective, attaining neither artistic nor financial success, and in 1921 converted to a monthly magazine.[17]

Other tabloids appeared in Chicago during the period to 1921. Some lasted only a few months, while others continued for a year or longer. In 1888 Oscar Durante started a second newspaper, *Il Corriere dell'Italia*, which presented essentially the same format as *L'Italia*. National and European (mostly Italian) news appeared on page one along with special features. In *Il Corriere* these took the form of "Telegraphic Dispatches," the most recent news from Italy; news of local people and happenings in various towns and provinces of Italy, and information about Chicago's Italians filled page two; pages three and four contained advertisements. Lasting less than a year, *Il Corriere dell'Italia* was evidently intended as a mid-week companion—on Wednesday—to the Saturday *L'Italia*. It could not compete, however, with *Il Progresso Italo-Americano* in coverage of Italian news or with *L'Italia*'s emphasis on local happenings, and its circulation never amounted to much.

On June 26, 1888, two of Durante's former associates from *L'Italia*, Dr. Giuseppe Ronga and Carlo Gentile, launched a new journalistic venture, *Il Messaggiere Italo-Americano*. The directors outlined the newspaper's goals in the first issue, promising to "describe the life of the Italians who live in this country, in all of their manifestations: intellectual, artistic, commercial, industrial." To this end the journal would note "the needs, the pains, and the aspirations" of co-nationals who, in America, fought "the arduous struggle for existence." The editors solicited communications, correspondence, and articles but made no mention of payment for materials used. Gentile and Dr. Ronga vowed that their paper would be neither spiteful nor personal, neither boring nor tedious. "We will attack only when attacked; we will offend no one; we will not judge with partisan spirit, . . . we will be subservient to no one; nor suffer pressures from anyone." Hoping for approval and acceptance, the editors "presented" their paper to the public "without pretense."

*Il Messaggiere Italo-Americano* exhibited livlier writing and a more polished style than most colonial papers. It closely resembled a European journal in character and format, with humorous pieces and regular articles that received light and ironic treatment. Apparently neither its humor nor its sophistication appealed to immigrants, for it lasted less than two years. Gentile published another short-lived venture, *La Colonia*, which appeared from 1889 to 1892.

Publishers of unsuccessful Italian-language newspapers, like Gentile, often sought to recoup some of their losses and remain in business by fooling the public. They simply changed the name, but seldom the appearance or policy, of their paper. Giuseppe Gaya, for example, directed *L'America* from 1891 to 1892 and when it failed to attract subscribers, altered the name to *La Fantasma*, which survived from 1892 to 1893. In similar fashion An-

tonio Ferrara's *Il Lucano* became *L'Independente* in 1908. Both
tabloids featured writing done in a humorous manner reminiscent
of *Il Messaggiere Italo-Americano*, but immigrants seemed to be
no more disposed to accept a light, witty treatment of "colonial
vicissitudes" (Ferrara's term for immigrant adjustment problems)
than they had been twenty years earlier.

Publicized aspirations motivating the founding of new papers
changed but little in the twenty years after 1888. Thus in announc-
ing the first issue of *Il Secolo*, appearing February 2, 1908, the
publishers promised to do all in their power to raise the moral and
intellectual conditions of immigrants, defend their rights, and
remove all dishonest and undesirable elements in the Italian community. Such high ideals did not inspire all publishers, some of
whom blackmailed community leaders by threatening to disparage
them through news stories and editorials. Paolo Parise, publisher
of *Il Movimento* (which in 1916 became *Il Giornale di Chicago*),
won renown of sorts for the number of times he was accused of
journalistic blackmail. It is interesting to note, however, that these
"gutter sheets" appealed to as few immigrants as did many of the
more literary papers.[18]

American critics complained, justifiably, about the number of
columns devoted by the Italian-language press to medical advertisements—"as much as a fifth of their space," according to
Robert F. Foerster—but Italian tabloids held no preeminence in
this respect. Frank Luther Mott, the foremost authority on American journalism, noted that patent-medicine advertisements "occupied a large space" in commercial columns of American papers.
Decisions concerning advertising space as well as style and content
of news stories rested with the paper's editor, who represented
the most important factor in his journal's success or failure. He
formed the mainspring of the entire operation to a far greater
extent than did his American counterpart. Generally owner and
publisher as well as editor, he often served also as chief (sometimes
the only) reporter, typesetter, proofreader, circulation agent, dis-
tributor, and salesman.[19]

The fortunate editor-publisher owned a printing press. He then printed his own paper, of course, and made additional profits by publishing Italian-language books and journals of less-successful publishers. Durante and Bertelli enjoyed this enviable position. Durante's firm printed Italian-American journalist Luigi Carnovale's book, *Il Giornalismo degli emigrati italiani nel Nord America,* in 1909. Bertelli printed the newspaper *Il Secolo* and, until 1913, *La Parola dei Socialisti.* In that year the Italian Socialist Federation established a cooperative publishing company (the Italian Labor Publishing Company) to print the paper and replaced Bertelli with Dr. A. Molinari as editor. After World War I Bertelli sold his plant and moved to New York City, where he founded a short-lived socialist daily.[20]

American papers profoundly influenced all foreign publications with innovations such as large, bold headlines and brief articles, special features, photographs and cartoons; all foreign-language papers that survived imitated them, although no Italian-language newspaper in Chicago found itself able to attempt a daily publication during the period to 1920. Most appeared once a week. While successful Italian-language papers of Chicago, including *L'Italia,* often started as journals written in the European style, they soon began to adopt American standards in content and appearance and featured sensational news stories—often reprinted directly from American newspapers. Unsuccessful newspapers generally did not adjust, or did not last long enough to adjust, to American techniques. Like American newspapers, the Italian-language press also experienced the often disastrous effects of technological changes. New, expensive, and intricate machinery, for example, required highly trained, and hence highly paid, personnel. New equipment and higher labor costs forced small and generally unremunerative papers of the pre-World War I era to consolidate into larger units with greater purchasing power.[21]

Nearly all Italian-language periodicals faced another serious lack, that of competent reporters. Even writers for the more successful papers supplemented meager salaries with money provided

by the Italian consul, who subsidized journalists in order to keep
items favorable to Italy and appeals for remittances constantly
before readers.[22]

In addition to their concern over immigrant welfare and other
worthy causes, all Italian-language newspapers in Chicago vigorously, often desperately, worked toward the goal of financial success, as indicated by circulation figures. Editors who placed literary
excellence before sensational news and frequent indications of
loyalty to Italy generally lasted a short time. To maintain healthy
circulations, papers had to provide information that immigrants
considered to be both desirable and necessary and which they
could not obtain elsewhere. In the early days of settlement in
Chicago, for example, Italian papers emphasized news of the
various villages in Italy, which represented the homeland for many
of the city's immigrants. These items gradually disappeared after
1900, replaced by national news of Italy and the United States and
pieces dealing with Italian colonies in other American cities. At
the same time that *L'Italia* satisfied the needs of its readers for
news of the homeland, it encouraged immigrants to adjust to their
American surroundings by acquiring citizenship, attending school,
entering politics, and resisting padrone domination.[23]

Most Italian-language papers tried to encourage immigrants to
adopt habits acceptable to urban Americans, particularly in the
early years of immigration. Newspapers censored adult Italian
males who married teen-age girls, parents who kept their children
out of school in order to put them to work, excessive drinking, and
personal dirtiness (reportedly "vulgar" by American standards).
Mothers nursing babies on streets provided a "shameful spectacle,"
commented one journalist; besides being "not a nice thing to do,"
the scene gave Americans "another point on which to jeer at Italians." Indeed, lamented *L'Italia* on August 4, 1894, "when will
Italian parents stop making such a disgraceful show of themselves
for American amusement and condemnation?"[24]

Italian-language periodicals faced many problems in the pursuit
of their material, aesthetic, and social aspirations. In addition to
lack of adequately trained personnel, relatively small circulations,

insufficient funds to hire or train workers, and limited prestige and authority, journals regularly lost readers as the larger American environment absorbed immigrants. The second generation cared very little about foreign-language papers. As a result, short-lived ventures with frequent turnovers in papers and staff typified the colonial press.

The second generation's lack of interest in Italian-language newspapers caught the attention of the *Chicago Herald* as early as 1887, when it noted that the children of Chicago's Italians, "acquiring the language as they do, readily become, as they grow up and select their own journals, readers of the native press." In 1922 the *Bulletin* (published by the Foreign-Language Information Service) noted not only that American-born children of immigrants preferred to read American papers, but also that the foreign born themselves "as soon as they have acquired sufficient English, turn to the American papers for American and general news, depending on the press of their language for little more than news of the home country." The same situation existed among non-Italian groups. The Mary McDowell Papers report an interview with officers of a Lithuanian organization. Asked what Lithuanian newspapers they read, the immigrants replied that "they read American newspapers. More news in them, they maintained. Once in a while someone brings around a Lithuanian paper and they read it." [25]

Despite all its shortcomings and inadequacies, the Italian-language press made a number of valuable contributions. For the generally illiterate "Southern" peasant (who had little opportunity to gain adequate schooling, at least until returned emigrants helped bring about much needed reforms), the newspapers satisfied a desperate need for reasonably accurate information about the old homeland and the new. Written simply and idiomatically with a mixture of Italian and English words and phrases, the foreign-language press unintentionally aided the immigrant's adjustment to the profusely illustrated and also simply and idiomatically written popular American press.

The Italian-language press also functioned as guide, coordinator

and promoter of national (Italian) pride. It served as an intermediary between the uneducated, frightened (and to many Americans, frightening) immigrant masses and the institutions and
inhabitants of their new homeland. The papers acted as a bridge
between life in familiar Italian villages and that in strange American cities. In addition, they provided identifiable leadership for
Chicago's Italian neighborhoods and voiced demands and complaints of individuals and groups. The maximum impact and value
of colonial papers lay within the ethnic community as the main
link between tradition and new experiences. When editors tried
to exert influence outside this sphere, they and their papers invariably failed.

## III

Many newcomers sought to solve life's complexities by joining
benefit groups. These were not, however, "transplanted" institutions
carried by "Southerners" to the United States. In the "South,"
where strong family ties ensured aid in times of need, group life
featured recreational activities in a few social clubs (*circolo
sociale*), most of which had small memberships and limited community importance.[26]

The mutual aid society (*società di mutuo soccorso*), although
known in Italy, existed almost exclusively among middle classes,
and especially among artisans, in urbanized areas of the northern
and central parts of the Kingdom. By the 1890's, it had begun to
appear in the "South," as J. S. McDonald has pointed out, but
not in those portions of the "South" from which emigration flowed.
The development of mutual aid societies among Italians in the
United States contrasted with that in the homeland. In Italy, benefit
groups closely intertwined with the growth of labor unions; societies were, in the words of labor economist Daniel L. Horowitz,
"the linear predecessors of the trade unions in Italy." Societies in
the United States, on the other hand, concentrated on insurance
and social functions, helping newly arrived immigrants to deal
with sickness, loneliness, and death rather than labor organization.[27]

Benefit societies in the United States antedated the period of large-scale immigration from southern and eastern Europe. By the middle of the nineteenth century, assessment mutual aid methods found popularity with working-class Americans, native as well as foreign born, with groups like the Mechanics Mutual Aid Society (founded in 1846) providing strong competition for regular life insurance companies. Benefit societies in the United States apparently grew out of English "friendly societies," which provided working-class points of view plus sickness, old-age, and funeral benefits, features from secret societies, ideas about organization and self-government, and an interest in social activities, ritual, and symbolism. "The prototype societies," according to insurance historian J. Owen Stalson, "were active in England while we were still colonies." American groups, however, developed a stronger social and fraternal character than English friendly societies. In a highly mobile country such as America, vast numbers of the native born as well as immigrants from Europe found themselves uprooted from familiar surroundings, people, and life patterns. For them the lodge filled a great social void. Furthermore, the practice of "passing the hat" for unfortunate group members guaranteed aid in the event of need at minimum expense for all concerned, at least during the early years of the society when members were young and vigorous, and death or illness appeared to be problems of the distant future.[28]

Immigrants (and native Americans) who joined mutual benefit organizations contributed small monthly sums, usually from twenty-five to sixty cents, to guarantee that the group would look after them when they were sick and provide a decent burial when they died. In addition, societies required all members to attend funeral services or pay a fine as penalty for nonattendance. In this way the organization assured each member of a proper burial and a well-attended service, with the result that funerals tended to become social events. Over the years the burial service grew into an opportunity for old acquaintances to gather at irregular intervals and to reminisce about old days. Since young and vigorous members predominated, most deaths resulted from accidents or disease

growing out of employment conditions. Societies also generally
handled other related activities, especially the payment of sickness
and accident expenses.[29]

In 1919, the State of Illinois Health Insurance Commission published the findings of an investigation into the benefit provisions
of foreign societies in Chicago. It studied 33 Italian societies (of
an estimated total number of 80 in the city). Of these, 28 provided
sickness and accident benefits, 25 offered death benefits, 16 included funeral benefits ("these related to flowers, carriages, and
the like furnished when a member dies and to the announcement
made through the press"), 11 provided medical benefits, and none
offered hospital benefits. Of the 28 societies that featured sickness
and death benefits, 22 required a waiting period up to one week
before commencing payments, 5 a waiting period of more than
one week, and 1 did not report. The benefit period of 22 societies
lasted from thirteen to twenty-six weeks, while the other 6 offered
periods from six to thirteen weeks. Benefits paid ranged from $5
to $10 per week by 8 societies; the other 20 offered $5 or less per
week. In addition, 12 of the 28 societies made provisions for an
additional period of reduced benefit payments; of these 10 offered
half the usual weekly amount, and 2 provided some other (un-
specified) reduced rate.[30]

In 1866 northern Italians organized and composed the membership of the first mutual aid society formed among Italians in Chicago, the *Unione e Fratellanza.* More groups formed in the 1880's
and 1890's, when "Southerners" poured into the city. Among early
organizations were the Umberto I Society (1881), *Corte Assunta
No. 50* (1886), *Re d'Italia* (1887), and *Trinacria Fratellanza
Siciliana* (1892). Italian benefit groups generally had strong religious connections and many were linked directly with the parish
church, with church membership a prerequisite to society membership. In early years of settlement, societies formed typically
on the basis of place of origin—either town or province of birth,
and often the group named itself after the patron saint of the
home village—for example, *Società S. di Nicosia, S. Cristoforo di
Ricigliano, Santo Stefano di Castellone, San Vito di Rapone.*[31]

Because of the number of small, financially weak, and short-lived groups, it is difficult, if not impossible, to determine accurately the number of societies in existence or membership totals. The Illinois Health Insurance Commission investigation of Chicago's mutual aid societies, for example, counted 80 Italian groups in 1919. A City Department of Public Welfare study in the same year claimed that the correct total was 110, but included 28 lodges of a fraternal organization—the *Unione Siciliana*—in its figure. Completely at variance with these estimates was that of the Italian consul, Luigi Provana del Sabbione, who in 1912 stated that within the city there existed approximately 400 mutual aid groups. Unfortunately, he presented his total without documentation to indicate how he reached this surprisingly high number. Vincent E. Ferrara, who arrived in Chicago in 1901, joined the *Unione Siciliana* in 1914, and became Supreme Secretary of the organization nine years later, believed that there might have been "as many as" 160 benefit groups in existence during the decade 1910–20, an estimate that appears to be more reasonable. Membership figures are equally difficult to pinpoint, but—as was true in New York City during this same period—probably about half of Chicago's adult Italian males had membership in at least one society.[32]

Despite the profusion of organizations, with new groups coming into existence only to go out of business rather quickly, the general tendency was toward consolidation. The small size of the average group typically resulted in its early demise, as the management of benefit societies often proved to be ignorant of basic insurance practices. Unsound investments and depositing of the society's funds in private banks that went bankrupt also played a part. Perhaps the most important cause of the disappearance of foreign societies was the absorption of mutual aid groups into fraternal organizations. The member benefited from this change, for he gained entrance into a "larger and more stable organization."[33]

Thus financial considerations speeded the process of consolidation of small mutual aid societies into larger units, generally fraternal insurance groups organized on regional or even national lines. One, the *Unione Siciliana* (Sicilian Union), absorbed vari-

ous benefit groups based on village or province of origin in Sicily
to create a powerful regional organization, which in 1910, according to an Italian government study, totalled 800 members. (As an
example of the difficulties involved in accurate determination of
membership, a pamphlet published in Chicago in 1908 credited
the *Unione* with "a membership of more than 1300.") In the
following years Italians as well as Sicilians joined the *Unione;*
as a result, by 1925 the organization became national in character
and members renamed it the Italo-American National Union. The
stated purpose in the change of name was "closer unity among
those of our race into one homogeneous group, which would be
a credit to ourselves, to America, and to Italy." An unstated reason for the name change arose from the entanglement of the
*Unione* with organized crime in Chicago. By 1928 the Society
included 4000 adult members in 39 Chicago lodges (and 1000
children in a juvenile auxiliary), and owned cash assets of $176,-
169.58 with $5,317,900 of insurance in force. Lodges also formed in
other Illinois cities, and in Indiana, Michigan, and Ohio.[34]

The Columbian Federation (*La Federazione Columbiana delle
Società Italo-Americane*) organized in Chicago on October 10,
1893, with delegates sent by Italian societies from all over the
United States. It is still in existence. Another and more powerful
national organization, the Order Sons of Italy in America, formed
in New York City in June, 1905; it did not appear in Chicago until
November, 1924. Both the *Unione Siciliana* and the Order Sons of
Italy in America were fraternal insurance organizations. Another
fraternal organization in Chicago was the *Unione Veneziana*
(Venetian Union), which incorporated in 1924.[35]

Each society, mutual aid or fraternal, had its own doctor, and
many also employed an attorney. The group's doctor and lawyer
generally belonged to the membership of the organization (although some served more than one society). Their duties consisted of looking after medical or legal interests and needs of
fellow members. In this way members enjoyed advice and aid
in times of stress, and the society doctor or lawyer was assured of
customers and income regardless of whether or not he could attract

other clients. Fraternal orders paralleled mutual aid organizations in most respects. Indeed, the Illinois Health Insurance Commission stated that benefit societies were "merely local fraternals organized on a race (or language) basis." The Commission differentiated between societies and fraternals with the statement that "the former are small and much more unstable than the latter and are entirely unregulated under the insurance laws of the State." [36]

Mutual aid groups were purely voluntary and cooperative enterprises that operated on unsound actuarial principles and could not be called "insurance companies." The method by which benefit societies met obligations usually was to assess members in order to raise the needed amount of money. When a death occurred, for example, the society might find its cash on hand unequal to the cost of burial; then each member contributed a proportionate amount to cover funeral expenses. The same process applied for any shortages in meeting payments for sickness benefits or other group costs. The society therefore held each member responsible, in the event that the group could not meet its obligations. Some fraternals employed the same techniques. For young, vigorous members, this method appeared to be a safe and inexpensive way to provide for insurance needs. Assessments could be kept at a low level, however, only if the average age of the society's members remained constant. "Once recruitment lagged and the age structure changed, the mortality rate climbed, and the assessments must be increased or benefits cut, or else the organization faced bankruptcy. With one society after another, the early faith that regular infusion of 'new blood' would keep the association financially healthy, proved fallacious." The alternative was fixed-premium insurance, which collected more money in the early years of the policy so that a reserve fund could be accumulated to make up for increased costs involved in later years. The Italo-American National Union, the Sons of Italy, and other organizations turned to approved insurance practices, such as risk selection, level premiums, and setting up reserves. [37]

Immigrants who went without sufficient food and lived in miserable lodgings in order to save every penny for the anticipated

return to Italy or to purchase property or a business in Chicago
either could not afford to belong to mutual aid groups or preferred
to depend on other resources in times of distress. In the event of
sickness or death, voluntary contributions through colony-wide
fund-raising activities met their needs. On the other hand, upwardly mobile newcomers preferred to obtain insurance protection
from established American companies. "As substantial corporations
with fixed premiums, the industrial firm had an air of stability and
business efficiency," historian Morton Keller has pointed out, which
was not to be found in mutual benefit groups or fraternal societies.[38]

In order to attract and hold membership, fraternals and mutual
aid groups expanded their services from the basic benefit functions
to include social ones as well, among them provision for recreational facilities and special annual events, such as picnics, dances,
and religious celebrations. According to Italo-American National
Union Supreme Treasurer Vincent E. Ferrara, three reasons for
his organization's success in holding membership were its early
recognition of the importance of providing for social requirements
as well as financial necessities of members, its sound insurance
practices, and its ardent Italian nationalism, even when Sicilians
composed the entire membership.[39]

Since members overwhelmingly favored social activities, societies
gradually placed a heavy emphasis on such events. "Because of
jealousy, or the ambition of some factotum," however, each group
went its own way to hold dances, picnics, banquets, and other
celebrations independently. As a result, reported *La Tribuna
Italiana Transatlantica* in 1906, "on the same day, there would be
three or more picnics or dances held by as many different Italian
societies." To end this confusion and duplication, the city's leading
organizations combined in the spring of 1906 into "one brotherhood under the name of the United Italian Societies," in order to
coordinate social activities. The venture proved to be popular and
successful. Two years later the United Italian Societies initiated a
campaign to raise funds "to put up a building for the use of affiliated societies," and thus Italian Hall was constructed at Clark

and Erie streets. Member societies used the building for meetings, banquets, and dances; by the late 1920's these groups had a combined membership that reached between five and six thousand.[40]

While mutual aid societies and fraternals added social activities to basic benefit functions, some organizations formed and existed to serve social or recreational needs only. One such group, the Alpine Gun Club, organized in May 1892, as a nonprofit social group established "for pleasure, amusement, social and educational purposes." The group's principal activity consisted of trap shooting, first at temporary sites at Lake George in Indiana and Summit and Long Lakes, Illinois. In 1910 the club selected a permanent site at English Lake, Indiana, on the banks of the Kankakee River, where the group's first clubhouse formally opened. Originally the club existed exclusively for male members, but the rules were gradually relaxed, and in 1915 members voted to share the clubhouse and facilities with families and guests. In 1921 the Alpine Gun Club joined with an older social club, the *Legione dei Trampi* (Legion of Tramps, organized in 1865) to cosponsor a yearly masquerade and banquet held on Shrove Tuesday, which the Gun Club had sponsored independently for a number of years. All segments of the city's Italian population took part in this celebration, and it soon became a major social event for the Italian community. Other groups serving strictly social or recreational functions included the Maria Adelaide Club, the Italian Pleasure Club, and the *Nuova Lega dei Trampi* (formed in 1902).[41]

Other societies originated with military, political, religious or anti-religious objectives. Italian military organizations in Chicago included the *Bersaglieri di Savoia,* the *Bersaglieri e Carabinieri,* the *Reali Carabinieri,* and the *Marinai;* the first two were also mutual aid organizations. These groups celebrated Italian national holidays, such as September 20, the day in 1870 when Rome became the capital of United Italy; they also marched proudly with other Americans on Memorial Day. The many Italian political clubs in the city included the Lincoln Italian Republican Workers Club, McKinley Italian Club, Italian Political Club and Benevolent Society, Aetna Republican Club, Italian Progressive Democratic

League of Cook County, and Italian Progressive Republican Club of the Nineteenth Ward.[42]

Anti-clericals in the community, including socialists, liberals and nationalists, formed the Giordano Bruno Anti-Clerical Society in 1907. The group remained in existence for about a year and then disappeared until May, 1913, when it reappeared for a brief time. According to an article in *La Tribuna Italiana Transatlantica* on December 28, 1907, the Bruno Society was created "to combat religious superstition and priestly exploitation" of community residents. On May 10, 1913, *La Parola dei Socialisti* stated that the first aim of the group consisted of "an incessant campaign of anti-clericalism, . . . to rid the Italian immigrant of all the superstition and ignorance in which he is kept by the papists." The organization failed to stay in existence because of internal disputes, bickering, and criticism. Liberals like Alessandro Mastro-Valerio, for example, found that they abhorred the ideas and methods of socialist fellow members more than they disliked Catholic priests.[43]

The Italian-language press played an intimate role in the existence of the community's organizations. Generally societies found their budgets too small to permit their own news disseminating services. Even those groups that could furnish newsletters for their members looked upon Italian-language journals as a useful means of communicating with the rest of the Italian colony. Thus Italian newspapers reported items concerning the establishment of benefit societies, and news of their elections and operations, picnics, banquets, dances, and other social events. In addition, the papers publicized the societies' fight against legislation intended to restrict immigration, and their support of efforts to eliminate crime among Italians.[44]

Italian societies and the press joined together each year to celebrate not only September 20, but also the anniversaries of battles fought in the struggle to achieve Italian unification, birthdays of heroes of unification like Garibaldi and Mazzini, and the birthday of the reigning monarch of Italy. Another project of the press and societies, the building of monuments and statues to commemorate famous Italians, depended on contributions from the Italian colony.

Tabloids in Chicago and elsewhere initiated or supported plans for memorials to Columbus, Verdi, Dante, and Garibaldi.

Often such rallies opened with great fanfare and enthusiasm; actual construction usually lagged, as did collection of money. The campaign for a statute to Garibaldi, for example, commenced on April 30, 1887, with a call for a monument to be erected in his honor. Earlier in the month a statue of Garibaldi had been dedicated in New York's Central Park, and this event spurred Italian pride in Chicago. Societies supported the campaign, which continued sporadically during the following years. Efforts intensified in 1888—and again in 1890, 1899, and 1900. In October 1901, societies and press announced jointly the erection of Garibaldi's statue in Lincoln Park, fourteen years and several fund-raising campaigns after the initial rally.

Societies also participated actively in celebrating American holidays like Independence Day and Memorial Day. They feted Columbus' discovery of America and worked to make October 12 a state holiday. By 1910 fifteen states, including Illinois and New York, had officially designated it as such, and societies increased their efforts to have Columbus Day proclaimed a national holiday. As early as 1898 *La Parola dei Socialisti* took note of this movement (without condemning it) and publicized the attempt "to have October 12 . . . a national holiday. It is promoted by the United Italian Societies. . . . It seems that a petition will be sent to Washington. No harm done!" These efforts continued during succeeding years.

Press and societies did not limit their activities to the celebration of holidays and the raising of memorials. All of Chicago's Italian papers carried subscriptions for the benefit of needy Italians, whether they lived in America or in Italy. In the early years of the twentieth century, for example, a number of devastating earthquakes occurred in Italy, each of which elicited sympathy and generous financial support from the Italian press and societies in Chicago. Periodicals proclaimed it a patriotic duty for Italians living abroad—that is, in the United States—to help the homeland in times of trouble and hardship. Names of subscribers and amounts contributed appeared in community journals. Although individuals usually gave small sums, societies sought to outdo each other in donations, some of which reached large totals. After the San Francisco earthquake, the *Unione Siciliana* collected $200 at a single meeting in May, 1906, to help Italian victims of that catastrophe. Societies and press also devoted time, effort, and money to help individual Italians in financial or legal difficulties, as much to defend the good name of Italy and of Italians in Chicago as to aid the needy.

In the process of collecting money for monuments and for relief purposes, societies ignored or underemphasized beneficial neighborhood and civic activities. That this neglect was not a universal failing of Italian emigrants but, in fact, was a reaction to particular conditions facing newcomers is indicated by the activities of Italian societies in Latin America. There, while taking part in patriotic celebrations and erecting monuments to Italian heroes, societies concentrated on building or supporting the construction and maintenance of schools, hospitals, and other institutions. Three categories of Italian schools, for example, functioned in Argentina: parochial, private, and those set up by mutual benefit societies. In Chicago the availability of public schools made society-sponsored schools unnecessary. In the absence of a social-insurance system in the United States (and also in Argentina), however, the insurance function served by mutual benefit societies and fraternal organizations became necessary and vital to immigrant members. Monument building, patriotic celebrations, and other manifestations of loyalty to the homeland, on the other hand, cost immigrants time, effort, and money they could ill afford to squander.[45]

Yet even these activities served a purpose. Projects with tangible results—and the more immediate the better—helped to develop a feeling of identity within the Italian colony for newly arrived immigrants, along with a sense of community pride and rapport. National self-consciousness and group identity, as social historian Caroline F. Ware accurately observed, were "the product of American conditions, not importations from abroad." Efforts to adjust to American middle-class attitudes forced upon immigrants some

sense of ethnic self-awareness, for, as Miss Ware noted, "Nationalism, on the whole, has been a product of the middle class, while
the peasant has known only his family and his village." Thus in
America, immigrants widened their provincial horizons and began
to think of themselves as Italians (or Poles, Germans, Slavs, etc.)
with bonds of pride and parentage linking them to the heroes of
their homeland.[46]

This feeling of ethnic pride showed clearly in a description by
Alessandro Mastro-Valerio in *La Tribuna Italiana Transatlantica*
of his concept of Italian nationalism: "The monument of Garibaldi
in Lincoln Park, the Dante Alighieri Society of Chicago, the
celebration of the historic date of September 20 and other patriotic
dates, and the protests to the Board of Education [to promote
the naming of a public school after Garibaldi] are demonstrations
of our nationalism." Through such activities the immigrants gained
self-respect and confidence in "their" glorious past while they faced
a strange and often hostile environment. Italian newcomers learned
to respect their homeland's history; they could not or would not
recognize that much of this "history" was factually distorted or
even mythical. It began to form a significant part of their personal
and cultural background, providing an opportunity to gain equal
footing with Americans and newcomers of other backgrounds who
indicated pride in the country of their own origin.[47]

## IV

Unlike societies and newspapers, the Catholic Church existed for
newcomers, and had formed an integral part of their lives, before
they left Europe. Yet it, too, underwent changes in the new world.
Italians found the Church in America to be a cold and puritanical
organization, controlled and often operated by the hated Irish,
even in Italian neighborhoods. Devout Catholics and critics of religion alike resented Irish domination of the Church. They demanded Italian priests and control of churches in their neighborhoods. *La Tribuna Italiana Transatlantica* charged that "Irish
priests work among the Italians not to save them from sin but

through fear of losing fruitful clients." Liberals and nationalists resented the Roman Church's opposition to Italian unification and its continued refusal to recognize the Kingdom's existence.[48]

While they attacked abuses of the Church both in Italy and the United States, Italian-American critics generally remained loyal Catholics and rallied to the support of the "Italian Church" against Irish "usurpers" and Protestants. Indeed, one Protestant clergyman who worked zealously to convert Italians complained that Italian-language editors who talked and acted like "rationalists, atheists, free-thinkers and the like," called themselves Catholics, strongly opposed Protestantism, and urged Italians to "stand fast to the traditions of their fathers' religion." [49]

By 1900, nevertheless, Italians appeared to be so dissatisfied that many Catholics believed the situation posed a serious threat to the Church's future in the United States. Laurence Franklin wrote an article for *Catholic World,* which appeared in April 1900, and showed how Italian disillusionment developed. He contrasted the religious turmoil among immigrants in the United States with conditions in Italy. "At home a chapel or church stood at their very door," Franklin pointed out. "Their parish priest was their personal friend, who had baptized them at their birth, taught them their catechism, and watched over them like a father or elder brother." In an American city, on the other hand, "they are suddenly thrown back upon themselves, without either tradition or public opinion to foster their sense of moral and social responsibility. . . . No church is to be found in the long row of tenements which form their horizon line, and the priests whom they meet speak another tongue." As a result of these factors, "like sheep without a shepherd, they too often go astray, wandering into some other fold, through interest or ignorance." [50]

In the following years the Italian immigrant "Problem" remained a source of deep concern within the Church. By early 1914 the *Catholic Citizen* of Milwaukee concluded that the religious conditions of Italian immigrants and their children in the United States was "our biggest Catholic question," a view widely held among American Catholics. Between the beginning of the century and

1921, various aspects of the "Italian Problem"—including discussions of religion in the homeland, parochial education in America, the need for Italian-speaking priests, and analyses of proposed solutions to the "Problem"—received frequent and persistent examination in the Catholic press.[51]

Protestants saw in Catholicism's difficulties an ideal foundation for proselytizing. They lost no opportunity to proclaim Protestant loyalty to the Italian Kingdom, in obvious contrast to the attitude of the Catholic Church. Protestant clergy condemned the papacy as a reactionary institution—"it could not be the papacy and be anything else"—and branded Catholicism as "a papal cult," "fetish materialism," "image worship and spiritualism," entirely opposed to the simple truths of the Protestant interpretation of the gospels.[52]

Some Protestant sects, especially Methodists, Baptists, and Presbyterians, worked actively among Italian immigrants in urban America, supporting a total of 326 churches and missions with more than 200 pastors, printing several Italian-language newspapers, and publishing a stream of books, articles, pamphlets, and leaflets in English and Italian.[53]

In Chicago at least fourteen Protestant churches or missions organized during the years after 1892, when the First Italian Presbyterian Church opened at 71 West Ohio Street. One of the more successful endeavors was the Moody Italian Mission, started in 1910 by volunteer workers of native American background. Originally the Mission formed as a Bible class meeting in conjunction with the Moody Sunday School. In September, 1914, the Executive Committee of the Moody Church appointed an able and ambitious Italian pastor, Antonio F. Scorza, to coordinate and direct the Mission's activities within the Near North Side colony of "Southerners" in the Milton Avenue area. In 1934 Scorza summarized the results of his years of dedicated effort: "Over two thousand Bibles and Testaments are on record as being given or sold"; an average of one thousand homes a year visited by gospel missionaries; a Sunday School and a Vacation Bible School maintained; "20,000 gospels or portions have been distributed, 75,000 'Way of Life' in Italian and about 60,000 periodicals and sound evangelical papers were also given out." Despite these extensive and costly efforts, the Mission gained meager returns.[54]

In the 24 years following the Moody Italian Mission's founding in 1910 (when "not a single Bible Christian could be found" in the community) Scorza reported that "one hundred thirty have united with our Church." A survey of Protestant work among Italians in Chicago (prepared also in 1934) by the Reverend Palmerio Chessa claimed that the membership of Moody Italian Mission "at the present is 200 communicants." These differing figures indicate the difficulties involved in attempting to determine the number of Italian converts to Protestant churches. Italian Protestant minister Constantine M. Panunzio, in the Methodist newspaper *La Fiaccola*, described the problem faced in New York City, where a situation similar to Chicago's existed:

> In a certain church, under the enthusiastic leadership of a pastor, 500 members were reported as belonging to the church. . . . Whenever an Italian church reports such a large number of members, either the printer made an error by adding a cipher, or the preacher has given the number of his constituency, and not of his members. When a successor was appointed to that field, he labored for a year, and by taking into account every last person who had been related in any vital way to the church and who could legitimately be counted as a member or even an adherent, he found 140. Another pastor went to the same field, and accidentally discovered that fully one-third, if not more, of those members were enrolled upon the books of another denomination. . . . It was exactly this state of things that led an able minister, who had opportunity to observe the whole Italian situation in a large city, to make this remark: "The Italian work in this city is a big farce." [55]

In Chicago, Pasquale R. De Carlo, Pastor and Director of St. John Presbyterian Institutional Church, estimated in the late 1920's that the total membership of all Italian Protestant churches and missions in the city approximated 4000. This figure, although pitifully small when compared with the total Italian population of the city (in 1930, first- and second-generation Italians numbered 181,-861), seems to be excessively optimistic. For Palmerio Chessa,

Assistant Pastor to De Carlo at St. John (and himself given to overly optimistic estimates of church memberships), in 1934 placed the number at 1214, in "seven organized Italian churches." In 1916 the state of Protestant proselytizing among Italians led *La Fiaccola* to lament that "not all the hoped-for results have as yet been attained." The De Carlo and Chessa figures show (although they were not intended to do so) that these objectives were not subsequently realized.[56]

Prejudices existing on both sides comprised one of the principal reasons for Protestant failure to attract Italian converts. One American clergyman, Philip Rose, who labored for many years among Italian immigrants, felt himself forced to advise those who would work with Italians that "such is the dislike of the word 'Protestant,' with which Italian-Americans have been imbued, it is better to emphasize our name of 'evangelical churches,' which is accepted with approbation." In its efforts to win over newcomers, one Protestant mission in Chicago went so far as to adopt the name "American Catholic Church." At the same time, according to Italian-born minister Antonio Mangano, "Within the Protestant field itself there are those who would discourage . . . attempts to evangelize the Italian." Two internal problems further hampered evangelical efforts: few American Protestants spoke Italian, and most American Protestant churches, located in middle-class native or "old" immigrant communities, had little contact with Italian immigrants. Encounters between newcomers and natives indicated that Americans feared and disliked Italians.[57]

Efforts of sincere and dedicated Protestant denominations to convert Italians were further weakened by the activities of Holy Roller fringe groups that preyed on the ignorance of the peasants to further the personal financial gain of the minister or group rather than to assure the salvation of cult members. One such preacher, G. Lombardi, a consumptive in whose eyes "burned the fire of madness," operated a store-front church at 256 West Grand Avenue. *La Parola dei Socialisti* described in the issues of February 25 and March 20, 1908, visits to services held in Lombardi's church. "What a scene!" commented the paper's reporter. "Here lay a girl in a faint, there a man in convulsions; everywhere the wailing of children. Above all the noise ran the persistent, shrill, maddening refrain of the tubercular leader: 'May His holy name be praised!' " Lombardi received ample rewards for "making the Holy Ghost descend into the bodies of his proselytes," ruefully admitted *La Parola*. "Two weeks ago a laborer gave to this exhorter the sum of $400, which must have represented many a sacrifice. The laborer said that the Holy Ghost had ordered him to do so. Last week another Italian contributed $1000, likewise commanded by the Holy Ghost." Other Italian-language newspapers of Chicago reported similar examples of "religious buffoonery," in the words of *La Tribuna Italiana Transatlantica*.[58]

In addition to establishing churches and missions, Protestant denominations sought to aid the adjustment of Italians and their children by establishing social settlements in ethnic areas. Protestant settlement houses devoted considerable time, effort, and money to Bible classes, preaching, and conversion activities. These efforts, however, met with strong immigrant resistance and suspicion that carried over to other settlement functions. Emphasis on evangelical activities severely limited the acceptance and use of facilities in general. Successful settlement houses either stressed their nondenominational character (like Hull House, the first and most influential settlement in Chicago, established in 1889) or, like Chicago Commons (established by Congregational minister Graham Taylor), did not emphasize religion, recognizing that "church and settlement has each its distinctive sphere and neither can take the place of the other without losing its own place." Taylor in fact proclaimed that the settlement house must disavow "being in any sense a substitute or a rival of the church or the mission." According to his biographer, Louise C. Wade, Taylor desired to bring "Protestant, Roman Catholic, Jew and Ethical Culturist" together in one settlement house in an "all-embracing framework of neighborship and fellow-citizenship." The course followed by Hull House and Chicago Commons proved to be successful, as Italian immigrants and their American-born children came to depend upon the advice of settlement workers and to make extensive use of settlement facilities. Olivet Institute, on the other hand, emphasized proselytizing activities and experienced great difficulty in persuading "Southern" residents in the Near North Side community to use the settlement's social and educational facilities. According to its director, Wallace Heistad, conversion efforts met with even less success.[59]

In contrast, as many as 31 different Italian organizations used Hull House in a single year. These included nationalist groups such as the Fiume National League and the Greater Italy Dollar Loan Committee, religious organizations like the Italian branch of the International Bible Students' Association, theater groups such as the Novella Dramatic Club and the Eleanora Duse Dramatic Club (which existed for Italian men and women from 18 to 50 years of age), and local units of organized labor such as an Italian local of the Amalgamated Clothing Workers of America. A number of benefit societies and social clubs also made use of Hull House facilities, including *Allienza Riciglianese, San Conone, Società Venefro,* Italian Odd Fellows Chapter 948, and the Giordano Bruno Anti-Clerical Society. Italian women and children participated there in a variety of clubs, classes, and recreational services. More than half the members of the Hull House Boys' Club during its early years of existence were of Italian birth or extraction.[60]

Contacts with Protestant settlements, social workers, public school teachers, ministers, and missions profoundly influenced some Italians, who turned to Protestantism because it seemed to be one road to Americanization. Protestants believed that conversion formed an integral and essential element of immigrant adjustment; as one minister proclaimed in 1906, "If the immigrant is evangelized, assimilation is easy and sure." Nevertheless, despite costly and prodigious efforts by non-Catholic churches and settlements, relatively few Italians converted; those who did quickly transferred to American congregations.[61]

The tendency of many newcomers simply to turn away from all religious activities created a greater menace to the Church than did

Protestantism. Undoubtedly what Father Joseph Schuyler calls "the stress of disorganization," the  impact of migration, and the influence of the American environment distracted many immigrants from traditional organizations like the Church.[62]

Appearances to the contrary, most of Chicago's Italians remained nominally or actually loyal to the Church, but in a way differing from other Catholic groups (like Irish- or Polish-Americans). National consciousness, which developed among all three groups in the United States, strongly influenced ethnic attitudes toward religion. While for Irish and Polish Catholics, religion made up a central aspect of national loyalty, for Italians Catholicism and nationalism were opposing forces. Thus bourgeois and proletarian papers alike condemned the Pope's temporal claims in Italy. Papers like *L'Italia, Il Progresso Italo-Americano,* and *La Tribuna Italiana Transatlantica* opposed the Church, in this instance, primarily out of loyalty to the Kingdom. In October, 1890, Oscar Durante stated in *L'Italia* that he—and, he believed, a majority of Italian immigrants in Chicago—fully supported the state in disputes between Italy and the Church, for "the Pope . . . is the relentless enemy of our unity and liberty." (The Protestant *La Fiaccola* and the left-wing *La Parola dei Socialisti* and *Il Proletario* also fully upheld the Kingdom, partly to embarrass the Church and partly to further their own particular objectives.)[63]

Italian denial of papal worldly pretensions along with graphic (and generally accurate) descriptions of priestly imperfections did not, however, signify a rejection of the Catholic faith, although *New World,* the official newspaper of the Chicago Archdiocese, and the Church hierarchy concluded that it did: "For irreverence, hostility and blasphemy," charged *New World* editors, "the Italian Liberal probably excels all other individuals of his class." Ardent and verbose liberals and nationalists like Alessandro Mastro-Valerio felt shocked and insulted to find themselves accused of being anti-Catholic. On June 18, 1904, Mastro-Valerio responded angrily in *La Tribuna Italiana Transatlantica* to criticism from *New World:* "We refute the insinuation that this newspaper occasionally attacks the doctrine of the Church because it is not the truth. . . . [Such statements] show the [*New World*] editor to be a fanatic Irishman." [64]

Lacking an ardent core of nationalism, religion for Italians demanded neither extreme fervor nor public proclamations of faith and loyalty. Critics pointed to Italian addiction to festivals, processions, and feasts as perversions of religion; yet to Italians these celebrations formed an integral part of Church traditions, whether participants were northern Italians from the Illinois-Franklin streets area or "Southerners" from the city's Near West Side. Immigrants celebrated these functions not only in an effort to reestablish those elements of religion that had strongly appealed to them in the homeland, but also to counteract Irish influences, which seemed to them to make the American Church impersonal, indifferent, and rigid.[65]

In the years after the turn of the century, the Church indeed began to provide effectively for the religious needs of Italian-Americans. The most significant manifestation of this new concern appeared in the establishment of a number of national parishes served either by Italians or by Irish-Americans who spoke Italian. As a result of such actions the "Italian Problem" began to ease, although the defection of a sizable minority indicated that it had not been completely solved. Nevertheless, as Father Henry J. Browne has shown, by 1900 the critical period had probably passed.[66]

Construction began in 1880 on Assumption of the Blessed Virgin Mary, located in the northern Italian neighborhood on West Illinois Street near Orleans Street. Reverend Sosteneus Moretti of the Servite Order organized the congregation and said the first Mass in the basement of the church on April 17, 1881. Reverend Thomas Moreschini, O.S.M., joined Father Moretti in 1883, and the two oversaw completion of the church building in 1886. On the Feast of the Assumption, August 15, 1886, Archbishop Feehan dedicated this, Chicago's first Italian parish. In 1892 Father Moretti, then 84 years old, died and Father "Tom" Moreschini became Pastor of Assumption, assisted by three fellow Servite Fathers, Reverend Joachim Tonissi, who had served at the church since 1887, Reverend Peregrine Giangrandi, newly assigned to the parish from Rome, and Reverend Frederick S. Angelucci, recently transferred from London.[67]

A second Italian congregation, St. Mary of Mount Carmel, formed in 1892 on the city's Far South Side at Sixty-seventh and Page streets, under the pastorship of Reverend Serafino Cosimi, C. R. Residents of the large and rapidly expanding Near South Side and Near West Side Italian districts existed without their own parish churches until the end of the decade. During the 1880's and early 1890's, those who wished to attend mass or who desired their children to learn the catechism had to choose between traveling several miles to the Assumption Church or attending a non-Italian neighborhood church—perhaps the Bohemian (and later Polish) St. Wenceslaus, or the Irish Holy Family. In 1892 a Jesuit priest, Father Paul Ponziglione, who taught at Ignatius College (which was connected with Holy Family Church) founded a parochial school for Italian children on Forquer Street, which he named Guardian Angel School. Two years later the Servite fathers of Assumption Church established a short-lived mission in a rented hall on Ewing Street, near Guardian Angel School. Father "Tom" Moreschini and then (after he contracted a serious case of bronchitis) Father Giangrandi celebrated Mass there for several months on Sundays and Holy Days. The mission closed after less than a year of operation when Father Giangrandi's superiors sent him to teach classics to students of the Servite Order in Granville, Wisconsin.

In 1898 Archbishop Feehan appointed Father Edmund M. Dunne to found a parish for West Side Italians. Father Dunne purchased land on Forquer Street (adjacent to the existing parochial school) for the construction of a new church and rectory. On September 10, 1899, Father Dunne celebrated the first Mass at Guardian Angel Church. Four Italian priests assisted Father Dunne during his five-year pastorship, but Italian nationalists like Mastro-Valerio objected strenuously to the presence of an Irish priest, even one who spoke fluent Italian. They rejoiced when in 1903 the ambitious and able Father Dunne was promoted to the position of

Chancellor of the Archdiocese of Chicago (he later became Bishop of Peoria, Illinois). Italian-born Pacifico Chenuil of the Scalabrini Fathers became the pastor of Guardian Angel parish.[68]

In the same year that the newly built Guardian Angel opened on the West Side, Father Orazio Mangone bought an old Protestant church, St. Clemens, located at Eighteenth and Clark streets in the Near South Side and converted it into a Catholic Church, Santa Maria Incoronata. In 1904 the congregation moved to a newly constructed church building on Alexander Street near Wentworth Avenue, built under the guidance of Father Mangone's successor, Riccardo Lorenzoni. In the years between 1903 and 1919, eight more Italian parishes were founded in Chicago: St. Michael and Santa Maria Addolorata (1903); St. Philip Benizi, St. Anthony de Padua, and Holy Rosary (1904); Our Lady of Pompei (1910); St. Francis de Paula (1911); and San Callisto (1919).

The great amount of residential mobility characteristic of the ethnic colony formed one major problem faced by the Church in its efforts to win the allegiance of Italian newcomers in Chicago and elsewhere in urban America. This constant movement made the formation and maintenance of a stable congregation difficult to achieve. An additional complication was the fact that many immigrants, at least in their early years of settlement, intended their stay in the city to be temporary and regarded themselves as members of an Italian village church rather than of the national parish in Chicago. Such immigrants saw no reason to contribute financially to a church in Chicago, since they expected to use its facilities only until they returned to Italy. In actuality, of course, they generally settled permanently in the city.[69]

In order to gain and hold the support of immigrants and their children, the Church in the United States found it necessary to offer a variety of services and facilities that were partly or entirely of a nontheological nature, unnecessary in the static, unchanging homeland village. Among these new facilities were missions, clubs, lay societies and organizations, and Sunday schools. These expanded functions formed part of a general movement in the American Catholic Church, during the period from the 1890's to

World War I, to provide social services in order to keep Slavic as well as Italian immigrants within the fold. Thus the Servite and Scalabrini fathers operated missions in the suburbs (particularly Melrose Park) as well as in the city, many of which grew into national parishes. Mother Frances Xavier Cabrini and her Missionary Sisters of the Sacred Heart established and operated Columbus Extension Hospital (now Mother Cabrini Memorial Hospital), for poverty-stricken West Side Italians, and the Italian Orphan Asylum and Industrial School. Among the lay groups designed to serve social and (indirect) religious functions were settlement houses, the Holy Name Society, the Knights of Columbus, the Catholic Order of Foresters, Young Ladies Sodality, church-sponsored mutual aid societies, dramatic clubs, and playground and gymnastic classes.[70]

Chicago Catholics expressed deep concern because most Italian parents sent their children to public rather than to parochial schools. In 1899 editors of *New World* complained: "The Italians will not send their children to the parochial schools if they have to pay for them." Italian-language papers tended to support and encourage Italian nonsupport of parochial education, although not for economic reasons. Liberals, along with Protestants and socialists, attacked the entire concept of Catholic schools, which they viewed as a means through which the Church sought to control men's minds. They called upon Italians to send their children to public schools, stating: "Religion should be taught in your homes in the sanctity of your family." [71]

For the average immigrant, economic considerations and availability rather than the fear of Church domination determined the decision to enroll his youngsters in Chicago's public school system. Newcomers made full use of Sunday schools established at Guardian Angel, Santa Maria Incoronata, and other churches to provide for the religious training of children educated in public schools. In 1903 more than 1400 children each week attended the Sunday-school classes conducted at Guardian Angel, which required the services of more than 125 volunteer public schoolteachers under the direction of William Bogan, principal of Lane Technical High

School, who later became Superintendent of the city's public school system (and the first Catholic to hold that office). By 1913, according to Father W. H. Agnew, S.J., the average Sunday-school attendance had risen to somewhere between 2500 and 3000. Sunday schools were not, however, limited to Italian areas. In 1906, for example, the Archdiocese of Chicago reported the existence of 477 Sunday schools staffed by 1856 teachers who instructed 63,648 students. According to Sister Ann Edward Scanlon, the church placed Sunday schools in districts where residents could not afford to support a parish school. "When parish schools were built the Sunday school method was discarded." (For Italians, this replacement has transpired since the 1920's).[72]

Despite all efforts, a number of Italians did leave the Church. The full extent of this exodus is difficult to determine, but it was apparently never as extensive as contemporaries assumed. While most Italians used national parishes in significant numbers when these churches became available, many others attended non-Italian churches in the community. Thus even after Guardian Angel and Our Lady of Pompei were constructed, many West Side Italians continued to attend St. Wenceslaus, Notre Dame, and Holy Family churches. As the original German congregation of St. Francis of Assisi began to decline rapidly in the years around 1900 the parish clergy decided that—rather than close the church—they would open membership to neighborhood Italians. Hence, while St. Francis was not officially listed as an Italian national parish, in effect it became one. Some Italian churches, on the other hand, lost their strictly Italian character as upwardly mobile parishioners left the colony and members of newer immigrant groups took their places. Mexicans, without a church of their own, attended Guardian Angel and Our Lady of Pompei; St. Francis de Paula (located at Seventy-eighth Street and Ellis Avenue) absorbed an area containing English-speaking Catholics from St. Lawrence parish.[73]

The Church intended national parishes to fulfill the religious needs of non-English-speaking newcomers. That they did so is seen in membership of Italian parishes, which reached a peak during the high point of Italian immigration into Chicago and included approximately 75 per cent of the combined immigrant and American-born population of the city in 1910. Italian parish membership declined (in proportion to the total population) in the following years as war and restrictive immigration laws shut off the flow of newcomers in need of priests who could speak Italian. George Cardinal Mundelein, who became Archbishop of Chicago in 1916, strongly discouraged establishment of additional national parishes, and in subsequent years the Church added only one Italian church, San Callisto (1919), to those already in existence. This did not, however, cause an imbalance, because the virtual end of immigration removed the need for more Italian parishes. Second-generation Italians, who shunned Italian-language newspapers, societies, and other community institutions and facilities as being undesirable and "old country," also turned away from the national parish in favor of American churches at the same time that they moved out of the colony and into neighborhoods earlier settled by "older" waves of Catholics (generally Irish or German). The second generation, it should be noted, doubled during the decade 1910–20 while foreign-born Italians increased by only one fifth. The departure of second-generation and upwardly mobile newcomers from national parishes and ethnic colonies is seen in the decline of Italian church membership figures between 1920 and 1927, as the exodus from the community increased in size.[74]

Despite the eventual loss of adjusting members to American churches or to "old" immigrant churches, the Italian national parish filled a vital need by aiding immigrants to accommodate to their new homeland. In the ethnic parish, newcomers from different localities in Italy found that they had to forget or suppress old-world prejudices against outsiders (that is, anyone from another town or province) in order to form the desired national church. Thus while southern Italians predominated in the West Side community served by Holy Guardian Angel and Our Lady of Pompei, many Sicilians and some northern Italians also resided in the area, as well as Slavic groups and—after 1910—Mexicans. The mainland "Southerners" themselves formed no homogeneous group, for they arrived from every province, but especially from Cosenza, Aquila,

## Table 10

CHICAGO'S ITALIAN CATHOLICS, 1890–1927

| Italian Parishes | | | Italian Population | | |
|---|---|---|---|---|---|
| No. of Parishes | Membership | Year | Foreign Born | American Born | Total |
| 1 | 3,000 | 1890 | 5,685 | 7,924 | 13,609 |
| 4 | 11,000 | 1900 | 16,008 | 10,476 | 26,484 |
| 10 | 56,000 | 1910 | 45,169 | 29,774 | 74,943 |
| 12 | 72,650 | 1920 | 59,854 | 64,330 | 124,184 |
| 12 | 68,000 | 1927 | — | — | — |

Sources: Marvin Reuel Schafer, "The Catholic Church in Chicago, Its Growth and Administration," unpublished Ph.D. dissertation, University of Chicago, 1929, 50, collected from yearly parish reports to the Chancellory Office of the Archdiocese of Chicago. U.S. Bureau of the Census, *Eleventh Census of the United States, 1890. Population,* I, 672, 708; *Twelfth Census . . . 1900. Population,* I, 798; *Thirteenth Census . . . 1910. Population,* I, 946; *Fourteenth Census . . . 1920. Population,* II, 934. "School Census of 1898," City of Chicago, Board of Education, *Proceedings, July 13, 1898, to June 28, 1899* (Chicago, 1899), 256. Note: According to the *Fifteenth Census . . . Population,* II, 316, Chicago's Italian population in 1930 totalled 181,861 and included 73,960 foreign born and 107,901 American born.

Campobasso, Caserta, Abruzzi and Reggio-Calabria. In Chicago they joined together in the same parish.

One result of this mixing in the immigrant colony as a whole as well as in the church showed in the shift in choice of marriage partners over the years. During early years of settlement, weddings generally took place between partners from the same province and even the same town in Italy. As time passed one or both mates came of American-born parentage; even where partners came from the same province, there was a greater tendency to marry outside the home village. Holy Guardian Angel parish marriage records illustrate these points:

In 78 of the marriages taking place in 1906 that involved partners from the same Italian province, both came also from the same town. By 1920 this similarity in origin occurred in only 27 cases. The growth to maturity of the second generation is seen in the increase in marriages in which one or both marriage partners had

## Table 11

COMPARISON OF MARRIAGES PERFORMED AT
HOLY GUARDIAN ANGEL CHURCH, 1906 AND 1920

| | 1906 | | 1920 | |
| --- | --- | --- | --- | --- |
| | Marriages Performed | Per Cent | Marriages Performed | Per Cent |
| Bride and groom born in same Italian province | 103 | 52 | 45 | 31 |
| Bride and groom born in different Italian province | 52 | 26 | 28 | 19 |
| Bride and groom born in U.S. | 2 | 1 | 15 | 10 |
| Bride or groom born in U.S. | 34 | 17 | 47 | 32 |
| Marriage with non-Italian | 7 | 3 | 9 | 6 |
| Bride or groom of Italian extraction, but born outside U.S. or Italy | 2 | 1 | 2 | 2 |
| Total | 200 | 100 | 146 | 100 |

Source: Holy Guardian Angel Church, manuscript parish marriage records,
Note: Marriages were performed at Guardian Angel parish as early as 1899.
but 1906 was the first year in which both place of birth and marriage age were
recorded (place of birth first appeared July 6, 1902, and marriage age September
10, 1905).

been born in the United States—from 36 in 1906 to 62 in 1920. An
interesting sidelight is that, although Guardian Angel was located
in a "Southern" community, 13 marriages in 1906 involved natives
of northern Italy. In one the bride was American born, in another
she was a "Southerner," while in the other eleven both partners
were northern Italians. By 1920 northerners either had moved from
the parish or were marrying elsewhere, since in that year only two
weddings involved them and in both the bride came from northern
Italy while the groom was a "Southerner."

Significantly intermarriage with non-Italians had begun to take
place at least by 1906. In that year seven weddings involved non-
Italians. The partners were:

> Giuseppe Oliva, of Camponarello, Avellino, age 37, and Kate
> Curtin, of Ottawa, Illinois, age 39;
> James Tortorelli, of Chicago, Illinois, age 21, and Mamie
> Dolan, of Chicago, Illinois, age 19;

Vivenzo Pascale, of Montesano, Salerno, age 28, and Mary Hill, of Harrodsburg, Kentucky, age 21;

Alessandro D'Guida, of Oliveto Citra, Salerno, age 56, to Lenie Whisunaut, of North Carolina, age 30;

Antonio Anicello, of Chicago, Illinois, age 18, to Ester Nordby, of St. Paul, Minnesota, age 18;

Riccardo Napoleone, of Malito, Cosenza, age 24, to Kattie Leonard, of Chicago, Illinois, age 28;

Rocco Gragido, of Basilicata, age 36, to Lena Reckroot, of Chicago, Illinois, age 22.

Not only did "Southerners" at this date wed non-Italians (including Anglo-Saxons and Scandinavians), but they also married non-Catholics. Thus Lenie Whisunaut was listed in the marriage records as a Baptist, Ester Nordby as a Methodist, and Lena Reckroot simply as a Protestant, with no mention of their converting to Catholicism. In each of the seven intermarriages taking place in 1906, Italian men married non-Italian women. By 1920 this pattern had changed when four of nine intermarriages involved non-Italian men:

Francis P. Sullivan, of Tipperary, Ireland, age 31, and Rosa Mercurio, of Chicago, age 25;

John Psicalino, of Greece, age 24, and Francesca Gagliardi, of Chicago, age 17;

Louis Garano, of Chicago, age 25, and Dorothy Clara Nye, of Logansport, Indiana, age 26;

Edward G. Sullivan, of Riverside, Illinois, age 22, and Vitella Meccia, of Chicago, age not listed;

Joseph Pentz, of Elizabeth, New Jersey, age 21, and Maria Franzo, of Pittsburgh, Pennsylvania, age 21;

Giuseppe Indelicato, of Marsala, age 27, and Pearl Klodzinski, of Chicago, age 20;

Salvatore DeCola, of Chicago, age 28, and Sylvia Baldwin, of Morocco, Indiana, age 24;

Nicola Daddabo, of Bari, age 24, and Maria Estrada, of Guadalajara, Mexico, age 19;

Francesco Minnitti, of Reggio Calabria, age 31, and Ida Schneider, of Limoges, France, age 21.

Italians married three non-Catholics in 1920 but in each case the partner—John Psicalino, Dorothy Clara Nye, and Sylvia Baldwin —converted to Catholicism.

Marriage with non-Italians extended beyond the West Side colony. Sicilian-born Vincent E. Ferrara related in an interview that in 1911, when he was 23 years old, he married a non-Catholic girl who lived in the same Near North Side neighborhood as he. His wife, although Swedish, had grown up among Italians and spoke the language fluently. Ferrara further stated that nearly all the ambitious young Sicilian men he had known in his youth had married non-Italians. Evidence indicates that during the years prior to 1921, a small but significant number of Italians intermarried with non-Catholics (Scandinavians and Anglo-Saxons) as well as with German, Polish, and Irish Catholics.[75]

Weddings involving Italian police officers reflected the tendency of the upwardly mobile men to marry outside the ethnic group. Of 35 Italian city policemen who married during the period between 1900 and 1920, non-Italians were chosen by 21, and two of those who married Italian women later obtained divorces and remarried non-Italian women (in both cases women of Slavic background). In addition, these weddings generally took place outside the Italian community and even outside the city—in Waukegan, Illinois, and Crown Point, Indiana, among other locations—indicating that Italian parish records do not fully reflect the extent of intermarriages taking place during the period prior to 1921. Many Italian political leaders and criminal bosses also married outside the ethnic group. Albert J. Prignano, a political figure, married a former singer, Jean Gibson (née Beardmore), while James Colosimo took for his second wife an Ohio-born girl of Anglo-Saxon background. John Torrio married a Kentucky native, and Brooklyn-born Mae Capone was of Irish extraction.[76]

# V

While each community institution or organization—press, society, church (Protestant and Catholic), immigrant bank, and labor agency—served vital functions during the early stage of immigrant adjustment, each, with one exception, declined to the advantage of an American counterpart after that period of service had been completed. The tremendous amount of immigrant mobility comprised the principal reason for the waning of community institutions. "A given race, closely settled and extensively organized," wrote Illinois Health Insurance Commission investigator Jakub Horak in 1919, "sooner or later scatters and perhaps surrenders its locality to another" ethnic element. As a result, mutual aid groups, padrone systems, Italian banks, and Italian-language newspapers rapidly disintegrated.[77]

While the roles of other institutions decreased as Italians and their children made use of American newspapers, insurance companies, banks, and trade unions (and in the process forsook foreign counterparts), the importance of the Catholic Church increased. In contrast to other immigrant agencies, the American equivalent to the national parish formed part of a larger institution, not a foreign and competing agency. The Catholic Church remained flexible enough to provide for the social and religious needs of new arrivals from overseas as well as long-time colony residents and immigrant inhabitants of outer city and suburban neighborhoods. Hence Italians who exhibited mobility by moving from nationality parishes merely transferred, in many cases, to American Catholic churches in new neighborhoods. Second and third generations viewed the Church as the only "traditional" institution that offered anything of use or value.

As immigrants and their children moved away from the ethnic colony and into American institutions, they found the Church to be one organization that existed in the new neighborhood in much the same form as it had in the old locality. Their former (national) church had used the Italian language in sermons and confessions; priests in the new parish conducted these and other services in English. In both churches, the liturgy of the mass was in Latin, while rituals and vestments were similar or identical.

As former residents left the ethnic neighborhood, the Catholic Church remained behind and attempted to help new waves of immigrants (generally from Latin America) to adjust to their new homeland. National parishes also provided at least one Mass in English or Spanish, with others in Italian, so that individual churches kept their self-identity. Many second-generation Italian residents of Austin, Wilmette, or Cicero, along with numbers of immigrants, returned to Guardian Angel, Assumption, or other core area national churches for Sunday mass, marriages, baptisms, and confirmations, thus fulfilling their religious obligations in a comfortable and familiar environment with priests they had known for long periods of time. Some made use of their national church as a cultural crutch and journeyed back to the core area each Sunday until they felt confident enough to attend the church in their new home locality.[78]

Identification with the colony, and use of its facilities and institutions, not only indicated a growth away from homeland outlooks, but also formed for many newcomers a vital step in assimilation. While we now recognize that immigrant institutions speeded the process of acculturation, contemporary opinion held that the opposite was true. In the period to the end of World War I, natives measured immigrant accommodation to the United States in terms of Americanization (which meant the degree of Anglo-Saxonism), or the "melting pot" concept. Immigrant institutions appeared to retard assimilation; hence Americans and second-generation Italians regarded them with derision and contempt. Historical perspective has made it possible for scholars to revise this view, as the values and (often unintentional) aids to assimilation offered by immigrant institutions have become more intensively studied and documented and their functions better understood and appreciated.[79]

# 7

## Decade of Transition:
## From World War to Depression

The Italian government declared war on Austria-Hungary in May, 1915, fully expecting Italians living overseas to return to defend the mother country. Throughout hostilities, the Kingdom hoped for both financial aid and manpower from across the Atlantic, and anticipated that newspapers and societies would support its needs and lead immigrant colonies in fulfilling them. While press and societies consistently publicized and encouraged the Italian war effort, most Italian-Americans reacted with indifference to Italy's plight. The average immigrant might feel some pride in occasional Italian military successes, but he did not believe that he ought to serve in the Italian army. Colonial periodicals claimed (probably at the consul's insistence) that all able-bodied immigrants should recross the ocean and join the fighting as members of the Italian armed forces; but most papers found it inexpedient to emphasize this unpopular theme.[1]

Homeland Italians reacted with anger and contempt to immigrant disinterest. In May, 1917, the Reverend Augusto Giardini, a Protestant minister and a recent arrival from the Kingdom, expressed this attitude when he complained that "Mother Italy" needed her sons at her side on the Isonzo, and not a safe distance away on the Hudson. Editors of the Methodist paper *La Fiaccola* thought it necessary to explain in a postcript to Giardini's comments that certain factors brought about this seeming disinterest of immigrants toward Italy's struggle. Newcomers in America, the journal pointed out, had acquired homes and families in the United States. To them, "any number of sentimental considerations," such as defending "the graves of their fathers," could not equal the "needs of their children." In any case, guilty consciences could be salved by financial contributions to the Italian war effort and postwar Italian requirements.[2]

Socialists and anarchists opposed both American and Italian involvement in the conflict, but the bulk of the foreign-language press, societies, and immigrants loyally supported the American war effort. Chicago's Italians contributed money to the Liberty Bond campaign, labored in factories producing war materials, and served in the American armed forces. Following the United States' declaration of war on Germany (April 6, 1917), city Italians volunteered for service in army, navy, marine, and army airforce units. During hostilities Italian-American soldiers joined artillery, infantry, engineering, and other units of the 33rd Division, including the 131st and 132nd Infantry regiments, 122nd Machine Gun Battalion, 108th Ammunition Train, 108th Supply Train, 122nd and 149th Field Artillery regiments, and 108th Engineers.[3]

Graham Taylor, who worked as chairman of a draft board on Chicago's West Side (Local Board 39), noted that, while a few Italians "preferred to go back to Italy to fight," most willingly registered and served in the armed forces of their adopted country. Italians throughout the country exhibited this readiness to go to war under the American flag. They enrolled in military outfits "more than any other immigrant nationality," according to Philip M. Rose, and "twenty thousand gave their lives." George Creel, as Chairman of the United States Committee on Public Information, responsible for uniting public opinion behind the war effort, estimated that more than 300,000 Italians served in the army during the war; "Italians are about 4 per cent of the whole population, but the list of casualties shows a full 10 per cent of Italian names."

During the last four months of the war, twenty-four of Chicago's Italians from various parts of the city died in service:[4]

Samuel Basone, 919 Cambridge Avenue
Pasquale Carravatta, 836 Garibaldi Place
James Catalano, 116 South Sangamon Street
Andrew Cina, 1755 Ashland Avenue
Charles J. Corsiglia, 2742 North Sacramento
Nick Cuza, 248 Alexander Street
Guerrini D'Avolio, 1110 South Morgan Street
Charles Domiane, 1008 Cambridge Avenue
F. Fontana, 734 East 104th Street
Joseph Greco, 505 South Campbell Avenue
Fred Guido, 1452 Komensky Street
William R. Lamberti, 3351 North Troy Street
James Manguso, 1162 West Erie Street
John Mazzali, 332 West Chicago Avenue
Ignazio Miozi, 655 Vedder Street
Joseph Nevara, 3052 South St. Louis Avenue
Louis Noterdonado, 448 North Curtis Street
Joseph Picrucce, 1367 Fulton Street
Frank B. Potampa, 2712 South Kildare Street
Thomas Saffore, 3723 South State Street
John C. Scalzitti, 2426 North Tripp Avenue
Xaxier Sieradi, 1735 Wabansia Avenue
N. Zucchero, 611 Sholto Street
Antonio Zullo, 1142 West Taylor Street

The war had a profound and lasting effect upon the city's Italian colony. Sacrifices on the battlefield increased ethnic pride and prestige at home, while the virtual end of immigration after 1914 and the resultant sharp decrease in new arrivals to be assimilated hastened the decline of the community and its institutions. The cessation of immigration ended the constant refilling of labor reserves and combined with military manpower needs to provide Italians with a large number of jobs at—in the words of Robert Foerster—"unprecedentedly high wages." [5]

The general prosperity that began during World War I and continued until late 1929 (except for the recession of 1920–21) facilitated the upward movement of Italians and other "new" im-

migrant groups. Writing early in the 1920's, Oscar Durante noted
that Italians had risen to occupy prominent positions in business,
politics, and the professions. This improved economic status
brought about greater self-esteem in the community: "No longer
do Italians attempt to conceal their origins or change their names." [6]
During the 'twenties the increased affluence of many immigrants
made possible, even speeded, the dispersal of Italians throughout
all parts of the city and its suburbs. Along with the passage of
legislation restricting further immigration, residential mobility
depopulated the ethnic community and lessened its importance.

## II

Characterizing the "Southern" colony of the Near North Side in
1928, an Italian priest noted that "since the war there has been a
great change and it is no longer an Italian community." He continued, "Many of the people, as they have been able to afford it,
have moved farther north, especially the young people who
marry. They establish their homes north and west of the neighborhood in which they were born, and bring up their families more
nearly according to the standards which they learned at school."
In the process, they abandoned Italian-language newspapers for
"newspapers in English," and old-world foods for "food which is
no longer strictly Italian." Their new way of life indicated that
"the old colony is disappearing, and their old country ways are
becoming fused with the customs of their adopted country." While
these remarks applied specifically to one district, they accurately
described changes occurring in other ethnic enclaves.[7]

With few new arrivals from overseas, and with increased con-
version of the area to business use, the Italian colony in the lower
Loop had lost more than three fourths of its population by 1930.
Hull House and Chicago Commons districts remained in existence,
but the proportion of Italians rapidly declined. In the old Near
West Side Italian quarter (east of Halsted), the number of
"Southerners" decreased by almost two thirds in the decade fol-
lowing 1920, from 2753 to slightly more than 1000. During the

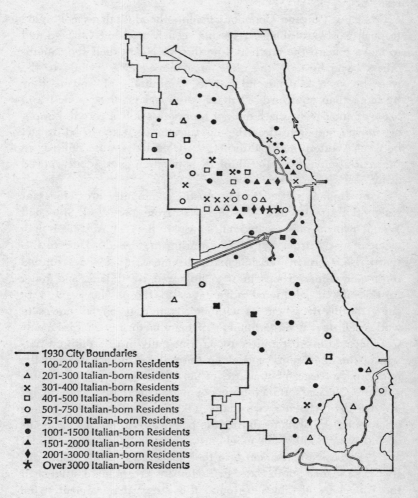

9. Italians in Chicago, 1930

same decade, the heavy concentration of Italians between Halsted and Racine diminished by more than half, from 7931 to 3683, while blocks farther west showed a dramatic increase in Italian residents.[8]

From the Chicago Commons neighborhood, Italians continued to push westward along streets between Kinzie and Chicago and to move toward the north and northwest. Nearly half the "Southerners" who lived in the older area moved away, while to the west, between Ashland and Leavitt, the number of Italians grew by more than one third. That this dispersal involved a desire to leave ethnic enclaves and did not represent solely a core-to-periphery move is apparent from the fact that the old established district between Western and California, itself located several miles from the central city, lost a fourth of its population as residents moved away.

Many Italians settled in the Austin community area. Pleasant residential streets drew "Southerners" from the West Side and West Town colonies, located miles away to the east. Austin's Italian element soared from 739 to 3042 during the decade. Despite this sharp rise, Germans, Irishmen, Englishmen, and Swedes formed the major ethnic groups in 1930, followed by Italians and Jews. Austin offered additional advantages to those who wanted to enjoy the district's benefits without commuting long distances to work each day. A large number of manufacturing establishments were located in Austin after 1900, principally in the southern portion of the community and along the railroad, which formed the northern and eastern boundaries of the township.[9]

While Chicago's Italian-born population increased from 59,854 in 1920 to 73,960 ten years later, all of the city's settled Italian colonies lost inhabitants during the post-war era. Former residents of the Near South Side neighborhood moved into more distant areas. Extensive movement also took place away from ethnic districts in the Far South Side. F. R. Jenkins, a graduate student at the University of Chicago, found this outward movement to be true in the West Englewood community, which he studied in the mid-'twenties for the Local Community Research Committee. Jenkins noted "a rise in the economic status of some original settlers, coupled with the incoming of more wealthy Italians" which, by 1925, resulted in the shifting of that ethnic group "to a section farther south than the original settlement." Because of the movement of this more ambitions element of the population, he declared, "the original settlement is deteriorating and new property is depreciating in value." [10]

During the 'twenties, approximately one fourth of the residents left the heart of the "Southern" colony on the Near North Side (Milton, Cambridge—formerly Gault Court—and surrounding streets). As a result of this exodus, according to a long-time (German-born) inhabitant commenting in 1926, "only the rough class" remained behind as "the good Italians" moved west and north. Italians scattered throughout the north and northwest sides of the city, with new concentrations forming in Lincoln Park, Lake View, and North Center areas. A German store owner who had lived in North Center for more than thirty years found "Southerners" to be fully acceptable as neighbors. "All the Italians who have moved into our neighborhood," she maintained, "are ambitious and home loving people, young ones with families, who can speak enough English to carry on a little business of their own or work well enough for some other man. I have always found them honest, but then so are my Swedish and Polish customers." A thirteen-year-old boy whose family had recently left the "Southern" community and settled on School Street summed up the attitude of those who moved out of ethnic enclaves into American neighborhoods. Cambridge Street, he said, "isn't as nice as it was when our parents first went there, for today many Mexicans and colored people have filled up the old Italian streets." Ironically, these sentiments echoed those spoken years before by northern European residents who moved from the Near North Side and other sections of Chicago in order to escape contact with Italians.[11]

The wish for better living conditions led Italians, as well as other Chicagoans, to leave the city for new homes in nearby suburbs.[12] Italians moved into industrial suburbs—Chicago's "satellite cities"—at least as early as the 1890's, but did not begin to locate in many of the better residential communities to the west and north until after World War I. By 1929 there were Italians living in every suburb of the metropolitan area.

In the autumn of 1894, Our Lady of Mount Carmel church was established as a mission for the numerous Italian residents of Melrose Park. Nine years later San Rocco opened its doors in Chicago Heights, the first Catholic church in the village. By 1905, religious processions and feasts celebrated at these two parishes had become yearly events, rating coverage in the *Chicago Tribune*, *Chicago Chronicle*, and other city newspapers as well as Italian-language journals. In following years Italians continued to pour into Cicero, Melrose Park, Chicago Heights, and other industrial suburbs, where they generally lived in neighborhoods with a sizable Italian element.[13]

Although most Italian "satellite city" residents worked in factories or on construction projects, and achieved only a modest degree of upward mobility by American standards, some, like Joseph Imburgio (who later changed his name to Bulger) realized significant financial success. In 1918, at the age of eighteen, Bulger arrived in Melrose Park with his four siblings and widowed mother from his native New Orleans. Two years later he married Elsie Tomm, the daughter of a Melrose Park jeweler. Following his marriage, Joe Imburgio Bulger left his job as a clerk in the Citizens State Bank of Melrose Park for real-estate and insurance businesses and local politics. According to the Chicago Crime Commission, Bulger "often boasted that he had made his first million dollars by the time he was thirty years of age"—that is, during the 1920's. In the following decade he served as president of the Italo-American National Union and as Mayor of Melrose Park. In 1938 he earned a degree from Chicago's John Marshall Law School and turned to the practice of law. His activities increased in importance over the years and at the time of his death in an air crash in 1966, Bulger was (in the words of the Chicago Crime Commission's *Report* for 1967) "an attorney for numerous powerful crime syndicate leaders" and "dominated the affairs of tax-supported bodies in Melrose Park and Cicero." The institutions referred to were the Clyde Park District in Cicero and the Veterans Park District in Melrose Park.

The youngster who, during World War I, had worked after school and on weekends as a waterboy on the New Orleans docks, gained wealth and power in Chicago, although not, apparently, by means of qualities lauded in Horatio Alger's novels.[14]

Wilmette, Evanston, Kenilworth, River Forest, Oak Park, and other north shore and western suburbs attracted middle- and upper-income Italians who wanted to live in essentially "American" communities that also offered such advantages as large houses and lots, better schools, and lower taxes than did Chicago. Among the hundreds of suburban Italians who traveled to work in the city were professional men like Vincent Marzano of Kenilworth, physician and surgeon, who practiced medicine at 5044 Sheridan Road on Chicago's Far North Side; Dr. Frank J. Fara, a Berwyn resident, who kept his office at 3341 West Twenty-sixth Street; and attorney Rocco R. Covello, who lived in Oak Park and worked in the Loop. Businessmen included Jacob F. Battistini, of River Forest, who headed three Chicago fruit and vegetable companies; Oak Park's Joseph Soravia, department head, Sears, Roebuck and Company; William Quattrocchi, vice-president and treasurer of the Marb-L-Cote Company, who commuted from Winnetka; and Frederick G. Salerno, one of Chicago's most successful Italian executives, who traveled to the city from Wilmette.

Born in 1877 in Cosenza in the Italian "South," Salerno arrived in Chicago when he was a boy. At the age of twelve he began to work as a pan greaser in a small local biscuit company. Over the years he moved to the presidency of the Sawyer Biscuit Company. In 1933 Salerno and R. Lee Megowen, secretary-treasurer of the Sawyer Company, formed the Salerno-Megowen Biscuit Company. Their firm, originally located at 4500 Division Street, grew into one of the nation's largest bakeries.[15]

Most Italian migration to middle- and upper-income suburbs took place during the 'twenties. Joe Delvecchio operated a meat market at 1031 Polk Street in 1923, and lived at 815 Miller near his place of work. By 1929 Delvecchio commuted to his job from Oak Park. Contractors Paul V. Colianni and Joseph Dire, who owned and operated several businesses located in Chicago, among them two railroad construction firms (Colianni & Dire and the Western Contracting Company), also settled in Oak Park. Dire moved from 1225 Congress Street between 1923 and 1929. His business partner, who won election as a Sanitary District Trustee in 1930 and figured prominently as a Cermak supporter, moved from the Congress Hotel in the Loop. Others who, during this period shifted residences but not businesses to northern and western suburbs (principally Evanston, River Forest, Oak Park, and Wilmette) included Arthur M. Brianza, dentist; Enrico Ditorrice, grocer; Ralph Pacini, owner of a statuary company; Alfonso and Biaggio Alfini, monument makers; Eugene Mancinelli, jewelry-store owner; Victor F. Lassagne, patent attorney for the International Harvester Company; Dario L. Toffenetti, founder and owner of Chicago's Triangle Restaurants; and Frank H. Gazzolo, president of a drug and chemical company.

While economic success and desire for better living conditions encouraged the movement of many upwardly mobile Italians to the suburbs, not all departed from the city. Most of those who remained resided in outer areas of Chicago. One highly successful Italian, Joshua D'Esposito, lived on the periphery at 6936 Sheridan Road. Born in Sorrento, D'Esposito arrived in the United States in 1897 at the age of eighteen and began his employment as a draftsman for the Pennsylvania Railroad, rising to the position of chief draftsman in 1907. He moved to Chicago in 1913, became assistant chief engineer of the Chicago Union Station Company in 1914, assistant manager of the Emergency Fleet Corporation of the United States Shipping Board during World War I, and in 1919 chief engineer in charge of construction of the Union Station Building, completed in 1925. At one time a messenger boy, Chicago-born Albert H. Fabbri of 4741 North Paulina Street became a successful industrialist, serving as president of Northwestern Expanded Metal Co. and of Northwestern Steel Products Co. In 1930 Dr. Lisi Cipriani (Ph.D., University of Chicago) counted Italian business and professional men in Chicago and identified 4500 firms or men. She limited her study largely to lawyers, doctors and merchants located in ethnic neighborhoods, but made no attempt to include industrialists and businessmen connected with American firms. She ignored, among others, Salerno, Toffenetti, Fabbri, and D'Esposito.[16]

Italians engaged in political or criminal activities generally remained in the city, except for those who based their operations in suburban communities. Many stayed in or near the core areas. The six Genna brothers, for example, grew up and lived in the Near West Side colony (where four died violently between May 1925 and January 1926), while First Ward political leader Daniel A. Serritella lived at 1142 South Michigan Avenue in the Near South Side. A few of the more successful criminals settled in pleasant residential districts in distant sections of the city or suburbs. Among these were John Torrio, who lived at 7011 South Clyde Avenue, and Joseph Aiello of the O'Banion organization, who selected a residence on Chicago's Far West Side at 205 Kolmar Avenue in West Rogers Park. Wealthy, prominent gangsters with families, like their counterparts in the world of legitimate business, preferred to live outside the city. According to United States Treasury agent Elmer L. Irey, they favored Berwyn, "where the boys did no business in return for unmolested living privileges." Irey referred particularly to Frank Nitti, supposedly Capone's successor, as well as other criminal bosses. In less-favored suburban areas on the West and South sides, particularly Cicero, the Torrio-Capone organization did a great deal of "business" during the 1920's.[17]

## III

Italians realized incredible financial success from organized crime. At a time when "American" Italians (those born or raised in the United States) were arriving at maturity only to find economic advancement made difficult—but not impossible—by inadequate education, "undesirable" social and ethnic backgrounds, and lack of political connections, a new field of endeavor appeared, requiring as qualifications only ambition, ruthlessness, and loyalty. With its fast, lush monetary opportunities, prohibition provided a powerful attraction for many qualified young men who felt irresistibly

drawn to this novel form of economic enterprise. "Prohibition is a
business," maintained "Scarface Al" Capone. "All I do is to supply
a public demand. I do it in the best and least harmful way I can."
He and others like him undoubtedly convinced themselves that
they worked simply as labor and distribution organizers in a
strongly competitive field. Criminals could persuade themselves
of their value to society and the business world because the
liquor trade provided a service that rich and poor alike desperately
wanted and willingly paid for. Prohibition "opened up a new
criminal occupation, with less risk of punishment, with more cer-
tainty of gain, and with less social stigma than the usual forms of
crime like robbery, burglary, and larceny." [18]

Under the leadership of John Torrio and his successor, Capone,
Italians exerted a powerful economic and political influence in
Chicago, and made a spectacular and notorious entrance into the
mainstream of city life and consciousness during the 'twenties.
Their glittering successes and extravagant excesses, and the extensive publicity accorded their actions by the press, diverted public
attention from widespread but less sensational accomplishments
of Chicago's law-abiding Italians.

James Colosimo's funeral on May 15, 1920, signified a major
turning point in the emergence of Italians in organized crime and
indicated the growing influence of gangsters in city politics. The
elite of Chicago's officialdom attended the ceremony. Three judges,
eight aldermen, an assistant state's attorney, a congressman, and
a state representative served as honorary pallbearers, along with
gamblers, vice-resort operators, and racketeers. The event proved
to be, in the words of Chicago Crime Commission Executive Director Virgil W. Peterson, "a public announcement that the criminal
world ruled the city, and political success depended upon the
favor of those in control of gambling and vice. The voice of the
general public which abhorred such criminal-official alliances was
weak and politically insignificant." Chicago had "capitulated to the
underworld." [19]

Following Colosimo's burial, John Torrio—also an honorary
pallbearer—quickly consolidated his control over the Levee and

moved to extend his influence throughout the city as well as South Side and West Side suburbs. The former Colosimo lieutenant established a highly efficient city-wide "syndicate" to operate breweries and convoys of trucks needed for the manufacture and distribution of beer, a product for which Chicagoans exhibited a powerful craving. During the initial period, many pre-prohibition brewery owners apparently formed partnerships with gangsters. Others employed underworld leaders as "fronts" while continuing to operate their companies; these seemed to comply with legislation prohibiting the manufacture of alcoholic beverages for general consumption. In short order the criminal elements established their supremacy, at least partly because of the unwillingness of legitimate owners to continue their involvement when police enforcement became more effective and the prospect of jail terms, consequently, more likely.[20]

Between 1920 and 1923, Torrio brought a measure of peace among warring criminal factions, and elevated himself to a position of dominance by convincing his fellow gangsters of the advantages of cooperation as opposed to competition. He presided over the city's division into spheres of influence, keeping most of the South Side under his personal control. Realizing that violence harmed his business, he avoided conflicts whenever he could. As John Landesco pointed out, however, "when murder must be done, it was done deftly and thoroughly." Torrio acted quickly, for example, to discourage two free-lance bootleggers, Morrie Keane and William Egan, who attempted to invade his territory in December 1923. Their venture ended violently, with two bullet-ridden bodies sprawled by a roadside—a lesson not lost on other overly ambitious hoodlums. Torrio's success, however, rested on more than strong-arm methods. He provided his bootlegging associates with protection from the law, and with lavish outlays of money purchased the cooperation of local politicians and police officers. "Immunity from punishment," concluded Landesco, "appears to be an almost indispensable element in maintaining the prestige and control of a gangster chief." [21]

The "syndicate" operated quietly, efficiently, and profitably in

Chicago under the benign eyes of grafting politicians and police, during the years of the second Thompson administration. According to newspapermen Lloyd Wendt and Herman Kogan, "as long as Thompson was in office, despite all his fuss about driving out the criminals, this alliance progressed smoothly, in the business-like way Torrio hoped it would." In his techniques of organization, Torrio was "not unlike a master politician, using the powers of patronage and favor when it suited his purpose, punishing when his purpose was thwarted, breaking and upsetting alliances when an underling sought to defy him." A United States District Attorney admitted that "as an organizer and administrator of underworld affairs, Johnny Torrio is unsurpassed in the annals of American crime; he is probably the nearest thing to a real mastermind that this country has yet produced." Writing at the end of the Capone era, Walter Noble Burns judged that Torrio "would have been an outstanding success in any field of endeavor," possessing as he did a remarkable degree of "poise, sound judgment, finesse, shrewd diplomacy, common sense, and clear vision. He was, in his way, a genius." To Elmer Irey, who succeeded in accumulating enough evidence in the 1930's to send Torrio to jail (for two and a half years) for tax violation, "he was the smartest and, I dare say, the best of all the hoodlums. 'Best' referring to talent, not morals." [22]

The election of William E. Dever as Mayor in April 1923, upset this harmonious arrangement and resulted in Torrio's retirement two years later. The refusal of Dever and his chief of police, Morgan A. Collins, to cooperate with Torrio destroyed the old system of official protection and damaged the prestige and control of the "syndicate" chief. On May 19, 1924, Chief Collins directed a secret and highly successful raid on the Sieben Brewery, which netted, along with the usual small-time crooks (truck drivers, gunmen, workmen), three major gang leaders including Torrio himself. Torrio's arrest and indictment proved beyond any doubt that the "syndicate" did not control the new city administration, a fact that encouraged ambitious underlings like Dion O'Banion and Hymie Weiss to challenge the established criminal hierarchy.[23]

The relative calm of the corrupt Thompson era ended abruptly. The "union of each for the good of all" under the guidance of Torrio gave way to the "war of each against all," in which yesterday's ally often became today's enemy. Between September 1923, and October 1926, an estimated 215 gangsters murdered each other in the struggle to seize control of local booze and beer businesses. Police accounted for another 160 outlaw deaths. One casualty was former altar boy Dion O'Banion, who bossed the so-called North Side gang at the time of his demise on November 10, 1924. Although the killers were never identified or apprehended, general gossip assumed them to be either members of the Genna clan, which had long feuded with O'Banion, or paid assassins employed by the Torrio-Capone organization. Dion's successor, Polish-American Hymie Weiss (born Wajciechowski), vowed to avenge his Irish friend's murder. On January 12, 1925, unknown assailants tried to kill Capone; later in the month Torrio suffered a near-fatal attempt on his life. In February, a thoroughly shaken Torrio appeared in United States District Court to face charges growing out of his part in the Sieben Brewery affair. Found guilty, he received a sentence of nine months in jail. The former overlord of crime uncomplainingly accepted the temporary safety that prison offered. Following his early release from jail, Torrio hastily departed from Chicago, abandoning the organization that he and Colosimo had taken years to build. The "syndicate" now functioned under the leadership of a new and hand-picked director, Al Capone, who assumed control of the empire while he was still in his twenties.[24]

The war for control of Chicago's underworld continued its violent course (in the process damaging the reputation of the city's reform mayor) until the rival factions finally concluded that the prize did not justify the cost. On October 21, 1926, representatives of the major gangs met to negotiate a settlement. This provided for a division of the city among rival organizations and an agreement not to operate outside the allotted territory. While Capone apparently obtained direct rights only to part of the West Side and the western suburbs, he continued to exert great influence on the

South Side. The powerful and cohesive organization bequeathed him by Torrio gave him a tremendous advantage over his major rivals, the North Side mob.

Lasting little more than five months, the truce of October 21 ended with the death of Vincent "the Schemer" Drucci at the hands of the police on April 4, 1927. As boss of the O'Banion gang, Drucci had abided by the terms of the October agreement. His successor, George "Bugs" Moran, refused to compromise with the Capone organization, a feeling shared by Moran's allies, Christian P. "Barney" Bertsche, Jack Zuta, and the Aiello brothers. The relative quiet of the interim period ended, and the gang wars progressed toward what newspaperman Denis Tilden Lynch (writing in 1932) termed the underworld's "most gory act of terrorism." On February 14, 1929, four men—two dressed like police officers—entered a garage at 2122 North Clark Street and murdered seven members of the North Side group. This St. Valentine's Day Massacre failed to eliminate Moran, who happened not to stop by the garage that particular morning. He left shortly afterward for the East Coast, and the once-strong North Side organization disintegrated. With all Capone's rivals removed from competition, "Scarface Al" ruled Chicago's underworld at the age of thirty-two, just ten years after his inauspicious arrival in the city.[25]

In appearance, personality, and behavior the "Big Fellow" (as Capone was known to friend and enemy alike) contrasted sharply with his predecessor. The slim, quiet, conservatively attired Torrio suggested a successful businessman—perhaps a banker—rather than the leader of a criminal gang. His reputation as a man who indulged in no debauchery reinforced this impression, although the organization he directed offered for sale every vice known to man. While his underlings beat, maimed, and murdered countless numbers of victims, Torrio despised violence and proudly boasted that never in his life had he fired a gun. The tall and husky Capone, on the other hand, fitted the gangster stereotype. He was loud, uncouth, and a flashy dresser. He enjoyed alcohol and women, and had a passion for gambling, once losing $500,000 in a day at the racetrack. Nothing in his manner or looks indicated the qualities of mind, the shrewdness, subtlety, and keen intelligence that enabled him to seize and maintain control over Chicago crime while still a young man. The "Big Fellow" also had the ability to withstand the pressures of his work and to face without visible fear the constant threat of violent death. To the underworld and the general public, Torrio's precipitous flight from Chicago after the attempt on his life dimmed the luster of his earlier achievements. In contrast, numerous assassination attempts never deflected Capone from his objectives.[26]

Capone, or "Al Brown," as he called himself at the time of his arrival from Brooklyn, began his career in Chicago as bodyguard for "syndicate" boss James Colosimo. After "Big Jim's" death in 1920, "Scarface Al" quickly moved upward in the organization and two years later emerged as chief lieutenant to Torrio. In 1923 Torrio felt his position threatened by the election of reformer William Dever, the Democratic candidate for mayor, who vowed to prosecute the major prohibition violators rather than the "small fry" operating in Chicago. Torrio soon found himself confronted with the problem of finding an alternate base of operations for metropolitan-area beer distribution and gambling, a base that could not be touched by the militant new city administration. Cicero offered an ideal location. It lay adjacent to Stickney, where Torrio already operated several houses of prostitution; and of all Chicago suburbs, Cicero was most accessible to the Loop and other core areas of the city. In addition, the suburb itself promised to be a rich market for liquor and beer sales as well as gambling. With a population of 50,000 people (the majority of them of Slavic or German background) Cicero formed the largest urban area in the county (outside Chicago) and the fifth in size in Illinois.[27]

Torrio's forces moved into Cicero in the fall of 1923. Local political-criminal elements led by Eddie Vogel and Eddie Tancl, and Miles and William "Klondike" O'Donnell (whose gang supplied Cicero and Chicago's West Side with beer and other liquors), attempted unsuccessfully to block Torrio. Before the end of the year Torrio had imposed a compromise agreement that assured his gang a monopoly of gambling activities in the greater part of the town. Capone directed "syndicate" activities in the West Side suburb in his first independent "command" assignment. "Scarface Al" proceeded quietly and carefully at first, emphasizing the vital services he provided to the community through his beer-running activities. "It's a shame," he noted disapprovingly, "that a man should be denied a glass of beer after a hard day's work," a line of argument designed to appeal to the residents of the working-class suburb. Cicero's mayoralty election of April 1, 1924, provided an opportunity for Capone to gain control of the entire town. Through fraudulent registration, bribery, ballot-box stuffing, kidnapping, slugging, and shooting, Capone "elected" his candidate over an opposition equally corrupt but less resourceful.[28]

In following years Capone emerged as the "feudal baron of Cicero" (in the words of his biographer Fred D. Pasley). In addition to Cicero, the "syndicate" allegedly controlled Burnham, Chicago Heights, Melrose Park, Stickney, and other nearby towns. Mayor Dever's action in attempting to eliminate crime and corruption in the city drove the Torrio-Capone forces into the suburbs, where they carried on their illegal and highly profitable business openly and without effective opposition from county officials, among them Anton J. Cermak, President of the Cook County Board of Commissioners. The captivity of Cicero continued even after the election of Republican "Big Bill" Thompson as mayor in 1927 prepared the way for Capone's return to Chicago. John Lyle, Judge of the Municipal Court (and a publicity-conscious reformer) recalled in 1960 that "Cicero besmirched and looted, would in the end, have revenge on its prime minister of evil." Evidence captured in raids on Capone-controlled Cicero gambling houses and speakeasies made possible the conviction of the "Big Fellow" for income tax evasion in 1931. During the six years between Torrio's retirement and Capone's conviction, "Scarface Al" directed an organization that exceeded that of his predecessor in extent, influence, power, and wealth.[29]

Capone, Torrio, Drucci, the Aiellos, the Gennas, and other "Southerners" acquired millions of dollars during prohibition years.

No accurate measure of their wealth exists, but estimates of the Capone "syndicate's" gross annual income ranged from $100,000,000 to over $300,000,000 by the late 1920's. Beer and other alcoholic beverages accounted for about 60 per cent of each year's intake, with gambling, prostitution, and other activities bringing in smaller but still significant amounts. Thus records seized by United States Bureau of Internal Revenue agents showed net profits in excess of $500,000 for a single Capone-controlled gambling house, The Ship, during an 18-month period in 1925–26. On Chicago's Near West Side the Genna brothers, at the height of their power and glory, employed hundreds of neighborhood "Southerners" to distill alcohol in their own homes. This particular business enterprise resulted in a highly lucrative operation with gross sales of $350,000 a month, and total assets valued at $5,000,000.[30]

For American gangsters and especially second generation "Southerners," prohibition formed a Golden Age, when ambitious youngsters could amass wealth and power beyond their wildest dreams. Practical considerations rather than moral values shaped the attitude of ethnic district youths toward criminal activity, declared John Landesco. On the basis of extensive interviews conducted during the late 'twenties with youth gang members, Landesco concluded that "where the choice of a young man is between a low paid job as an unskilled laborer and good wages for driving a beer truck, a stigma is soon attached to legitimate employment." [31]

During prohibition, professional criminals—pickpockets, extortionists, safecrackers and others—abandoned their former practices in the Italian community and joined the growing ranks of bootleggers. The last vestiges of the Black Hand disappeared as members (allegedly among them the Genna brothers) entered the "syndicate." Many legitimate businessmen found the lure of fast money too powerful to resist. John Landesco noted that the Aiellos, who later became prominent members of the North Side organization, worked initially in business, first appearing in the city's bootlegging activities as suppliers of sugar "on a large scale to wholesalers." To laboring-class "Southerners," the "syndicate's" eagerness to buy the product of home stills offered a quick and easy way to augment family incomes.[32]

Journalistic accounts of Chicago crime in the prohibition era generally ascribed control and direction of the production of bootleg booze in the city's Italian neighborhoods to the *Unione Siciliana* (after 1925 the Italo-American National Union). Before World War I this organization enjoyed a prestigious reputation for its opposition to immigrant colony crime as a supporter of the White Hand Society. By 1929 Fred D. Pasley would write that the Union "comprises some 15,000 Sicilians, disciplined like an army; implacable of purpose; swift and silent of deed; the Mafia of Italy transplanted to the United States." Walter Noble Burns claimed that "its members distilled the greater part of the basic alcohol used in the whisky, brandy, rum, and gin sold in Chicago and held a monopoly on the sale of sugar and yeast used by Sicilian distillers." Rumor held that ample profits led to a tug-of-war between rival criminal elements in 1928 over control of the Union, the two main protagonists being the Aiellos and Capone. A number of murders took place, including those of Antonio Lombardo, Pasqualino Lolardo, Joseph Giunta, and Joseph Aiello, all presidents of the Italo-American National Union or aspirants to that position. The Capone faction emerged victorious.[33]

In contrast to years before 1920, the greater part of illegally gained cash during prohibition came from outside the ethnic group. Chicagoans decried the violence and bloodshed, the debasement of public officials, the involvement of the *Unione Siciliana*, and the enrichment of social undesirables. At the same time city residents subsidized the "syndicate" by patronizing its establishments (speakeasies, gambling parlors, and houses of prostitution), drinking its booze and glorifying its criminals. Foremost among these antiheroes, of course, was Al Capone.

The general public admired Capone's audacity, respected his power, and envied his wealth. Many people saw the gangster chieftain's life as one of glamour, danger and excitement, far removed from the sweat and drudgery of daily labor. Millions of

Americans ignored his crimes and lionized him for "disdaining a law that was becoming increasingly unpopular; they sympathized when he objected to being called a bootlegger and a racketeer" and offered no objection when he described his activities as being those of a harassed businessman. During the days of his glory, Capone received fan letters from all over the world. Foreign authors traveled thousands of miles to interview him and write books and articles about his place in American life. In 1931 Frederick Lewis Allen observed that Capone, by the end of the preceding decade, had grown "as widely renowned as Charles Evans Hughes or Gene Tunney. He had become an American portent." [34]

Significantly, Italian-language newspapers devoted less space to crime during the 1920's (when Italians scaled the heights of criminal success) than they had earlier to Black Hand activities. Any readers who depended solely on *L'Italia* or *La Tribuna Italiana Transatlantica* for news during prohibition years remained ignorant of the actions and notoriety of John Torrio and Al Capone. The attempts to murder the "Big Fellow" and Torrio in January, 1925, for example, received no mention in Italian periodicals. While Italian journals did report the St. Valentine's Day killings, they indicated no connection between that event and organized crime. This deliberate policy of silence reflected the middle class aspirations and orientations of newspaper publishers and their intention to minimize the sordid and unpleasant aspects of Italian-American life in the city. Chicago's Italians who had departed from the immigrant quarter in search of acceptance and respectability, or who planned to do so, saw in "Scarface Al" and other gangland figures a constant source of chagrin and embarrassment. Giovanni E. Schiavo's paean of praise for Italian-American achievements, *Italians in Chicago*, completely ignored the city's wealthiest and most widely known Italian, although the book appeared in 1928 when Capone had reached the height of his power.[35]

To many ethnic colony residents, Capone appeared to be a benefactor. In Chicago and Cicero he supplied the needy with coal, groceries, clothing, and other necessities. Capone's benevolence, like the criminal organization that he headed (and that provided

the cash for his welfare activities) reached beyond his fellow
"Southerners." The "Big Fellow" opened his wallet and his "syndicate" to anyone, regardless of race, creed, or color. Novelist
Mary Borden, who in 1930 visited her native Chicago after an
absence of twelve years, described Capone as "an ambidextrous
giant, who kills with one hand and feeds with the other." The
gangster chief's concern for the plight of poor Chicagoans was
more than the outpouring of a generous spirit. Along with his
multifarious illegal activities, Capone functioned as a political
boss and knew that favors lavished on voters and potential voters
often paid dividends on election day.[36]

## IV

During the 1920's Italians realized no political achievements com-
parable to their spectacular successes in Chicago crime. There
emerged no candidate who combined the qualities of personality
and political acumen necessary to win a major office. Only one
office seeker attempted to become Chicago's first Italian mayor.
In 1923 Bernard P. Barasa entered the Republican primary after
his good friend "Big Bill" Thompson decided not to stand for
reelection.

Chicago's Italian-language press greeted the announcement of
Barasa's candidacy with strong approbation. All Italians, proclaimed *L'Italia* on February 4, must support "the election of
Barasa as mayor of Chicago" for the honor of the group. *La
Tribuna Italiana Transatlantica* extended its "sincere and warm
wishes for victory" and described "great enthusiasm in the colony
for Judge Barasa." During the campaign, the press maintained a
steady chorus of support, expressing the conviction that "Italians
will perform their duty and vote for Barasa." As the primary of
February 27 approached, the newspapers announced that Barasa
had gained widespread support outside the Italian community.
*L'Italia* predicted that "individuals of every nationality" would
vote for the Municipal Court Judge, while *La Tribuna Italiana
Transatlantica* foresaw the support of "Americans, Italians, and

voters of other extractions and of every social class, of every party
and political faction and of every religious creed." [37]

On election day Italians trooped to the polls and loyally voted
for Barasa, who received 113 of 123 votes in Precinct Nineteen of
Ward One (a heavily Italian area), all but 1 of 200 votes in Precinct Four of Ward Twenty-six, 156 of 170 in Precinct Eleven of
Ward Thirty-one, and 334 of 365 in Precinct Eighteen of Ward
Forty-two. Except for Negroes, who supported him because of
his widely known association with Thompson, Barasa held little
appeal for non-Italians and placed last in a field of four candidates.
He received 47,685 votes out of a total of 304,600. Italian-language
journals portrayed Barasa as a trailblazer who, although himself
unsuccessful, had prepared the way for his fellows. Since 1923,
however, no Italian candidate has followed Barasa's lead in bid-
ding for the position of mayor of Chicago.[38]

During the decade Italians achieved modest, although still significant, political gains. Four Democrats and three Republicans
won seats in the State House of Representatives. In 1926 Republican James B. Leonardo became the first member of his ethnic
extraction to enter the State Senate. Four years later another Republican, Daniel A. Serritella, joined him in the upper chamber.
That same year, Democrat Paul V. Colianni, also a prominent
railroad contractor, became the first Italian elected to the office
of Sanitary District Trustee. Albert J. Prignano and William V.
Pacelli won election (in nonpartisan contests) to the City Council
from the Twentieth Ward, while Joseph "Diamond Joe" Esposito
of the Twentieth Ward and Daniel A. Serritella of the First served
as Republican Ward Committeemen. Serritella was also City Sealer
in William Hale Thompson's third mayoral term, a post held by
another Italian colony politician (and alleged Capone cohort)
during "Big Bill's" second term. Two Democrats and four Republicans of Italian background, including Bernard P. Barasa, occupied
seats on the Municipal Court during the 'twenties. Italians also
held a variety of appointive offices, among them Assistant Attorney
General of Illinois and Assistant State's Attorney.[39]

One Italian politician never ran for elective office and remained

unknown to American voters. Michael Merlo, a shadowy figure in
local politics, reputedly ranked as a major power in city crime
during the early 1920's. According to one journalist, "Mike" Merlo,
labor leader of prominence and President of the Board of Directors
of the *Unione Siciliana,* "was head of the Mafia of Chicago." His
influence seemed limitless, that of "a god of the Mafiosi. His will
was theirs." The Italian press indicated no criminal activities linked
to Merlo and the *Unione,* but *La Tribuna Italiana Transatlantica*
made clear in an obituary that Merlo had figured powerfully and
pervasively in the colony's affairs and had served as "the acknowledged, widely accepted and respected head of Chicago's Italian
Democratic Party organization with great influence in municipal,
county, state and federal Democratic politics." [40]

A number of successful Italian politicians had connections with,
or were identified with, criminal elements. Many had grown up in
the same neighborhoods and attended the same schools as their
gangster acquaintances. Most ethnic community youth who pur-
sued careers in law became professionally familiar with still other
criminals. Those who desired political office found underworld
leaders to be useful friends or contacts. Gangster-controlled votes
held the balance of power in many core-area wards, where a favorable nod could ensure a profitable career for an aspiring politician just as readily as a frown could ruin him. During the late
'twenties in the Near West Side, for example, Italians placed members of the group in the City Council at least partly because of
underworld pressure. The Twentieth Ward elected Chicago-born
Albert J. Prignano as Alderman in 1927. Once in office, according
to the *Chicago Tribune,* he alternated between political independence (he enraged his ward boss Morris Eller by a willingness
to cooperate on occasion with reformers) and subservience to the
Capone organization.[41]

Standing for reelection two years later, Prignano received what
equaled a kiss of death for a West Side politician—the Municipal
Voters' League endorsement ("in spite of some bad votes," noted
the League *Report* of 1929). William V. Pacelli ran as Prignano's
major opponent in the 1929 campaign. According to Fred D.

Pasley, a reporter for the *Chicago Tribune* and the *Chicago Herald and Examiner,* Pacelli entered the aldermanic race "at the behest" of City Sealer Daniel A. Serritella, also a crony of Capone. Pacelli relinquished a safe seat in the State House of Representatives, which he had held since 1924, in order to return to Chicago and restore some semblance of order to Twentieth Ward politics. On the basis of his record in Springfield and his identification with "the notorious Eller gang," Pacelli was described as "totally unfit for office" by the Municipal Voters' League. Similar words of condemnation in Chicago newspapers did not prevent Pacelli from winning the tumultuous and violent "nonpartisan" aldermanic election on February 26, 1929, by a margin of nearly five to three over Prignano (4879 to 3166); the third candidate, Martin Klass, received 376 votes. Roland V. Libonati took Pacelli's place in the State House, beginning a long career as State Representative, State Senator, and member of the United States House of Representatives. Prignano returned to elective office in 1934, when he won a seat in the State House of Representatives, a position that he occupied until his assassination on December 29, 1935. Although they differed in party affiliation (Prignano a Democrat, Pacelli and Libonati Republicans), the three politicians had one factor in common, according to the city press: they were friends of "syndicate" boss Al Capone, although Prignano reportedly decided in 1935 that as State Representative and Twentieth Ward Democratic Committeeman he no longer needed to cooperate with Capone's successor, Frank Nitti. Prignano apparently embarked upon an independent course, which, before the year's end, culminated in a clash with Nitti and the death of the self-proclaimed ward boss.[42]

"Diamond Joe" Esposito, another Near West Side resident and one of the most powerful Italian politicians in the city, also reputedly hobnobbed with criminals. Like his friend "Diamond Jim" Colosimo, Esposito operated a well-known restaurant, Bella Napoli Cafe, at 850 South Halsted Street, where Chicago's social and political prominenti dined in the company of underworld chieftains. The Bella Napoli served an important function in Esposito's ward activities during the 'twenties. Like other successful local bosses, Esposito attended christenings, weddings, and funerals, found jobs for the faithful, and provided food for the needy. Many of these activities, and other community affairs, could be handled in his restaurant or with its facilities.

Rumor held that Esposito, once indicted for murder but freed because of insufficient evidence, operated as the political power behind the "terrible Gennas." Within the Republican Party, "Diamond Joe" was a prominent member of the anti-Thompson faction led by United States Senator Charles S. Deneen. The Italian-language press accorded the West Side leader wide coverage and fulsome praise. *La Tribuna Italiana Transatlantica* proclaimed him "the greatest politician in Chicago" when he became one of Illinois' 29 presidential electors in November 1924. While he did not reach the heights of success claimed by community journals, Esposito figured as a popular and influential personage in Near West Side and Republican Party events until March 21, 1928, when he was murdered near his home at 800 South Oakley Boulevard. Like Colosimo's assassination, "Diamond Joe's" death remained unsolved, although the killing formed one of several acts of violence in Chicago occurring shortly before the April 10 primary. Italian-language newspapers reacted with shock and disbelief to the news about Esposito. Commenting on the murder, Oscar Durante of *L'Italia* complained bitterly about Chicago's excessive violence and denied vehemently that Esposito had involved himself in bootlegging or any other criminal activity.[43]

The generally accepted view of Italian voting patterns—that criminal elements strongly influenced core-area wards, and illegal activities often decided the outcome of elections—seems to be accurate, but incomplete. Ethnic rivalries, specifically between Italian residents of the Forty-second Ward and Irish boss Dion O'Banion, frequently interfered with underworld plans. O'Banion reputedly carried the votes of the Forty-second and Forty-third wards "in his pistol pocket," and delivered them regularly to Democratic Party candidates. In the 1924 presidential election (during O'Banion's most powerful period), the Irish boss handed the Forty-second to John W. Davis, the Democratic candidate. Italian precincts in the ward, however, went overwhelmingly to Calvin Coolidge—the Eighteenth by a count of 430 to 74, and the Twentieth by 513 to 155.[44]

According to newspapermen Lloyd Wendt and Herman Kogan, Al Capone operated in the First Ward much as did O'Banion on the Near North Side. In the First, however, Capone continued the tradition established long before by "Big Jim" Colosimo of cooperating with the ward's Democratic politicians and supporting machine-backed candidates in exchange for a free hand in the conduct of bootlegging, vice, and gambling operations. As described by Wendt and Kogan, Capone "made it clear" that Kenna and Coughlin "would get the gangland vote and remain clear of interference as long as—Capone was never the most eloquent of men—'Ya keep ya nose clean, see?'" The story went that after one audience with Capone, Coughlin emerged sweating and shaken and blurted, "My God, what could I say? S'pose he had said he was goin' to take over th' organization! What could we do then? We're lucky to get as good a break as we did." [45] Wendt and Kogan did not discuss the political aspects of this arrangement, but its effects showed clearly in the 1924 election when—in contrast to O'Banion's experience and the general trend of Chicago's Italian vote—First Ward Italians supported the Democratic Party's presidential candidate. Even more striking was the 1927 mayoral contest, because of its crucial importance to the city's bootleggers.

During the 1927 campaign, Capone's group contributed amounts estimated between $100,000 and $260,000 to the Republican ticket, headed by William Hale Thompson. In some wards Capone's men used threats and beatings to encourage support of Republican candidates. Apparently in keeping with the long-term arrangements made with Kenna and Coughlin, Capone, himself a Republican, made no attempt to influence the First Ward vote and permitted it to go to the Democratic candidate, Dever. Dever's margin there of 7145 votes (he totaled 11,076 to Thompson's 3931) was the largest he obtained in any ward. All Italian precincts voted for him. Instead of operating in the First Ward, the Capone gang swung into combat in the West Side; and with a new ally, Vincent "the Schemer" Drucci, who at that point headed the O'Banion gang, set out to influence votes in the Near North Side as well.[46]

To Italians and other ethnic voters and to the underworld, enforcement or non-enforcement of the liquor law formed the election's key issue. The incumbent mayor, Dever, personally disliked prohibition; in 1923 he had supported the "wets," and at least partly because of this stand he won large totals in immigrant areas, carrying every one of 27 Italian precincts located in the First, Twentieth, Twenty-fifth, Twenty-sixth, Twenty-seventh, Thirty-first, and Forty-second wards. As mayor, however, he considered his duty to be enforcement of the law. His personal popularity declined steadily as a result. In the 1927 campaign Dever called for a modification of the Volstead Act to permit the manufacture and sale of beer and light wines, a position that lost its appeal when placed against Thompson's extravagant promises to reopen establishments closed by Dever and "open 10,000 new ones." Attempting to return to the office he had occupied from 1915 until 1923, "Big Bill" lost no opportunity of attacking Dever's enforcement of the Volstead Act and of proclaiming himself to be "as wet as the Atlantic Ocean." Parched Chicagoans rallied to his cause. In words sure to appeal to moderate drinkers and bootleggers alike, Thompson vowed to "break any cop I catch on the trail of a lonesome pint into a man's house or car." His promise of a "wide open town" held special attractions for the underworld.[47]

Widespread violence and corruption marked the campaign. Drucci himself was one of many casualties, dying from police bullets under highly suspicious circumstances. Both sides resorted to demagogic appeals, lies, distortions, and misrepresentations. Thompson railed against the "trust press," blaming it for helping his Democratic opponent by deliberately printing lies about him. The former mayor emphasized his record, particularly as "Big Bill the Builder," and boosterism—"Throw away your hammer, and get a horn!" was a favored slogan. Dever retaliated by point-

ing out that the Thompson years had provided very little con-
structive physical growth, and the buildings for which Thompson
took credit had been erected during Dever's mayoralty. The deliberate injection of racism comprised one of the sordid campaign's
least savory aspects. A Thompson slogan, "America First," which
he used to remind German and Irish voters of his wartime opposition to Great Britain, received a publicized interpretation by
Dever as "Africa First." Democrats conducted a whispering campaign to exaggerate and sensationalize Thompson's very real appeal
to Negroes. His formidable strength in black wards became, when
described in the Democratic campaign, seriously threatening to
white Chicago. On the eve of the election, Democratic Party boss
George E. Brennan proclaimed that "Nature never makes a mis-
take. Mayor Dever will be re-elected . . . for the reason that this
is a white man's town." [48]

On election day, according to an ardent Thompson supporter,
Capone's strong-arm squad performed valiantly against its Democratic opposite. "Capone's men, an army of them spread through
the 'bad lands' of the West Side" on election eve and morning,
related the partisan. "There were none more ferocious in political
or bootlegging warfare, none better trained," he continued. "They
were enlisted against the 'Dever and Decency' gunmen. Their
orders were to meet and beat the enemy at the enemy's own game.
They did. Steal the election from Thompson? Not where the
Capone mob was marshaled!" [49]

The desperate Democratic racist strategy had little effect. Prohibition outweighed all other issues for white ethnic groups, and
Thompson enjoyed strong support among Italians, Poles, Germans,
and other immigrant voters. While Coughlin and Kenna succeeded
in keeping First Ward residents in line behind the Dever candidacy, Italians in West Side and North Side wards shifted from
Dever, whom they had supported in 1923, to Thompson. In the
process Dever, who had carried the 27 precincts examined in 1923
with an incredible 79 per cent of the Italian vote, won only eight
of them in 1927 and received 46 per cent of the Italian vote (these

precincts were selected for study not only because they had a majority of Italian-American voters, but also because precinct lines remained unchanged for both elections).

Factionalism typified Chicago politics in the 1920's. Both major parties had split into antagonistic wings that did everything in their power to defeat other candidates within the same party. In 1923 State's Attorney Robert E. Crowe, an anti-Thompson Republican, dashed "Big Bill's" hopes for a third consecutive term as mayor; he prepared a grand jury investigation of charges against Fred Lundin, a friend and political associate of the mayor, and twenty-two other politicos, of defrauding the school board of more than one million dollars. The school scandal broke late in January, just prior to the mayoral primary election, and Thompson felt obliged—as Crowe undoubtedly intended—to withdraw his name from the February 27 primary, the only alternative (his advisers informed him) to a humiliating defeat in the general election. The Crowe-Barrett candidate (Charles Barrett was another anti-Lundin party leader), Arthur C. Lueder, went on to win the party nomination, but lost overwhelmingly to Democrat William E. Dever in the April 3 contest. In time-honored Chicago tradition, Thompson and his faction provided no assistance to Lueder, if they did not actually work for Dever's election. Lueder proved unable to carry the city's three Negro wards, which were traditionally Thompson Republican strongholds, and lost every one of 27 Italian precincts to Dever (in the primary, Thompsonite Bernard Barasa carried all these precincts). By 1927 political expediency had forced 1923's bitter enemies to join forces. Thompson and Crowe merged their influence while Lundin, Thompson's former political friend but no longer the power he had been in Republican affairs, affiliated himself with Governor Len Small. The principal opposition in the February 1927 primary, however, came from another faction within the party, led by United States Senator Charles S. Deneen. Edward R. Litsinger, a prominent Deneen leader and a member of the Board of Reviews, lost by more than a two-to-one margin to Thompson (342,337 to 161,947).[50]

The Democratic Party appeared to present a more united front.

## Table 12

CHICAGO MAYORAL ELECTION, 1923 AND 1927:
ITALIAN PRECINCT VOTE

| Ward | Precinct | 1923 | | | 1927 | | |
|---|---|---|---|---|---|---|---|
| | | Dever | Lueder | Cunnea | Dever | Thompson | Robertson |
| 1 | 19 | 453 | 47 | 1 | 552 | 157 | 8 |
| | 20 | 323 | 30 | 5 | 392 | 65 | 6 |
| | 25 | 175 | 48 | 13 | 192 | 168 | 7 |
| | 26 | 261 | 69 | 12 | 248 | 157 | 7 |
| 20 | 1 | 218 | 104 | — | 85 | 201 | 7 |
| | 2 | 300 | 94 | 3 | 219 | 170 | 25 |
| | 3 | 336 | 121 | 14 | 222 | 232 | 1 |
| | 4 | 306 | 71 | 17 | 106 | 215 | 23 |
| | 5 | 282 | 55 | 8 | 232 | 151 | 2 |
| 25 | 2 | 240 | 45 | 11 | 119 | 80 | 6 |
| | 4 | 306 | 60 | 13 | 219 | 176 | 16 |
| 26 | 1 | 365 | 20 | 13 | 169 | 202 | 9 |
| | 2 | 227 | 6 | 6 | 126 | 170 | 8 |
| | 3 | 196 | 70 | 40 | 184 | 222 | 8 |
| | 4 | 394 | 25 | — | 189 | 269 | 13 |
| | 5 | 436 | 3 | 2 | 138 | 271 | 27 |
| 27 | 1 | 389 | 111 | 9 | 239 | 257 | 24 |
| | 2 | 196 | 80 | 14 | 196 | 205 | 4 |
| | 3 | 275 | 65 | 5 | 195 | 192 | 15 |
| | 4 | 300 | 129 | 3 | 201 | 254 | 26 |
| 31 | 10 | 289 | 69 | 13 | 84 | 225 | 1 |
| | 11 | 329 | 52 | 14 | 128 | 178 | 13 |
| | 12 | 217 | 129 | 11 | 108 | 284 | 10 |
| | 13 | 395 | 78 | 4 | 78 | 290 | 5 |
| 42 | 18 | 217 | 70 | 14 | 85 | 151 | 22 |
| | 20 | 215 | 93 | 9 | 48 | 303 | 15 |
| | 21 | 178 | 53 | 19 | 121 | 238 | 4 |
| Totals | | 7818 | 1797 | 273 | 4875 | 5483 | 312 |

Sources: City of Chicago, Board of Election Commissioners, *Official Precinct Voter Registration Lists* and MS of Official Election Returns for the April 3, 1923, and April 5, 1927, Municipal Elections.

1923 Candidates and Party Affiliations: William E. Dever, Democrat; Arthur C. Lueder, Republican; William A. Cunnea, Socialist.

1927 Candidates and Party Affiliations: William E. Dever, Democrat; William Hale Thompson, Republican; J. Dill Robertson, Independent.

The formerly powerful Harrison wing had gone into a decline,
Boss George E. Brennan retained a reputation for influence, and
Dever would run as the incumbent mayor. The aging Brennan,
however, had lost control of his organization, and Dever only
reluctantly agreed to seek another term. Anton J. Cermak, a rising
force in city politics, loathed the Party's Irish hierarchy and with
the aid of Harrisonites secretly and effectively worked to ensure
Dever's defeat. According to political scientist Alex Gottfried, the
prohibition issue caused Cermak to support the Republican Party.
Claiming that Dever had betrayed the cause of "personal liberty,"
Cermak aligned himself with Thompson in wards under his control. Perhaps the race issue aided Dever among some white voters;
but it worked to his disadvantage among black Chicagoans who
flocked to the polls to show their approval of "Big Bill." The combination of his appeal to black and white ethnic groups, the
Cermak defection, and the activities of Capone henchmen enabled
Thompson to win a plurality of 83,038 despite the presence of a
third candidate on the ballot (J. Dill Robertson, a member of the
Lundin wing of the Republican Party, who hoped to drain enough
votes from "Big Bill" to cause his defeat).[51]

Once again in office, Thompson fulfilled his "wide open town"
pledge. Reporter Henry Justin Smith noted a few years later that
"every vice, every parasite, every swindle, came back." Gambler
and vice-resort operator Jack Zuta, a Jewish member of the North
Side gang, contributed $50,000 to "Big Bill's" campaign, explain-
ing to his friends that he would quickly recoup that amount when
his candidate took office. Capone also received ample reward for
his investment in the Republican cause. In addition to permitting
the "Big Fellow" to move his business operations back to Chicago,
Thompson appointed a personal friend and political contact of
Capone, Daniel A. Serritella, to the post of City Sealer (inspector
of weights and measures). In 1928 Serritella became Republican
Committeeman in the First Ward. This post, along with his position in the mayor's cabinet and the contacts he established in the
labor movement as president of the Newsboys' Union and member
of the Chicago Council, American Federation of Labor, spot-

lighted Serritella as a promising young Italian politician. He proved to be a source of embarrassment when Thompson stood for reelection in 1931, for during the mayoral campaign Serritella and his chief deputy, Harry Hockstein, were indicted for conspiring with city merchants to defraud the people of Chicago through short weights and measures. Both found guilty, they drew sentences of a year in the county jail and fines of $2000. They appealed the decision, which Appellate Court overturned in November 1933, because of insufficient evidence. The affair, although eventually decided in Serritella's favor, had already damaged the reelection hopes of the man who had appointed him to office.[52]

Thompson's opponent in the 1931 mayoral election was Bohemian leader Anton J. Cermak, the man who four years earlier had helped "Big Bill" to win. Following the death of Democratic Party boss George E. Brennan in 1928, Cermak directed an anti-Irish revolt within the Democratic organization, which resulted in the creation of an awesome new political machine based primarily on the support of Chicago's "new" immigrants. Cermak proved his political perspicacity and skill when he provided a measure of political appointments and patronage to keep the still-powerful Irish element from bolting the party; but the Irish felt far from content with the Bohemian captivity of the Democratic machine. The wily Cermak emerged as the city's most effective political boss up to that time.[53]

Cermak and the Democratic Party benefited from the entrance of "new" immigrants into a dominant role in city politics. According to recent studies, ethnic voters in Chicago and other urban centers gradually identified the Republican Party with "intolerance, outmoded Puritan Mores, and insults to immigrants" during the course of the 'twenties. In contrast, Democrats appeared to concern themselves with "liberalization of immigration restriction, prohibition, and defense of minority groups." [54]

At least in part because of this orientation, the overall trend of ethnic voting in Chicago shifted from the Republican to the Democratic side, especially in the years after 1927. Italians, however, did not seem to conform to this pattern. Like members of other

ethnic groups, they strongly supported Democratic candidates Al
Smith (in the 1928 presidential election) and J. Hamilton Lewis
(in the 1930 race for a seat in the United States Senate). They
deviated from the "new" immigrant trend in 1931 by voting for
Thompson, who won 57 per cent of their vote totals while Cermak
received 43 per cent. This result led one recent writer to conclude
that Italians "followed a less rational course" than did other white
ethnic groups he examined.[55]

Despite seeming irrationalities, Italians exhibited a consistent
voting pattern. Throughout the late 1920's and early 1930's, Italian
voters supported "wet" over "dry" candidates regardless of party
affiliation. Since both candidates in the 1931 mayoral election ran
as "wets," prohibition became a minor issue and campaign oratory
focused on crime and corruption. Cermak frequently, vehemently,
and relentlessly denounced gangsters and lawlessness. He directed
his remarks against prominent criminals, many of whom were Italians, and he thereby offended the ethnic group as a whole. "Southerners" felt that Cermak deliberately insulted all immigrants from
the Italian Kingdom. The indictment of the popular Serritella on
election eve—an obvious move to discredit Thompson and boost
Cermak—combined with ethnic pride to induce Italians to vote
against the Bohemian (whom they had supported the previous
year in his successful race for the office of President of the Cook
County Board of Commissioners). In 1932 Italians returned to the
Democratic fold when they cast more than 60 per cent of their
votes for Franklin Delano Roosevelt.[56] After decades of following
a relatively independent course, Italians joined the new ethnic
coalition within the Democratic Party. Astute and ambitious Italian-American politicians, like Roland Libonati, recognized this
tendency and switched their own party loyalties during the 'thirties.

## V

Throughout the 1920's the continued existence of precincts with
large concentrations of Italian voters seemed to prove that old
ethnic colonies persisted in size and strength much as they had

before the war. With additional immigration precluded by law, these precincts retained Italian majorities only because large-scale migrations of still newer immigrant groups did not take place, although Negroes began to displace Italians in the Near North Side district centered around Cambridge and Milton avenues. During the decade the total population as well as the Italian segment residing in these areas actually decreased. The vital core of the Near West Side colony, the center of social and economic activity in this period, was in the blocks between Van Buren Street and Roosevelt Road, Morgan Street and Racine Avenue. Italian voters played an important role in the local affairs of the Twentieth, Twenty-fifth, Twenty-sixth, and Twenty-seventh wards, which met at this point. Yet a steadily diminishing population wielded this influence. In 1910 the area housed 15,677 people; by 1920 it had 13,255, and ten years later, 8497. Italians comprised approximately three quarters of the inhabitants in 1920 and 1930, although American-born and foreign-born totals declined from slightly more than 10,000 to less than 6000.[57]

Those remaining in this location and other inner-city districts after upwardly mobile elements departed did not represent the whole range of the ethnic group. Residents included old people clinging to church and homeland cronies; merchants and small businessmen trying to maintain painstakingly built establishments and goodwill; petty hoodlums; local politicians, political appointees, and others seeking similar positions; and villagers resisting change or unable to face American urban life. Even in the 1920's Chicago's various "little Italies" contained a sprinkling of newly arrived immigrants beginning their assimilation process within inner-city colonies.[58]

Observers of core-area life generally recognized neither the dispersal taking place from ethnic settlements nor the atypical nature of remaining inhabitants. They focused upon the many undesirable traits and old-world habits that seemed to persist without change despite decades of effort by reformers. In the late 1920's Dr. Alice Hamilton, Hull House resident and pioneer in the field of industrial medicine, found Near West Siders who professed a belief in witchcraft and the ability of certain compatriots to cast spells. "Without the help of these mysterious and powerful magicians they believe that they would be defenseless before terrors that the police and the doctor and even the priest cannot cope with." Dr. Hamilton related that from the time of her arrival twenty-five years before, she had heard of, but apparently never witnessed, many weird and dramatic happenings involving "this hidden side of life in the Italian colony." Probably without the author's intent, "Witchcraft in West Polk Street" left the impression of a wide-spread neighborhood belief in the Evil Eye.[59]

Anna Zaloha's study conducted during the 1930's concerning the Italian district served by Chicago Commons also presented a lengthy discussion of the persistence of old world superstitions among Chicago's Italians. After relating several gruesome examples—which had been told her—of the working of the "Evil Eye," or *Malocchio*, and noting that some residents made a lucrative living from curing those who felt themselves to be cursed, Miss Zaloha pointed out that "not all the people believe in their power." Neither the Hamilton nor the Zaloha study attempted to determine whether former inhabitants who moved into American neighborhoods retained a belief in *Malocchio*, and both left unclear the extent of the superstition among core area Italians. Although fear of the Evil Eye probably existed there on a widespread scale, one cannot differentiate among those who truly believed in *Malocchio*, those who succumbed during moments of anxiety, and those who professed acceptance simply to be on the safe side. The questionnaire used by Miss Zaloha to examine old world customs indicated that even in core area colonies (which contained, by the 'thirties, the least progressive element of the city's Italians), fewer than one third of the interviewees reported experiences with the Evil Eye. Only 19 per cent of the families thought that "someone knew how to cure illnesses due to overlooking," while 14 per cent of the families claimed to contain a member who sustained injuries from Evil Eye machinations. Considering the unlettered and unsophisticated nature of many householders and tenants, one might expect a larger percentage of Evil Eye adherents. It must be noted that

Miss Zaloha based her generalizations on a study of 143 families, and her conclusions therefore did not necessarily apply to the whole area. Nevertheless, she selected the group carefully.[60]

In an unpublished autobiographical statement covering the years between 1927 and 1930, Mr. E. L. Hicks, who served as principal of a predominantly Italian public elementary school in the Near West Side, described a student body that reflected home environments filled with ignorance and superstition. These children saw school as a waste of time, filled with difficult tasks and meaningless lessons completely irrelevant to their needs, abilities, and interests. Frustrated, they expressed their contempt through misbehavior that included intimidation of teachers and fellow students, destruction of school property, and theft of equipment, which they sold or used in gang clubhouses. After their public-school education ended, many boys sought money and excitement in armed robbery, burglary, and car theft. Some eventually reached the county jail or the morgue.[61]

Although he never attended Mr. Hicks' school, Rocco Marc-antonio followed the pattern described by that disillusioned principal. Finding school not to his liking, Rocco left at the age of fourteen, in the sixth grade. Starting his new career in a minor way, he turned to mischief making and stealing from clotheslines. Soon he graduated to the "big money," learned to use a gun, and expressed contempt for the law: "Money buys any copper in this city." In the mid-'twenties Rocco helped organize the infamous Forty-two gang. John Landesco learned, through personal contact, the life story of each member of this largely Italian group and found that the hoodlums had participated in "all of the crimes of violence as well as all of the crimes of property." [62]

While youth groups occupied an important place in the lives of most colony children, the gang did not inevitably lead to adult careers in crime. Anthony Sorrentino, like the members of the Forty-two mob, grew up in the Near West Side. He recalled that "the little gang and the meager club room were the predominant influences" that shaped "personalities and characters" of his boyhood friends and himself. Sorrentino and his peers fought other gangs, stole lumber for their club-house and coal to heat it, and begged pennies for candy. The boys hung about together, finding mutual comfort from the agonies of school and the dreariness of their surroundings. Unlike Marcantonio, Sorrentino did not follow the easy path to habitual criminality. He continued his education, attending evening high school while working during the day as youth leader in the Chicago Area Project (a self-help community welfare organization). He went on to college and after graduating from the University of Chicago took a position as sociologist with the Institute of Juvenile Research of the Illinois Department of Public Welfare.[63]

As studies by Frederic M. Thrasher, Clifford R. Shaw, and others have amply demonstrated, corner gangs continued through the 1920's to attract a steady stream of members who felt drawn together by the social needs of youngsters growing to maturity in core-area neighborhoods. Unlike youth gangs, benefit societies and the foreign-language press declined during the decade as numerous prewar members and subscribers turned away from institutions that reminded them of the colony from which they had recently departed and which seemed alien to the middle-class life to which they aspired. At the same time, restrictive immigration laws reduced the steady flow of new clients who were essential to the continued functioning and prosperity of societies and journals. Few recent arrivals replaced the pre-1914 immigrant generation as it died out or outgrew its need of benefit groups and Italian-language tabloids.[64]

Between 1920 and 1930 at least ten papers ceased operations, including *L'Idea,* which claimed a readership of 34,000 in 1919. Even *La Tribuna Italiana Transatlantica* and *L'Italia* suffered setbacks. *La Tribuna* continued to exist, but with severely diminished influence and clientele, until 1935. *L'Italia,* the oldest and most respected of the city's Italian-language journals, also declined in circulation during the decade (from 38,426 in 1921 to 27,310 in 1930) even though it, like *La Tribuna Italiana Transatlantica,* inherited readers from defunct rivals.[65]

A similar pattern operated among the colony's mutual aid societies. The Italo-American National Union, the Venetian Fraternal Order, and the newly formed Order Sons of Italy in America, Grand Lodge of the State of Illinois (1924) absorbed previously independent benefit groups that suffered from declining memberships and increasing financial drains. In 1928 the Italo-American National Union had at least 27 old mutual aid societies and functioned as Chicago's richest and most powerful Italian fraternal organization.[66]

Even core area Italian churches experienced a decrease in ethnic-group support, although parish records indicate that former colony residents often returned to the neighborhood in order to get married or baptize infants before a familiar priest and among relatives and friends. The decline of the Italian national parish is seen in the figures from Holy Guardian Angel and Our Lady of Pompei. The former, located in the Near West Side's oldest Italian district, reached its peak in the years before World War I, although it retained some of its earlier vitality into the 1920's. Pompei Church, which opened in 1911, had passed its peak of activity by 1930.

## VI

Throughout the 1920's Italian community residents and institutions (press, societies, and Church) exhibited an overriding concern for the homeland and its new experiment in government. Bourgeois colonial papers found Mussolini to be an ever-popular topic. They devoted the better part of page one and portions of other pages to happenings in Italy, statements of Il Duce, Italy's new grandeur, and American and Italian-American reactions to the Kingdom. In the process, domestic American politics and crime, two extremely important subjects of pre-World War I news, received extremely reduced coverage. Chicago-area Italian Catholics approved of Benito Mussolini's efforts to bridge the chasm that had existed between the Vatican and the Italian government since the creation of United Italy in 1860. The reconciliation of February 11, 1929, in the form of a treaty and concordat by which the Church recognized the Kingdom's existence and the Italian occupation of Rome

## Table 13

MARRIAGES AND BAPTISMS PERFORMED AT HOLY GUARDIAN ANGEL
AND OUR LADY OF POMPEI CHURCHES, 1899–1930

| | Baptisms | | Marriages | |
|------|---------------|----------|---------------|----------|
| | Holy Guardian | Our Lady | Holy Guardian | Our Lady |
| 1899 | 118  |      | 11  |     |
| 1900 | 328  |      | 43  |     |
| 1901 | 456  |      | 64  |     |
| 1902 | 501  |      | 99  |     |
| 1903 | 681  |      | 159 |     |
| 1904 | 854  |      | 170 |     |
| 1905 | 886  |      | 172 |     |
| 1906 | 1029 |      | 199 |     |
| 1907 | 1175 |      | 229 |     |
| 1908 | 1237 |      | 173 |     |
| 1909 | 1229 |      | 206 |     |
| 1910 | 1518 |      | 263 |     |
| 1911 | 1115 | 507  | 200 | 83  |
| 1912 | 1032 | 670  | 162 | 124 |
| 1913 | 1037 | 788  | 193 | 134 |
| 1914 | 1074 | 763  | 215 | 167 |
| 1915 | 1009 | 985  | 151 | 168 |
| 1916 | 1044 | 1081 | 143 | 170 |
| 1917 | 845  | 1158 | 152 | 162 |
| 1918 | 833  | 1151 | 79  | 97  |
| 1919 | 686  | 1064 | 135 | 220 |
| 1920 | 615  | 1049 | 146 | 250 |
| 1921 | 640  | 1062 | 156 | 249 |
| 1922 | 557  | 1053 | 121 | 226 |
| 1923 | 539  | 1078 | 135 | 216 |
| 1924 | 538  | 1076 | 122 | 217 |
| 1925 | 488  | 977  | 94  | 183 |
| 1926 | 352  | 1048 | 88  | 195 |
| 1927 | 365  | 817  | 84  | 173 |
| 1928 | 367  | 775  | 74  | 141 |
| 1929 | 275  | 748  | 72  | 145 |
| 1930 | 193  | 740  | 46  | 151 |

Source: Based on parish records.
Note: Records for 1899 are incomplete.

in exchange for acceptance of the sovereign status of Vatican City, indemnities, and recognition of Catholicism as the state religion, met with wild enthusiasm among Chicago's Italians.[67]

While middle-class Italian-Americans and core-area residents differed in many respects, their views coincided with regard to Mussolini: both groups heartily endorsed him. Il Duce won immense popularity because he seemed to be dealing effectively with homeland problems (such as church-state relations, the Mafia, and radicalism). He thus provided, they felt, the ideal government for Italy. Schiavo noted that "since the advent to power of Mussolini, the 'patriotism' of the [Chicago] Italians has been fanned to an extent probably never reached before." Upwardly mobile Italians in Chicago desired respect and acceptance from the native community, but realized that many Americans viewed them with contempt. They supported and glorified Italy in large part to win American admiration for Italian contributions to civilization. Social historian Caroline F. Ware quoted a "strongly anti-Fascist Italian-American girl" who, in spite of her opposition to Mussolini and his program, declared, " 'You've got to admit one thing: he has enabled four million Italians in America to hold up their heads, and that is something. If you had been branded undesirable by a quota law, you would understand how much that means.' " Suburbanites and outer-city residents as well as Italians living in tenement districts took pride in Italy's increased international status under Mussolini, and magnified Italy's achievements as a defense against American derision for "new" immigrant groups.[68]

Mussolini's basic importance to Chicago's Italians centered in these hopes of being accepted as Americans by the rest of society. Italian-Americans no longer had to point to dead heroes and vanished glories, for in Mussolini Italy exhibited a swashbuckling leader who—as ardent antifascists Gaetano Salvemini and George La Piana have shown—received the admiration and respect of many Americans and Englishmen, although not always of homeland Italians. Edward Corsi pointed out that the praise lavished on Il Duce and his system by "the press and leaders of public opinion in this country," combined with Fascist propagandist activities among the immigrants, "tended to strengthen the immigrants' impression that Italy under Il Duce had come into her own." [69]

Admiration for Mussolini did not, however, carry over into any desire for importing Fascism into the United States. In 1928 Italian nationalist Giovanni E. Schiavo probed the attitudes of fellow members of the Italo-American National Union and of Chicago's Italians in general. "The real essence of the admiration of the local Italians for Mussolini," he observed, "is not of a political nature. The Italians of Chicago are not interested in the governmental experiments of Fascismo . . . . They see in Mussolini only the savior of Italy, and they admire him because of what he has been doing for the good of Italy . . . . But real devotion or allegiance to Mussolini, as some people have stated, is totally absent among the Italians of Chicago." [70]

Efforts to establish an Italian Fascist organization in Chicago met with massive indifference within Italian neighborhoods and violent opposition from radical elements, although the bourgeois press ardently supported the idea (the press depended heavily on the homeland government for financial backing during the 'twenties and 'thirties). Socialists, anarchists, and other radical groups offered the only organized opposition to Il Duce among Italians in America. So pervasive was immigrant disinterest toward American fascism that by 1929 the Fascist League of North America had fewer than 13,000 members scattered among some 120 branches. [71]

## VII

A number of factors combined to make the 'twenties a transitional period for Chicago's Italians. One of these, the virtual end of immigration, held particular significance because the ethnic colony and its institutions, especially the press and societies, could not survive the lack of newcomers. The cumulative effect, as sociologist Harvey Warren Zorbaugh noted in 1928, was that "the community without any influx from the old country is fast becoming Americanized." [72]

In the process of adjusting to American values and modes of behavior, Italians and their children moved out of colonies not only to peripheral areas of the city but also to suburbs. These locations included working-class towns, middle-income communities, and upper-income retreats. Italians who moved to such neighborhoods often continued to work in the city, and in many cases within an Italian district.

Italians shared in the decade's general prosperity, although not all group members partook equally of material gains. "Southerners" enjoyed soaring incomes derived from both legitimate lines of work and organized crime. Spectacular and violent, Italian participation in big-time crime resulted in tremendous financial successes. Under the guidance and leadership of Al Capone and other political-criminal bosses, Italians made important political gains and captured a number of elective and appointive positions.

The seeming accomplishments of Benito Mussolini in bringing order and prosperity to Italy and in curbing radicalism during the years following his rise to power met with widespread approval among groups in the United States and elsewhere (at least during the decade) and brought reflected glory to Italian-Americans.

Vestiges of old attitudes, ideas, and ways of life persisted in some core areas of settlement. Nevertheless, the progress made by the group in general was "amazing," as a priest of St. Philip Benizi parish observed in 1928 after a trip to Sicily. The Near North Side cleric perceived the factors that spurred the assimilation of generations of "Southerners" in Chicago and other American cities. While in the homeland, Sicilians "live in little, tumbled down shacks with no sanitation, light or adequate water supply"; in Chicago, "comparatively, they have everything. There they have no hope of ever realizing anything different—here there is a constant shifting of Sicilians to better neighborhoods as they save enough money to make the move." [73]

The priest touched on the essential point: experiences and opportunities in the new world, rather than old-world habits, formed the major force influencing the "Southern" assimilation process in urban America—a process which operated more rapidly and thoroughly than contemporaries realized. Until the end of the period of large-scale immigration, ethnic colonies, far from remaining fixed in location, shifted steadily away from the city core. At the same time they experienced a heavy influx of newcomers which counterbalanced the constant loss of residents who moved to American sections of the city. Since then ethnic areas have remained stationary and static. With the exception of the Church, community institutions have fallen into disuse. For example, more than 300 Italian-American residents of the Near West Side colony adjacent to the University of Illinois at Chicago Circle campus were interviewed during the summers of 1966 and 1967; not one belonged to an ethnic fraternal insurance organization (although some held insurance with American companies), and none read a foreign-language publication. Student interviewers found that young people continue to leave the area at the first opportunity. In 1967 one Near West Side teenager expressed amazement over the construction of townhouses on West Flournoy Street near Loomis, and of the movement of university professors and other middle-class Americans into the neighborhood. To his surprise, university personnel moved even into older houses and apartments. As soon as he could, he confided, he planned to move to a suburb, just as his brothers and sisters had done before him. The few Italian districts still in existence in Chicago continue to serve as staging areas for the trickle of newcomers from overseas. For most other residents, many of them elderly, the ethnic neighborhood is a secure, low-rent enclave in the midst of a bewildering and rapidly changing world.[74]

## ABBREVIATIONS USED IN NOTES

| | |
|---|---|
| AICLC | *Journal of the American Institute of Criminal Law and Criminology* |
| AER | *American Ecclesiastical Review* |
| AJS | *American Journal of Sociology* |
| *Annals* | *Annals of the American Academy of Political and Social Science* |
| ASR | *American Sociological Review* |
| *Boll. Emig.* | *Bollettino dell'Emigrazione* |
| Election Returns | City of Chicago, Board of Election Commissioners, MS of Official Election Returns |
| *Immigration Commission* | *Reports of the U.S. Immigration Commission* |
| *Industrial Commission* | *Reports of the U.S. Industrial Commission* |
| JAH | *Journal of American History* |
| NCSW | *Proceedings of the National Conference of Social Work* |
| *Precinct Lists* | City of Chicago, Board of Election Commissioners, *Official Precinct Voter Registration Lists* |

# Notes

## PREFACE

1. A sampling of available literature on Italians and other "new" immigrant groups includes: Frank Julian Warne, *The Immigrant Invasion* (New York, 1913); Samuel P. Orth, *Our Foreigners* (New Haven, Conn., 1920); Robert A. Woods, ed., *The City Wilderness* (Boston, 1898) and *Americans in Process* (Boston, 1902); Jacob A. Riis, *How the Other Half Lives* (New York, 1890); Richmond Mayo-Smith, *Emigration and Immigration* (New York, 1890); Madison Grant, *The Passing of the Great Race* (New York, 1916); Prescott F. Hall, *Immigration and its Effects Upon the United States* (New York, 1906); Edward A. Ross, *The Old World in the New; The Significance of Past and Present Immigration to the American People* (New York, 1914).

2. Joseph P. Fitzpatrick, "The Importance of 'Community' in the Process of Immigrant Assimilation," *International Migration Review*, I (Fall 1966), 5–16.

3. Giuseppe Giacosa, *Impressioni d'America* (Milan, 1908), 174–75.

## CHAPTER 1

1. Italy, Commissariato Generale dell'Emigrazione, *Annuario statistico della emigrazione italiana dal 1876 al 1925* (Rome, 1926), 149–51, 86–88; *Immigration Commission*, IV (1911), 153–54; L. Bodio, *Di alcuni indici misuratori del movimento economico in Italia* (Rome, 1891), 6; Arthur Train, *Courts, Criminals and the Camorra* (New York, 1912); Howard B. Grose, *Aliens or Americans?* (New York, 1906), 30.

2. U.S. Department of State, *Reports of the Consular Officers of the*

*United States* (Washington, 1887), 292; Edward A. Steiner, "The Man with the Pack," *The Pilgrim,* VIII (Mar. 1904), 3; J. S. McDonald, "Italy's Rural Social Structure and Emigration," *Occidente,* XII (Sept.-Oct. 1956), 437.

3. Paolo Emilio de Luca, *Della emigrazione Europea ed in particolare di quella italiana,* II (Turin, 1909), 181; Romolo Murri, "Gl'italiani nell'America Latina—impressioni di viaggio," *Nuova Antologia,* CLXIV (Apr. 1, 1913), 435–48; Anon., "The Immigrant in South America," *Blackwood's Edinburgh Magazine,* CXC (Nov. 1911), 608–18. Despite the title, this article examines only the problems faced by Italian immigrants in Argentina and Brazil and the reasons for the decline of Italian immigration to those countries.

4. Italy, Commissariato Generale dell'Emigrazione, *Annuario statistico,* 88; U.S. Commissioner General of Immigration, *Annual Report,* 1924, Table xiv-A, 115–17: "Immigrant aliens admitted, fiscal years ended June 30, 1899, to 1924, by country."

5. Robert S. Foerster, *The Italian Emigration of Our Times* (Cambridge, Mass., 1919), Chaps. V, VI, VII; Denis Mack Smith, *A History of Sicily. Modern Sicily: After 1713* (London, 1968), 469; Luigi Villari, *Italian Life in Town and Country* (New York, 1903), 3.

6. *Immigration Commission,* III, 359.

7. McDonald, "Italy's Rural Social Structure and Emigration," 439, 441–42, 453; Bolton King and Thomas Okey, *Italy To-Day* (New and Enlarged ed.; London, 1909), 111–12; Edward C. Banfield, *The Moral Basis of a Backward Society* (Glencoe, Ill., 1958), 10. Some others who accept the Banfield position are: Rudolph J. Vecoli, "*Contadini* in Chicago: A Critique of *The Uprooted,*" JAH, LI (Dec. 1964), especially 404–5; Herbert J. Gans, *The Urban Villagers: Group and Class in the Life of Italian-Americans* (New York, 1962), 203; Norman Kogan, *The Politics of Italian Foreign Policy* (New York, 1963), 4–5.

8. Statement by Dr. A. J. Lendino, quoted in William Foote Whyte, "Social Organization in the Slums," ASR, VIII (Feb. 1943), 36. Significantly, Dr. Lendino married a non-Italian.

9. William H. Keating, *Narrative of an Expedition to the Source of St. Peter's River,* I (London, 1825), 162–75, quoted in Bessie Louise Pierce, ed., *As Others See Chicago* (Chicago, 1933), 32–39; Homer Hoyt, *One Hundred Years of Land Values in Chicago: The Relationship of the Growth of Chicago to the Rise in Its Land Values, 1830–1933* (Chicago, 1933), Chaps. I–III; Bessie Louise Pierce, *A History of Chicago, Vol. I. The Beginning of a City, 1673–1848* (New York, 1937), 44, footnote 4; U.S. Bureau of the Census, *Eighteenth Census of the United States. Census of Population: 1960,* I, Part A, 1–66.

10. Homer Hoyt, *One Hundred Years of Land Values in Chicago,* 283–84; Irving Cutler, *The Chicago-Milwaukee Corridor: A Geographic*

*Study of Intermetropolitan Coalescence* (Evanston, Ill., 1965), 12–21; George E. Plumbe, *Chicago: The Great Industrial and Commercial Center of the Mississippi Valley* (Chicago, 1912); Center for Urban Studies, University of Chicago, *Mid-Chicago Economic Development Study*, III, *Technical Supplement, Economic Development of Mid-Chicago* (Chicago, 1966), 11–20.

11. William T. Stead, *If Christ Came to Chicago* (New York, 1964), 187, 24–25, 51, 74, 110, 123, 172, 175–76; Lincoln Steffens, *The Shame of the Cities* (New York, 1904), 163.

12. *L'Italia*, Apr. 1, 1893; *La Parola dei Socialisti*, May 31, 1913.

13. Denis Mack Smith, *Italy* (Ann Arbor, 1959), 242.

14. Local Community Research Committee, *Chicago Communities*, Vol. IV, "Armour Square," Document 9; Interviews, summers, 1966–67.

15. John Foster Carr, "The Coming of the Italian," *Outlook*, LXXXII (Feb. 24, 1906), 429.

16. For example: U.S. Commissioner of Labor, *Seventh Special Report. The Slums of Baltimore, Chicago, New York and Philadelphia* (1894); Robert Hunter, *Poverty: Social Conscience in the Progressive Era* (New York, 1904); Robert W. DeForest and Lawrence Veiller, eds., *The Tenement House Problem* (New York, 1913); Robert A. Woods *et al.*, *The Poor in Great Cities* (New York, 1895).

Articles in city newspapers included "In the Home of Italians," *Chicago Daily News*, July 16, 1887; "In an Italian Patch," *Chicago Herald*, July 17, 1887; "Foul Ewing Street," *Chicago Tribune*, Mar. 30, 1893; "Reigns Like a King," *Chicago Tribune*, Feb. 21, 1897. Not all articles in the American press criticized the immigrants, a fact recognized and appreciated by Italian-language papers: "A Splendid Article in the *Chicago Herald*," *L'Italia*, Nov. 29, 1890; "The *Chicago Tribune* in defense of Italians," *L'Italia*, July 15, 1911. There were, however, more unfavorable than favorable reports.

17. See "To the *Daily News* and all who are interested in Italians," *L'Italia*, July 23, 1887; "Reply to *The Tribune*," *L'Italia*, Nov. 1, 1888; "The Article in the *Chicago Mail*," *Il Messaggiere Italo-Americano*, July 17, 1888; "A Reply to the *Daily News*," *L'Italia*, Feb. 21, 1891; "Unclean Ewing Street," *L'Italia*, Apr. 1, 1893 (a reply to the *Chicago Tribune*). That this is still true of the Italian-American press is seen in present-day reactions to real or imagined slurs on the "Italian good name," such as *Fra Noi* (Chicago), Dec. 1966 and July 1967.

18. U.S. Commissioner of Labor, *Seventh Special Report*, and *Ninth Special Report. The Italians in Chicago, a Social and Economic Study* (1897); Chicago Department of Public Welfare, "Housing Survey in the Italian District of the 17th Ward," *First Semi-Annual Report to the Mayor and Aldermen of the City of Chicago* (Chicago, 1915); Frank O. Beck, "The Italian in Chicago," *Bulletin of the Department of Public Welfare, City of Chicago*, II (Feb. 1919), 5–32; Edith Abbott and Sophonisba P. Breckinridge, "Chicago Hous-

ing Conditions, IV: The West Side Revisited," AJS, XVII (July 1911), 1–34; Grace P. Norton, "Chicago Housing Conditions, VII: Two Italian Districts," AJS, XVIII (Jan. 1913), 509–42; Natalie Walker, "Chicago Housing Conditions, X. Greeks and Italians in the Neighborhood of Hull House," AJS, XXI (Nov. 1915), 285–316; Robert Hunter (for the City Homes Association), *Tenement Conditions in Chicago* (Chicago, 1901), 149.

19. Among others, *Boll. Emig., Bollettino del Ministero degli Affari Esteri*, and *Emigrazione e Colonie*.

20. Adolfo Rossi, *Un Italiano in America* (3rd ed.; Treviso, 1907); Giuseppe Giacosa, "Gli italiani a New York ed a Chicago," *Nuova Antologia*, XL (Aug. 16, 1892), 618–40, and *Impressioni d'America* (Milan, 1908); Alberto Pecorini, *Gli Americani nella vita moderna osservati da un Italiano* (Milan, 1909); Gaetano Conte, *Dieci anni in America* (Palermo, 1903); Alessandro Rossi, "L'America del Nord vista a volo d'uccello nel Gennaio 1897," *Rassegna Nazionale*, XCVI (1897), 455–69. Compare the discussion of Italians in Chicago in Luigi Provana del Sabbione, "Condizioni della Emigrazione nel R. Distretto consolare in Chicago," *Boll. Emig.*, No. 1 (1913), 27–33, and in Giacosa, *Impressioni d'America*.

21. U.S. Commissioner of Labor, *Seventh Special Report*, 23, 41, 89–90, 93–94; Hunter, *Tenement Conditions in Chicago*, 94, 149.

22. Abbott and Breckinridge, "Chicago Housing Conditions, IV: The West Side Revisited," 32–33.

23. Norton, "Chicago Housing Conditions, VII: Two Italian Districts," 509–10, 542.

24. Walker, "Chicago Housing Conditions, X: Greeks and Italians in the Neighborhood of Hull House," 315–16.

25. Giacosa, *Impressioni d'America*, 169.

26. I. W. Howerth, "Are the Italians a Dangerous Class?" *Charities Review*, IV (Nov. 1894), 40. The U.S. Bureau of Immigration published *Agricultural Opportunities. Information Concerning Resources, Products and Physical Characteristics* [of various states] (1912–20). Under the direction of Alessandro Mastro-Valerio, the Agricultural Section of the Italian Chamber of Commerce of Chicago was very active in its efforts to settle Italians in rural colonies located in the southern states.

27. Adolfo Rossi, "Per la tutela degli italiani negli Stati Uniti", *Boll. Emig.*, No. 16 (1904), 74–80; *Hull House: A Social Settlement. An Outline Sketch* (pamphlet dated Feb. 1, 1894), 21; Florence Kelley, "The Settlements: Their Lost Opportunity," *Charities and the Commons*, XVI (Apr. 7, 1906), 80; Alberto Pecorini, "The Italian as an Agricultural Laborer," *Annals*, XXXIII (Mar. 1909), 383–84.

28. John R. Commons, *Races and Immigrants in America* (New York, 1907), 133, 166.

29. *Ibid.*, 167–68.

30. U.S. Senate, *Report from the Committee on Immigration*, 54th

Cong., 1st Sess., 1896, Rept. 290, 9; Henry Cabot Lodge, "Efforts to Restrict Undesirable Immigration," *Century Magazine*, LXVII (Jan. 1904), 468.

31. *Industrial Commission*, XV (1901), 497. Mastro-Valerio had founded two agricultural colonies in Alabama; both failed. For a view similar to Mastro-Valerio's, see G. E. De Palma Castiglione, "Italian Immigration into the United States, 1901–4," AJS, XI (Sept. 1905), 183–206.

32. Giovanni Preziosi, *Gl'italiani negli Stati Uniti del Nord* (Milan, 1909), 81.

33. Foerster, *Italian Emigration of Our Times*, 370–72.

34. *Industrial Commission*, XIX (1902), 969–71.

35. Frank Thistlethwaite, "Migration from Europe Overseas in the Nineteenth and Twentieth Centuries," *Population Movements in Modern European History*, ed. Herbert Moller (New York, 1964), reprinted from *XIe Congrès International des Sciences Historiques, Stockholm, 1960, Rapports V: Histoire Contemporaine*, 91; Walter F. Willcox, *Studies in American Demography* (Ithaca, 1940), 159, 161, 169, 174. This is from Chap. X, "The Foreign-born," which is in large part a reprint of an earlier article by Willcox, "The Distribution of Immigration in the United States," *Quarterly Journal of Economics*, XX (Aug. 1906), 523–46.

36. Alberto Aquarone, *Grandi città e aree metropolitane in Italia; Problemi amministrativi e prospettivi di riforma* (Bologna, 1961), 19–23; Max Ascoli, "The Italian-Americans," *Group Relations and Group Antagonisms*, ed. R. M. MacIver (New York, 1944), 32–33.

37. Frank P. Sargent, "The Need of Closer Inspection and Greater Restriction of Immigration," *Century Magazine*, LXVII (Jan. 1904), 470.

38. Robert E. Park, "Cultural Aspects of Immigration. Immigrant Heritages," NCSW, XLVIII (1921), 494; Carr, "The Coming of the Italian," 429; Pauline Young, "Social Problems in the Education of the Immigrant Child," ASR, I (June 1936), 419–29. Page 420 discusses urban adjustment problems of rural Americans.

39. Richard G. Ford, "Population Succession in Chicago," AJS, LVI (Sept. 1950), 160.

CHAPTER 2

1. J. D. B. De Bow, *Statistical View of the United States, . . . Being a Compendium of the Seventh Census* (1854), 399; U.S. Bureau of the Census, *Eighth Census, 1860. Population*, 613; *Ninth Census, 1870. Population*, I, 390; City of Chicago, Board of Education, *School Census of the City of Chicago. Taken May, 1884. Total Population of the City. Over 21 Years and Under 21 Years of Age. By Ward and by Division of the City* (Chicago, 1884), 20–31.

2. *Ninth Census of the United States, 1870, Manuscript Federal Population Census Schedule*, microfilm No. M-593, rolls 198–211;

Richard Edwards, *Chicago Census Report; and Statistical Review, . . . Compiled from Actual Canvass, at the Request of the Mayor, City Council, Business Firms and Capitalists of Chicago* (Chicago, 1871).

3. *Ninth Census, 1870,* manuscript population schedules; Edwards, *Chicago Census Report.*

4. Homer Hoyt, *One Hundred Years of Land Values in Chicago: The Relationship of the Growth of Chicago to the Rise in Its Land Values, 1830–1933* (Chicago, 1933), 140.

5. Blocks 3 to 10 of Butler, Wright and Webster's Add. Comments in the chapter about Italian purchase or leasing of property are based on examination of real estate conveyances and plat maps.

   Hereafter Hull House, Near West Side and Nineteenth Ward will be used to identify the Italian community located west of the Chicago River between Harrison and Twelfth streets; while Chicago Commons, Seventeenth Ward and West Town will designate Italian areas west of the river between Chicago Avenue and Kinzie Street.

6. Edith Abbott, *The Tenements of Chicago, 1908–1935* (Chicago, 1936), 95, footnote 27; Jane Addams, *Newer Ideals of Peace* (New York, 1907), 67.

7. New York was a possible exception, but there is every reason to believe that the remarks following in the text apply to that city as well. See, for example, Leo Grebler, *Housing Market Behavior in a Declining Area* (New York, 1952), 135–37, 245–46, on Manhattan's lower east side Italian community during the period from 1910 to 1930.

8. This and the material to follow are based on City of Chicago, Board of Education, *School Census of the City of Chicago. Taken May, 1884,* 20–31.

9. "School Census of 1898," City of Chicago, Board of Education, *Proceedings, July 13, 1898, to June 28, 1899* (Chicago, 1899), 122. This valuable study details Chicago's ethnic population by election precincts.

10. Goodhue's Sub., Block 126; Adams and Parker's Sub., Block 103; Ogden's Sub., Block 124.

11. Grace P. Norton, "Chicago Housing Conditions, VII: Two Italian Districts," AJS, XVIII (Jan. 1913), 531; Abbott, *Tenements of Chicago,* 111.

12. Board of Education, *Proceedings, 1898–1899,* 188; Robert Hunter (for the City Homes Association), *Tenement Conditions in Chicago* (Chicago, 1901), 56, 188. On p. 184 Hunter noted that "other nationalities" also resided in districts of the city which he labeled "Italian," "Jewish," "Polish," and "Bohemian," but the text consistently ignored this qualification; so did the numerous tables. The book examined living and working conditions in "typical" Chicago slums.

13. Jane Addams, "The Housing Problem in Chicago," *Annals,* XX

(July 1902), 99–103; Joseph Kirkland, "Among the Poor of Chicago," *The Poor in Great Cities*, Robert A. Woods *et al.* (New York, 1895), 198–200; Hunter, *Tenement Conditions in Chicago*, 58–72.

14. Agnes Sinclair Holbrook, "General Comments," *Hull House Maps and Papers* (New York, 1895), 5; Hunter, *Tenement Conditions in Chicago*, 36.

15. Sophonisba P. Breckinridge, *New Homes for Old* (New York, 1921), 105. The significant role played by property ownership as a means of upward mobility applied also to "old" immigrants, as historian Stephan Thernstrom found: *Poverty and Progress: Social Mobility in a Nineteenth Century City* (Cambridge, Mass., 1964).

16. U.S. Commissioner of Labor, *Seventh Special Report. The Slums of Baltimore, Chicago, New York, and Philadelphia* (1894), 23; *Hull House Maps and Papers*, 6–7.

17. Mark H. Putney, *Real Estate Values and Historical Notes of Chicago. From the Earliest Period to the Present Time* (Chicago, 1900), 66; *Olcott's Land Values of Chicago and Suburbs*, V (Chicago, 1913), 80–81. Comments on land use in the chapter are based on examination of insurance atlases and maps.

18. Florence Kelley, "The Settlements: Their Lost Opportunity," *Charities and the Commons*, XVI (Apr. 7, 1906), 80.

19. *Olcott's Land Values*, V, 79–80.

20. Macalester's Sub., Blocks 1, 7 (sub-block 1) and 17; Laflin's Sub., Block 16; Gilpin's Sub., Blocks 14 and 15; Martin's Sub., Block 16.

21. Flournoy's Re-Sub. of Jones & Patrick's Add., Block 1. During the 1950's this block was purchased as part of a projected Medical Center District containing approximately 70 blocks and extending from Congress Street to Roosevelt Road (Twelfth Street), Ashland Avenue to Oakley Boulevard.

22. Ernest W. Burgess and Charles Newcomb, eds., *Census Data of the City of Chicago, 1920* (Chicago, 1931). This provides a population breakdown of the city's ethnic groups by census tracts.

23. City of Chicago, Department of Public Welfare, "Housing Survey in the Italian District of the 17th Ward," *First Semi-Annual Report to the Mayor and Aldermen of the City of Chicago* (Chicago, 1915), 74–75. For property ownership see Ogden's Add., Blocks 1 to 20.

24. Board of Education, *Proceedings, 1898–99*, 199–201; Burgess and Newcomb, *Census Data, 1920;* real estate conveyances. Of 166 lots located on both sides of Milton Avenue and the east side of Gault Court between Chicago Avenue and Oak Street, Italians came to own (many for only limited periods of time) a total of 113 in the years before 1930. Five of these lots were purchased before 1900, and another fourteen during the 1920's. Hull's Sub., Block 19.

25. U.S. Bureau of the Census, *Seventh Census of the United States, 1850*, 705; De Bow, *Compendium of the Seventh Census*, 399.

26. Vivien M. Palmer, "Study of the Development of Chicago's North-side," unpublished MS prepared for the United Charities of Chicago, December, 1932, 41–52, and sources cited there; Bessie Louise Pierce, *A History of Chicago, I. The Beginning of a City, 1673–1848* (New York, 1937), 179–85 and *II. From Town to City, 1848–1871* (New York, 1940), 13–24.

27. Palmer, "Study of the Development of Chicago's Northside," 54.

28. Department of Public Welfare, "Housing Survey in the Italian District of the 17th Ward," 74; *Warden's Report of the Work of Chicago Commons* (to the Board of Trustees) for the year ending September 30, 1920, 8; J. Du Bois Hunter, "Church and Immigrant," unpublished study prepared in 1913 for Chicago Commons, in the Chicago Commons Papers, Chicago Historical Society.

29. Edith Abbott, *Tenements of Chicago*, 112–13.

30. Paul Frederick Cressey, "Population Succession in Chicago: 1898–1930," AJS, XLIV (July 1938), 59, 61, 65–69, and "The Succession of Cultural Groups in the City of Chicago," unpublished Ph.D. dissertation, University of Chicago, 1930.

31. Samuel Lubell, *The Future of American Politics* (3rd ed. rev.; New York, 1965), 79 (the same statement appears in all earlier editions); Richard G. Ford, "Population Succession in Chicago," AJS, LVI (Sept. 1950), 156.

32. Norton, "Chicago Housing Conditions, VII: Two Italian Districts," 511.

33. For purchase of property by Italians in the Twenty-fourth Street and Oakley area see Child's Sub., Block 3.

34. Local Community Research Committee, *Chicago Communities*, "History of West Englewood Community, Chicago," Document 1a; John Drury, "Old Chicago Neighborhoods, VII. Grand Crossing," *Landlords Guide*, XXXVIII (Oct. 1947), 18–20; "History of Twenty Years Advancement of South End Suburbs, Industries, Business Houses, Schools, Churches, Homes, Clubs, and Associations," *Weekly Reporter* (Chicago), Oct. 24, 1913, Part 2, 10, 13, 15–16; Chicago Real Estate Board, *Chicago as an Industrial Center* (Chicago, 1901); *Diamond Jubilee of the Archdiocese of Chicago* (Desplaines, Ill., 1920); *St. Anthony of Padua Souvenir Book* (for dedication of a new church building, Aug. 20, 1961); real estate conveyances. While Italians began to buy land in Pullman and Roseland during the 1890's, extensive purchase of property did not take place until the years after 1905. Among others, see Kensington Sub., Blocks 2 to 9.

35. Burgess and Newcomb, *Census Data of the City of Chicago, 1920.*

36. Department of Public Welfare, "Housing Survey in the Italian District of the 17th Ward," 89. Stephan Thernstrom has also discovered a high degree of residential mobility among the laboring class in Boston; see "Urbanization, Migration, and Social Mobility in Late Nineteenth-Century America," *Towards a New Past: Dissenting*

*Essays in American History,* ed. Barton J. Bernstein (New York, 1968), 169.

37. Original manuscript returns of the 1900 census will not be available for use by researchers until 1972 at the earliest, and there is some question as to whether the National Archives can legally open the records then. See comments on this problem in *Historical Methods Newsletter,* II (Dec. 1968), 2–6.

38. See Chap. IV for a full discussion of the points mentioned here.

39. This and material following are based on official precinct voter registration lists prepared by the Board of Election Commissioners of the City of Chicago.

40. The Chicago Directory Company, *Plan of Re-numbering City of Chicago. A Complete Table Showing New and Old Numbers Affected by an Ordinance Passed by the City Council of the City of Chicago June 22, 1908, and as Amended by an Ordinance Passed June 21, 1909* (Chicago, 1909). The new house numbering plan affected the entire city except for that part bounded on the north and west by the Chicago River, on the east by Lake Michigan, and on the south by Twelfth Street.

41. Kimball Young, "A Sociological Study of a Disintegrated Neighborhood," unpublished M.A. thesis, University of Chicago, 1918, 38–39.

42. Reuben H. Donnelly, comp., *The Lakeside Annual Directory of the City of Chicago, 1915* (Chicago, 1915); *Assumption Church Diamond Jubilee, 1881–1951* (Chicago, 1951); *Chicago Tribune,* Feb. 9, 1921; Feb. 10, 1921.

43. The following material is based on Reuben H. Donnelly, comp., *The Lakeside Annual Directory of the City of Chicago* for the years from 1890 to 1920.

44. Edith Abbott, *Tenements of Chicago,* 22.

45. Chicago Traction and Subway Commission, *Report to the Honorable, the Mayor and City Council of the City of Chicago on a Unified System of Surface, Elevated and Subway Lines* (Chicago, 1916); Hoyt, *One Hundred Years of Land Values in Chicago,* 202–3, 225–27, 295.

## CHAPTER 3

1. *Immigration Commission* (1911), 41 vols., especially summary vols. I and II; Gertrude Eileen Sager, "Immigration: Based Upon a Study of the Italian Women and Girls of Chicago," unpublished M.A. thesis, University of Chicago, 1914, 26.

2. League for the Protection of Immigrants (later the Immigrants' Protective League), *Annual Report, 1909–1910* (Chicago, 1910), 28; *Immigration Commission,* II, 393; *Industrial Commission,* XV (1901), 432.

3. For a variety of opinions: *Industrial Commission,* XV, 430–32; John Koren, "The Padrone System and Padrone Banks," *United States*

*Department of Labor Bulletin,* No. 9 (Mar. 1897), 113, 115; F. J. Sheridan, "Italian, Slavic, and Hungarian Unskilled Immigrant Laborers in the United States," *United States Bureau of Labor Bulletin,* No. 72 (Sept. 1907), 437, 438, 440; M. Victor Safford, *Immigration* (Boston, 1912), 18; Charlotte Erickson, *American Industry and the European Immigrant, 1860–1885* (Cambridge, Mass., 1957).

4. U.S. Congress, *Report on Importation of Contract Labor,* I (1889), 406–7; U.S. Immigration Commission of 1891–1892, *Report on European Immigration to the United States of America* (1893), 28–39.

5. Sheridan, "Italian, Slavic, and Hungarian Unskilled Immigrant Laborers in the United States," 411–12.

6. Adolfo Rossi, *Un Italiano in America* (3rd ed.; Treviso, 1907), 65–71; *Industrial Commission,* XV, 432–33.

7. Koren, "The Padrone System and Padrone Banks," 117; Luigi Villari, *Gli Stati Uniti d'America e l'emigrazione italiana* (Milan, 1912), 245–53.

8. Costantino Ottolenghi, "La nuova fase dell'emigrazione del'lavoro agli Stati Uniti," *Giornale degli Economisti,* XVIII (Apr. 1899), 379; Grace Abbott, "The Chicago Employment Agency and the Immigrant Worker," AJS, XIV (Nov. 1908), 293.

9. *Il Messaggiere Italo-Americano,* July 13, 1888; *L'Italia,* Nov. 29, Dec. 6, 1886; Aug. 6, 1887; June 23, 1888; Mar. 19, Dec. 17, 1892; May 12, Aug. 18, 1894; Dec. 7, 1895; Feb. 4, 1899; May 4, 1901; Nov. 15, 1902; May 16, 1903; June 29, 1907.

10. *L'Italia,* Aug. 15, 1891; Aug. 24, 1894.

11. Labor camp abuses are described in the annual reports (1909–17) of the Immigrants' Protective League of Chicago.

12. Domenick Ciolli, "The Wop in the Track Gang," *Immigrant in America Review,* II (July 1916), 61–66.

13. Carroll Wright, "Ninth Special Report of the Italians in Chicago," *United States Department of Labor Bulletin,* No. 13 (Nov. 1897), 727.

14. Commissariato dell'Emigrazione, *Emigrazione e Colonie,* III (Rome, 1908), 122.

15. *Chicago Daily News,* July 22, 1887.

16. For efforts of padrone laborers to escape and return to Chicago, see *La Parola dei Socialisti,* Nov. 21, 1908. Padrone-related accidents and deaths are discussed in *Il Messaggiere Italo-Americano,* July 17, 1888; *L'Italia,* Aug. 18, 1894; June 29, 1901; Mar. 7, 1903. Other Italians lost their lives in factories. In general, primitive or nonexistent safety precautions caused or aggravated these incidents. *L'Italia,* Feb. 1, 1902.

17. Charles B. Phipard, "The Philanthropist-Padrone," *Charities,* XII (May 7, 1904), 470.

18. Sheridan, "Italian, Slavic, and Hungarian Unskilled Immigrant Laborers in the United States," 444.
19. *Immigration Commission*, II, 392.
20. Assembly of the State of New York, *Report of the Board of Statutory Consolidation*, II (Albany, 1907), 1976–78; General Assembly of the State of Illinois, *Laws of the State of Illinois Enacted by the Forty-sixth General Assembly, January 6-June 4, 1909* (Springfield, 1909), 216–17; Immigrants' Protective League, *Annual Report of 1910–1911*, 21.
21. Commissariato dell'Emigrazione, *Emigrazione e Colonie*, III, 115–16; *L'Italia*, Feb. 4, 1899.
22. Koren, "The Padrone System and Padrone Banks," 115–16; *Chicago Daily News Almanac and Year-Book for 1905* (Chicago, 1904), based on the Chicago School Census of 1904.
23. *Industrial Commission*, XV, 435–36.
24. U.S. Commissioner of Labor, *Ninth Special Report. The Italians in Chicago, A Social and Economic Study* (1897), 11, 49.
25. Edith Abbott, *The Tenements of Chicago, 1908–1935* (Chicago, 1936), 154.
26. Filippo Lussana, *Lettere di illetterati* (Bologna, 1913), 134; Paolo Emilio de Luca, *Della emigrazione Europea ed in particolare di quella italiana* (Turin. 1909), II, 175; Juvenile Protective Association Papers, located at the University of Illinois at Chicago Circle; *L'Italia*, May 24, 1902; Frank O. Beck, "The Italian in Chicago," *Bulletin of the Department of Public Welfare, City of Chicago*, II (Feb. 1919), 9.
27. *L'Italia*, July 31, 1909; Jan. 12, 1913; Mar. 31, 1918; *La Tribuna Italiana Transatlantica*, Mar. 27, 1920; Nov. 26, 1921; *The Official Catholic Directory*, XXX (New York, 1915), 54–61; City of Chicago, Board of Education, *Report of the School Census of May 2, 1912*, 12. See Frederick A. Bushee, "Italian Immigrants in Boston," *Arena*, XVII (Apr. 1897), 731, for a similar situation.
28. Pauline Young, "Social Problems in the Education of the Immigrant Child," ASR, I (June 1936), 419–29 and especially 420.
29. Jane Addams, "Foreign-born Children in the Primary Grades: Italian Families in Chicago," *National Education Association. Journal of Proceedings and Addresses*, XXXVI (1897), 104–12; Edith Abbott and Sophonisba P. Breckinridge, *Truancy and Non-Attendance in the Chicago Schools: A Study of the Social Aspects of the Compulsory Education and Child Labor Legislation of Illinois* (Chicago, 1917), 120–23.
30. From an unpublished autobiography by Anthony Sorrentino, in the possession of the author, Chap. II, "What It Means to Live in a Slum." Sorrentino related the experiences of several other slum area children in Chap. VII, "There Was a Child Went Forth."
31. Gertrude Howe Britton, *An Intensive Study of the Causes of Tru-*

*ancy in Eight Chicago Public Schools including a Home Investigation of Eight Hundred Truant Children* (Chicago, 1906); Abbott and Breckinridge, *Truancy and Non-Attendance in the Chicago Schools.*

32. Anna E. Nicholes, "From School to Work in Chicago. A Study of the Central Office that Grants Labor Certificates," *Charities and the Commons,* XVI (May 12, 1906), 231–32.

33. Beck, "The Italian in Chicago," 20; *L'Italia,* Mar. 23, 1889; Jan. 24, 1891; May 4, 1895; July 19, 1909; Mar. 29, 1914; Oct. 13, 1918; *La Tribuna Italiana Transatlantica,* May 27, 1905.

34. Antonio Mangano, "The Effect of Emigration Upon Italy: Toritto and San Demetrio," *Charities and the Commons,* XX (May 2, 1908), 172; Edward A. Steiner, *The Immigrant Tide: Its Ebb and Flow* (New York, 1909), 175; Victor Von Borosini, "Home-going Italians," *Survey,* XXVIII (Apr. 6, 1912), 792.

35. Robert E. Park, "Cultural Aspects of Immigration. Immigrant Heritages," NCSW, XLVIII (1921), 496.

36. Beck, "The Italian in Chicago," 13. See Humbert S. Nelli, "The Role of the 'Colonial' Press in the Italian-American Community of Chicago, 1886–1921," unpublished Ph.D. dissertation, University of Chicago, 1965, 65–66 and sources cited there.

37. Survey of Seventeenth Ward business and industry, 1913–14, in the Chicago Commons Papers, located at the Chicago Historical Society.

38. U.S. Commissioner of Labor, *Ninth Special Report,* Table I, "General Social and Economic Conditions, by Families and Individuals," 51–273. Much more limited was the 1911 *Immigration Commission* (XXVI, 255–57 and XXVII, 128–29, 137–41), which examined three "typical" Italian blocks. Even the U.S. Commissioner of Labor, *Seventh Special Report. The Slums of Baltimore, Chicago, New York and Philadelphia* (1894) based generalizations about Chicago's slum conditions on a small area in the vicinity of Hull House.

39. *L'Italia,* Feb. 4, 1917; Cook County, Office of the Recorder, Real Estate Conveyances.

40. John Palmer Gavit, *Americans by Choice* (New York, 1922), 32–33.

41. U.S. Department of Labor, *Ninth Special Report,* 376–77. Information on Italians covered by civil service comes from official records of the City of Chicago, Civil Service Commission.

42. Material about city firemen is from Civil Service Commission records, and from obituary notices such as those for Anthony Tossi, which appeared in *Chicago Daily News,* Aug. 19, 1967 and *Chicago's American,* Aug. 19, 1967. Comments about city police officers are based on official files of the City of Chicago, Policemen's Annuity and Benefit Fund, files of the Civil Service Commission and copies of police department records in the files of the Chicago Crime Commission. On the history of the Police Department during the period to 1887, see John J. Flinn, *History of the Chicago Police* (Chicago, 1887).

43. City of Chicago, Board of Education, *Proceedings* (for the years listed).

44. *Ibid.*, for the years 1897–98 to 1920–21 inclusive.

45. *Immigration Commission*, XXIX, 129–33; City of New York, Board of Education, *Civil List* for 1905 and 1915.

46. S. M. Franklin, "Elisabeth Martini, Architect," *Life and Labor*, IV (Feb. 1914), 40–43; Elisabeth Martini, "How I Became an Architect," *Life and Labor*, VII (Sept. 1918), 195–96; Beck, "The Italian in Chicago," 13.

47. Immigrants' Protective League, *Annual Report, 1909–1910*, 25–26; Belva Mary Herron, "Labor Organization Among Women, Together with Some Considerations Concerning Their Place in Industry," *University of Illinois Bulletin*, II (July 1, 1905), 29–35; Sager, "Immigration: Based Upon a Study of the Italian Women and Girls of Chicago," 22.

48. Alice Henry, *The Trade Union Woman* (New York, 1915), 137–41.

49. *L'Italia*, Nov. 12, 1892.

50. *Ibid.*, May 11, 1912; *La Parola dei Socialisti*, Apr. 24, 1915; Edwin Fenton, "Italian Immigrants in the Stoneworkers' Union," *Labor History*, III (Spring 1962), 188–207.

51. Among others: *L'Italia*, Jan. 6, 1894; May 13, 1905; Oct. 12, 1907; Dec. 12, 1908; May 11, 1912; Sept. 26, 1915; July 29, 1919; *La Parola dei Socialisti*, Oct. 10, 1910; Apr. 15, Aug. 19, 1911; Mar. 9, July 13, 1912; Feb. 15, 1913; Oct. 9, 1915; *La Parola Proletaria*, June 10, July 1, 1916; *La Fiaccola* (Socialist paper) Mar. 18, May 11, 1918; *Avanti!*, May 8, 1920; *Il Proletario*, Mar. 10, 1911; *The Carpenter* (for the years from 1899 to 1921); *Chicago Typographical Union No. 16: Centennial Book, 1852–1952* (N.P., N.D.); *The Bricklayer and Mason* (for the years from 1899 to 1921).

52. *L'Italia*, Aug. 27, 1901; *Chicago Tribune*, Aug. 23, 1910.

53. International Hod Carriers' and Building Laborers' Union of America, *Report of Proceedings* (for the years 1903–20) and *Official Journal* (for the years 1904–8); Arch A. Mercey, *The Laborers' Story, 1903–1953* (Washington, 1954).

54. International Hod Carriers' and Building Laborers' Union of America, "Report of Executive Board. Board Meetings for 1907," reprinted in *Official Journal*, VI (Oct. 1909), 216; "Sixth General Convention, Held at Elmira, N.Y., September 27 to October 1, 1909," reprinted in *Official Journal*, VI (Oct. 1909), 166; *Report of Proceedings, Seventh General Convention, Held at Scranton, Pa., September 11 to 14, 1911* (N.P., N.D.), 3–5.

55. Katherine Coman, "A Sweated Industry," *Life and Labor*, I (Jan. 1911), 13–15 (reprint of a statement of worker grievances); "Chicago at the Front. A Condensed History of the Garment Workers' Strike," *Life and Labor*, I (Jan. 1911), 4–13.

56. A. D. Marimpietri, *From These Beginnings* (Chicago, 1928), 14. On the conduct of the strike: *Chicago Daily Socialist, Chicago Tribune*,

*L'Italia, La Parola dei Socialisti* and *Il Proletario,* all for the period Sept. 30, 1910 to Mar. 1, 1911; *Life and Labor,* Jan.-Mar. 1911.

57. *Chicago Daily Socialist,* Oct. 17, 1910; Agnes Aitken, "Teaching English to Our Foreign Friends. Part II. Among the Italians," *Life and Labor,* I (Oct. 1911), 309; *La Parola dei Socialisti,* Oct. 29, 1910.

58. *Chicago Daily Socialist,* Nov. 19, Dec. 6 and 19, 1910; Jan. 7, 1911.

59. *La Parola dei Socialisti,* Jan. 28, 1911; "The End of the Struggle. The Chicago Garment Workers' Strike," *Life and Labor,* I (Mar. 1911), 88–89; Alice Henry, "The Hart Schaffner and Marx Agreement," *Life and Labor,* II (June 1912), 170–72; "Holding the Fort; the Chicago Garment Workers' Strike," *Life and Labor,* I (Feb. 1911), 48–51; Sidney Hillman and Earl Dean Howard, *Hart Schaffner and Marx Labor Agreements* (Chicago, 1914).

60. On organizational activities among Italians see Clara Massilotta, "We Can't Make Our Living. Girl Striker Tells of Life in Chicago's Garment Shops," *Chicago Daily Socialist,* Nov. 21, 1910; "The Girls' Own Stories," *Life and Labor,* I (Feb. 1911), 51–52.

61. Amalgamated Clothing Workers of America, *Proceedings of the Convention, First Biennial Convention* to the *Fifth Biennial* for union activities from 1914 to 1922 (the report for 1922 is entitled *Report of the General Executive Board to the Fifth Biennial Convention*).

62. Amalgamated Clothing Workers of America, *Documentary History, 1914–1916* (N.P., N.D.), 10–13; *La Parola dei Socialisti,* Sept. 6 and 13, 1913; Dec. 25, 1915; *L'Italia,* Sept. 26, 1915; *La Fiaccola* (Socialist), Mar. 18, 1918; Wilfred Carsel, *A History of the Chicago Ladies' Garment Workers' Union* (Chicago, 1940), 279–80.

63. *Chicago Daily Socialist* first reported the strike on Sept. 30, 1910, the day after it began, and coverage continued throughout succeeding events.

64. *La Parola Proletaria,* May 13, 1916; *La Parola del Popolo,* Jan. 28, 1922.

65. *Chicago Daily Socialist,* Jan. 16, 1911.

66. *La Parola dei Socialisti,* Aug. 22, 1914; *La Fiaccola* (Socialist), Mar. 16, 1918; *La Parola del Popolo,* Jan. 28, 1922.

67. Renaldo Rigola, *Storia del Movimento Operaio Italiano* (Milan, 1946), 9–22. David A. Shannon, *The Socialist Party of America: A History* (New York, 1955), 18–21, examines Chicago socialists' strong trade unionism and middle-of-the-road social-democratic attitudes.

68. The prominence and influence of intellectuals in Italian-American socialist activities since 1907 (when the Italian section of the Socialist Party was established in Chicago) is clearly—although unintentionally—presented in *La Parola del Popolo*'s special 336-page fiftieth anniversary issue (Dec. 1958-Jan. 1959). See also Edwin

Fenton, "Italians in the Labor Movement," *Pennsylvania History*, XXVI (Apr. 1959), 148.

CHAPTER 4

1. Giuseppe Giacosa, *Impressioni d'America* (Milan, 1908), 163; *L'Italia*, Nov. 1, 8, Dec. 13, 1886; Mar. 7, 1891; Oct. 13, 1918.
2. *L'Italia*, Aug. 17, 1889; Aug. 11, 1888.
3. *Ibid.*, Jan. 27, 1894; Jane Addams, *Democracy and Social Ethics* (New York, 1902), 259.
4. "School Census of 1898" in City of Chicago, Board of Education, *Proceedings, July 13, 1898, to June 28, 1899* (Chicago, 1899), 121–252; *Precinct Lists*, Apr. 6, 1898.
5. These and other statements in the chapter concerning precinct boundaries, as well as changes that took place over the years, are based on ward maps issued for each election by the Board of Election Commissioners.
6. John Palmer Gavit, *Americans by Choice* (New York, 1922), 80; Municipal Voters' League of Chicago, *Annual Report* for the years from 1896 to 1921. The name "Gianni Pauli" for Johnny Powers was that of Alessandro Mastro-Valerio, who referred to Powers' lieutenant James Bowler as "Gimmi Bolla" and the Nineteenth Ward Republican boss Christopher Mamer as "Cristo Mimo." *La Tribuna Italiana Transatlantica*, July 21, 1906; Feb. 28, 1920.
7. The Addams-Powers struggle for control of the Nineteenth Ward has attracted the attention of historians Anne Firor Scott, "Saint Jane and the Ward Boss," *American Heritage*, XII (Dec. 1960), 12–17, 94–99, and Allen F. Davis, "Jane Addams vs. the Ward Boss," *Journal of the Illinois State Historical Society*, LIII (Autumn 1960), 247–65 (much of the material in this article appears in Davis' *Spearheads for Reform: Social Settlements and the Progressive Movement, 1890–1914* [New York, 1967], Chap. VIII). Both view Miss Addams as a practical and realistic reformer who, according to Davis ("Jane Addams vs. the Ward Boss," 265) "battled Johnny Powers in the Nineteenth Ward, and knew . . . when to stop."
8. Municipal Voters' League of Chicago, *The Municipal Campaign, 1898* (Chicago, 1898), 6, and *Ninth Annual Preliminary Report* (Chicago, 1904), 9–10; Florence Kelley, "Hull House," *New England Magazine*, XVIII (June 1898), 565.
9. Jane Addams, "Ethical Survivals," *International Journal of Ethics*, VII (Apr. 1898), 276.
10. Jane Addams, "Why the Ward Boss Rules," *Outlook*, LVIII (Apr. 2, 1898), 879–82; Grace Abbott, *The Immigrant and the Community* (New York, 1917), 256–57.
11. Ray S. Baker, "Hull House and the Ward Boss," *Outlook*, LVIII (Mar. 28, 1898), 769–70; Kelley, "Hull House," 565.
12. Addams, *Democracy and Social Ethics*, 229–68 (quotations from

239, 267–68); Lloyd Shaw [?], *Illinois Democracy, 1818 to 1899. Prominent Democrats of Illinois. A Brief History of the Rise and Progress of the Democratic Party of Illinois* (Chicago, 1899), 350.
13. Baker, "Hull House and the Ward Boss," 770.
14. Municipal Voters' League of Chicago, *Minute Book,* entry for Apr. 13, 1896. The League Annual Reports for the years from 1896 to 1921 attest to reformers' inability to eliminate these leaders.
15. Jane Addams, *Twenty Years at Hull House* (New York, 1910), 315–16, 322; *Democracy and Social Ethics,* 247–48, 257–58.
16. Election Returns and *Precinct Lists* for Apr. 7, 1896.
17. Baker, "Hull House and the Ward Boss," 971; Kelley, "Hull House," 565.
18. *Chicago Tribune,* Jan. 26, 1898; Election Returns, Apr. 6, 1898.
19. *L'Italia,* Mar. 25, 1899; Mar. 29, 1902; Apr. 6, 1907; Apr. 10, 1909; Mar. 4, 1911; Feb. 16, 1919; *La Tribuna Italiana Transatlantica,* Feb. 18, 1905; Mar. 24, Aug. 11, 1906; Feb. 28, Oct. 2, 1920; Feb. 26, 1921; *La Parola dei Socialisti,* Aug. 8, 1908.
20. Kelley, "Hull House," 566; *Chicago Tribune,* Apr. 6, 1898.
21. Municipal Voters' League, *Sixth Annual Report* (Chicago, 1901), 13–14.
22. Election Returns, Apr. 4, 1905; *Chicago Tribune,* Apr. 5, 1905.
23. City of Chicago, Board of Education, *Proceedings, 1898–1899,* 187–89; City of Chicago, Board of Education, *Report of the School Census of 1914* (Chicago, N.D.), 19–23.
24. *Chicago Tribune,* Feb. 22, 1916; John Landesco, *Organized Crime in Chicago: Part III of the Illinois Crime Survey* (Chicago, 1929), 949.
25. Election Returns, Apr. 13, 1920; *Chicago Tribune,* Feb. 12, 1921; *Chicago Daily News Almanac and Year-Book for 1921* (Chicago, 1920), 820; Harold F. Gosnell, *Machine Politics; Chicago Model* (Chicago, 1937), 27–29.
26. Nineteenth Ward Non-Partisan Organization, letter dated Feb. 1, 1921, Papers of the Citizens' Association of Chicago and the Municipal Voters' League.
27. *Chicago Daily News,* Feb. 12, 1921; *Chicago Tribune,* Feb. 13, 1921.
28. *Chicago Daily News,* Feb. 12, 1921; *Chicago Herald and Examiner,* Feb. 13, 1921; *Chicago Tribune,* Feb. 13, 1921.
29. The Illinois Legislature approved Woman Suffrage legislation in June, 1913. For a summary of the law's major provisions see *Daily News Almanac and Year-Book for 1914* (Chicago, 1913), 491.
30. *Chicago Daily News,* Feb. 12, 1921; Virgil W. Peterson, *Barbarians in Our Midst: A Study of Chicago Crime and Politics* (Boston, 1952), 115; *Chicago Tribune,* Feb. 13, 1921.
31. *Chicago Tribune,* Feb. 18, 1921; *Chicago Daily News,* Feb. 18, 1921.
32. *Chicago Daily Journal,* Feb. 21, 22, 23, 1921; *Chicago Herald and*

*Examiner,* Feb. 23, 1921; *Chicago Tribune,* Feb. 22, 23, 1921; *La Tribuna Italiana Transatlantica,* Feb. 26, 1921. Voting statistics are from Election Returns, Feb. 22, 1921.

33. Graham Taylor, *Pioneering on Social Frontiers* (Chicago, 1930), 72–74. Taylor concisely summarized the events in the disputed 1897 aldermanic election as well as other problems faced and overcome in his struggle against political bosses of the Seventeenth Ward during the years to 1901, in testimony before the U.S. Industrial Commission, Feb. 12, 1901, "The Chicago Labor Disputes of 1900," *Industrial Commission,* VIII (1901), 547.

34. Taylor, *Pioneering on Social Frontiers,* 72, "New Hope in Our Ward Politics," *Commons,* VI (Apr. 1901), 15, and "How Neighborly Citizenship Counts," *Chicago Daily News,* May 3, 1913; Graham Romeyn Taylor, "Chicago Settlements in Ward Politics," *Charities and the Commons,* XVI (May 5, 1906), 185; Louise C. Wade, *Graham Taylor: Pioneer for Social Justice, 1851–1938* (Chicago, 1964), 128–33.

35. Landesco, *Organized Crime in Chicago,* 953.

36. *Daily News Almanac and Political Register for 1889* (Chicago, 1889), 155, which includes the 1887 aldermanic vote; *Daily News Almanac and Political Register for 1895* (Chicago, 1894), 312; Election Returns, Apr. 7, 1896 and Apr. 2, 1913.

37. Municipal Voters' League of Chicago, *The Municipal Campaign of 1897,* 7; Election Returns, Apr. 6, 1897; *Daily News Almanac and Political Register for 1898* (Chicago, 1897), 350; Graham Taylor, "Ward Politics Good and Bad—Challenge," *Chicago Daily News,* Mar. 5, 1910.

38. Taylor, *Pioneering on Social Frontiers,* 73; Election Returns, Apr. 6, 1897.

39. *Precinct Lists* for Apr. 6, 1897 election.

40. *Precinct Lists* and Election Returns, Apr. 8, 1895, Apr. 6, 1897, Apr. 4, 1911, Apr. 2, 1912.

41. Election Returns, Apr. 5, 1898, Apr. 2, 1913; Municipal Voters' League of Chicago, *The Municipal Campaign, 1898,* 5; *Daily News Almanac and Political Register for 1894* (Chicago, 1893), 318.

42. Election Returns for the years 1896–1920, and the Italian-language press. *L'Italia, La Tribuna Italiana Transatlantica* and other papers devoted a great deal of space in each election during the period to the activities of Italian office seekers.

43. *Daily News Almanac and Year-Book for 1920* (Chicago, 1919), 918, and *Daily News Almanac and Year-Book for 1925* (Chicago, 1924), 808.

44. U.S. Bureau of the Census, *Thirteenth Census of the United States: 1910. Population,* I, 1092–93, and *Fourteenth Census of the United States: 1920. Population,* II, 862–63, 872–73; Harold F. Gosnell, "Non-Naturalization: A Study in Political Assimilation," AJS, XXXIII (May 1928), 930–39, and "Characteristics of the Non-

Naturalized," AJS, XXXIV (Mar. 1929), 847–55; statistics and other data collected by Gosnell in the Charles E. Merriam Papers, University of Chicago.

45. Election Returns, 1896–1921, especially Apr. 1, 1919, Nov. 2, 1920, and Feb. 22, 1921; *L'Italia*, Apr. 1, 1905; Oct. 12, 1912.

46. *L'Italia*, June 25, 1904; *La Tribuna Italiana Transatlantica*, June 25, 1904; *Il Progresso Italo-Americano*, Oct. 10, 1904. Concerning Italian press attitudes toward other vital issues of the day, including prohibition and immigration restrictions, see Humbert S. Nelli, "The Role of the 'Colonial' Press in the Italian-American Community of Chicago, 1886–1921," unpublished Ph.D. dissertation, University of Chicago, 1965, 159–67.

47. *L'Italia*, Oct. 20, 1912; Election Returns, Nov. 5, 1912.

48. In contrast to the rest of the Italian-language press, socialist newspapers dismissed both candidates as "Wall Street Pawns" and urged the support of Debs. See *Avanti!*, Aug. 21, 1920.

49. Election Returns, Nov. 2, 1920.

50. The Italian "White Hand" Society in Chicago, Illinois, *Studies, Action and Results* (Chicago, 1908), 6–7.

51. Luigi Carnovale, *Il Giornalismo degli emigrati italiani nel Nord America* (Chicago, 1909), 25.

52. *L'Italia*, Nov. 9, 1919; *La Tribuna Italiana Transatlantica*, Mar. 8, Sept. 20, 1919; Sept. 11, 1920.

53. Giovanni E. Schiavo, *The Italians in Chicago: A Study in Americanization* (Chicago, 1928), 104, 169; interview held March 20, 1964 with an Italian-American leader in Chicago who requested that he remain anonymous.

54. Charles E. Merriam, *Chicago: A More Intimate View of Urban Politics* (New York, 1929), Chap. II; Fletcher Dobyns, *The Underworld of American Politics* (New York, 1932).

55. Landesco, *Organized Crime in Chicago*, 1027; Peterson, *Barbarians in Our Midst*, 106.

56. George Kibbe Turner, "The City of Chicago, A Study of the Great Immoralities," *McClure's Magazine*, XXVIII (Apr. 1907), 583–88; City of Chicago, Board of Education, *Proceedings, 1898–1899*, 117, 122.

57. *L'Italia*, Mar. 29, 1914; Lloyd Wendt and Herman Kogan, *Lords of the Levee: The Story of Bathhouse John and Hinky Dink* (Indianapolis, 1943), 329; Gavit, *Americans by Choice*, 372; *Chicago Tribune*, Feb. 21, 1897.

58. *L'Italia*, Jan. 1, 1898; Dec. 1, 1900; Mar. 21, 1903; Nov. 6, 1909; *La Tribuna Italiana Transatlantica*, Oct. 2, 1920.

59. John Landesco, "Crime and the Failure of Institutions in Chicago's Immigrant Areas," AICLC, XXIII (July-Aug. 1932), 239–40; *Chicago Tribune*, May 12, 1921. Ward boundaries, as fixed by the redistricting ordinance of July 22, 1921, are presented in detail in the *Daily News Almanac and Year-Book for 1925*, 886–91.

60. *Chicago Commons News Letter,* Summer 1906, 14; *Warden's Report of the Work of Chicago Commons* (to the Board of Trustees) for the year ending Sept. 30, 1920, 8.

CHAPTER 5

1. John Chetwood, Jr., *Immigration Fallacies* (Boston, 1896), 141–42; Arthur Train, *Courts, Criminals and the Camorra* (New York, 1912), 214; *Immigration Commission,* IV (1911), 209.

2. Isaac A. Hourwich, *Immigration and Labor: The Economic Aspects of European Immigration to the United States* (New York, 1912), 358–61; Eliot Lord, John J. D. Trenor and Samuel J. Barrows, *The Italian in America* (New York, 1905), 209–10, 216; William S. Bennet, "Immigrants and Crime," *Annals,* XXXIV (July 1909), 120–21; Arthur H. Warner, "Amputating the Black Hand," *Survey,* XXII (May 1, 1909), 167; Editor's Note to anonymous article, "The Black Hand Scourge," *Cosmopolitan,* XLVII (June 1909), 31.

3. Gaetano D'Amato, "The 'Black Hand' Myth," *North American Review,* CLXXXVII (Apr. 1908), 544; Tomasso Sassone, "Italy's Criminals in the United States," *Current History,* XV (Oct. 1921), 23.

4. Sabetta quote from *Chicago Record-Herald,* Mar. 26, 1910; Malato and de Stefano quotes from John Landesco, *Organized Crime in Chicago: Part III of the Illinois Crime Survey* (Chicago, 1929), 938, 941–42.

5. *L'Italia,* Dec. 7, 1919; Jan. 24, 1891; *Vita Nuova,* Apr. 1925.

6. *La Parola dei Socialisti,* Mar. 28, 1914.

7. *L'Italia,* Oct. 8, 1892.

8. John E. Coxe, "The New Orleans Mafia Incident," *Louisiana Historical Quarterly,* XX (Oct. 1937), 1067–1110; John S. Kendall, "Who Killa de Chief?" *Louisiana Historical Quarterly,* XXII (Apr. 1939), 492–530; A. Pierantoni, *I Fatti di Nuova Orleans e il Diritto Internazionale* (Rome, 1891).

9. *L'Italia,* Oct. 25, Nov. 1, Dec. 27, 1890; Mar. 7, 21, May 9, July 18, Sept. 12, Dec. 12, 1891; Feb. 6, Mar. 19, Apr. 16, 1892.

10. Several theories have been offered to explain the appearance of the term "Black Hand" to describe certain types of crime within the Italian colony. Perhaps the most acceptable was the one advanced by Gaetano D'Amato, a New York City Italian community leader and friend of police lieutenant Joseph Petrosino of New York's Italian detective squad. In a 1908 article, "The 'Black Hand' Myth," 548, D'Amato stated, "The term 'Black Hand' was first used in this country about ten years ago, probably by some Italian desperado who had heard of the exploits of the Spanish society, and considered the combination of words to be high-sounding and terror-inspiring. One or two crimes committed under the symbol gave it a vogue among the rapacious brotherhood; and, as it looked well and attracted attention in their headlines, the newspapers finally applied

it to all crimes committed by the Italian banditti in the United States."

11. *L'Italia*, Apr. 16, 1910; Aug. 10, 1901; *La Tribuna Italiana Trans-atlantica*, Feb. 8, 1908.

12. *L'Italia*, Feb. 4, 1911.

13. *L'Italia*, Apr. 1, 1911; *La Tribuna Italiana Transatlantica*, Nov. 9, 1907; Commonwealth of Massachusetts, *The Problem of Immigration in Massachusetts. Report of the Commission on Immigration* (Boston, 1914), 105–6.

14. *La Tribuna Italiana Transatlantica*, Nov. 9, 1907; *L'Italia*, Apr. 1, 1911.

15. The Italian "White Hand" Society in Chicago, Illinois, *Studies, Action and Results* (Chicago, 1908), 25–26.

16. *La Tribuna Italiana Transatlantica*, Nov. 16, 23, 1907; *L'Italia*, Nov. 16, 1907.

17. *L'Italia*, Nov. 30, 1907. For the appearance of the White Hand in New Orleans see *La Tribuna Italiana Transatlantica*, Dec. 7, 1907.

18. *La Tribuna Italiana Transatlantica*, Dec. 14, 28, 1907. See Italian "White Hand" Society, *Studies, Action and Results*, 21–22 for the organization's aims.

19. *La Tribuna Italiana Transatlantica*, Jan. 11, Feb. 1, 15, 22, Mar. 7, 1908; *L'Italia*, Feb. 15, Mar. 14, May 23, 1908.

20. Italian "White Hand" Society, *Studies, Action and Results*, 24. Also *Chicago Record-Herald*, Mar. 20, 1911; *La Parola dei Socialisti*, Mar. 28, 1914.

21. Local Community Research Committee, *Chicago Communities*, Vol. VI, "East Side," Document 8. See also Vol. VI, "West Englewood," Document 1a; *La Tribuna Italiana Transatlantica*, Nov. 9, 1907.

22. Landesco, *Organized Crime in Chicago*, 947–48, 953–54; Kendall, "Who Killa de Chief?" 504.

23. Robert A. Woods, ed., *Americans in Process* (Boston, 1902), 207–9; *The Problem of Immigration in Massachusetts*, 105.

24. Robert J. Alexander, *Labor Relations in Argentina, Brazil and Chile* (New York, 1962), 147–49, 162–65, and *Communism in Latin America* (New Brunswick, N.J., 1957), 155; Robert D. Ochs, "A History of Argentine Immigration, 1853–1924," unpublished Ph.D. dissertation, University of Illinois, 1939, 149–57; James Bryce, *South America, Observations and Impressions* (new ed.; New York, 1914), 320.

25. Charles Wagley, *An Introduction to Brazil* (New York, 1963), 181–83; Thomas F. McGann, *Argentina, the United States and the Inter-American System* (Cambridge, Mass., 1957), 193; Italian "White Hand" Society, *Studies, Action and Results*, 26.

26. John Landesco, "Crime and the Failure of Institutions in Chicago's Immigrant Areas," AICLC, XXIII (July-Aug. 1932), 244; *La Parola dei Socialisti*, Mar. 28, 1914.

27. *L'Italia*, Oct. 12, 1913; Nov. 2, 1919.

28. Samuel Paynter Wilson, *Chicago and Its Cesspools of Infamy* (11th ed.; Chicago [1910?]), 29.

29. Landesco, *Organized Crime in Chicago,* 937, 947–48; Arthur Woods, "The Problem of the Black Hand," *McClure's Magazine,* XXXIII (May 1909), 40.

30. Landesco, *Organized Crime in Chicago,* 946–47.

31. John Landesco, "Prohibition and Crime," *Annals,* CLXIII (Sept. 1932), 125.

32. Immigrants' Protective League, *Annual Report for the Year Ending January 1, 1913* (Chicago, 1913), 18.

33. *Immigration Commission,* XXXVII, 203–25; Immigrants' Protective League, *Annual Report, 1910–1911* (Chicago, 1911), 20–21, and *Annual Report for the Year Ending January 1, 1913,* 18–20.

34. *L'Italia,* Apr. 13, Mar. 23, 1912; May 5, 1915.

35. Gino C. Speranza, "What Italians Send Back," *New York Evening Post,* reprinted in *Immigration,* II (Mar. 1911), 269.

36. *Immigration Commission,* XXXVII, 203–4; Immigrants' Protective League, *Annual Report for the Year Ending January 1, 1913,* 19–20; Grace Abbott, *The Immigrant and the Community* (New York, 1917), 92–94.

37. *L'Italia,* July 21, 1894. The ordinance referred to was passed on Sept. 24, 1888. City of Chicago, *Proceedings of the City Council of Chicago for Municipal Year 1888–1889* (Chicago, 1889), 381.

38. Alessandro Mastro-Valerio, "Remarks Upon the Italian Colony in Chicago," *Hull House Maps and Papers* (New York, 1895), 138–39.

39. *La Tribuna Italiana Transatlantica,* May 23, 1903; Aug. 16, 1914; *La Parola dei Socialisti,* Apr. 18, 1908; Jan. 4, May 31, 1913; *La Parola Proletaria,* Aug. 26, 1916; *L'Avanti!,* Nov. 15, 1918; *Il Messaggiere Italo-Americano,* July 5, 1888; *L'Italia,* Jan. 28, 1899; Feb. 11, Nov. 5, 1905; Dec. 4, 1909; Apr. 13, 1912; Mar. 21, 1913; Apr. 26, 1914; May 5, 1915; June 3, 1917; Aug. 4, 1918; Nov. 23, 1919.

40. Landesco, "Crime and the Failure of Institutions in Chicago's Immigrant Areas," 240; Clifford R. Shaw and Henry McKay, *Juvenile Delinquency and Urban Areas* (Chicago, 1942); David Matza, *Delinquency and Drift* (New York, 1964), 65; Albert J. Reiss, Jr., and Albert Lewis Rhodes, "The Distribution of Juvenile Delinquency in the Social Class Structure," ASR, XXVI (Oct. 1961), 729–30.

41. Alberto Pecorini, "The Child of the Immigrant," *La Fiaccola* (Protestant paper), Aug. 31, 1916; William Foote Whyte, "Social Organization in the Slums," ASR, VIII (Feb. 1943), 38; *L'Italia,* Apr. 1, 1911.

42. City of Chicago, Department of Police, *Reports of the General Superintendent of Police of the City of Chicago, to the City Council, for the Fiscal Year Ending December 31, 1908* (Chicago, 1909), 34.

43. Chicago City Council, *Report of the Committee on Crime* (Chicago, 1915), 52–56.

44. Edith Abbott, "Recent Statistics Relating to Crime in Chicago," AICLC, XII (Nov. 1922), 330; Gino Speranza, "The Relation of the Alien to the Administration of the Civil and Criminal Law," AICLC, I (Nov. 1910), 563–72; Kate Holladay Claghorn, *The Immigrant's Day in Court* (New York, 1923), 205–6, 209–10, 222–23; Grace Abbott, *The Immigrant and the Community*, 124–29.

45. Bessie Louise Pierce, *A History of Chicago, Vol. III. The Rise of a Modern City, 1871–1893* (New York, 1957), 305; Herbert Asbury, *Gem of the Prairie: An Informal History of the Chicago Underworld* (New York, 1940), 142 ff.

46. Virgil W. Peterson, *Barbarians in Our Midst: A History of Chicago Crime and Politics* (Boston, 1952), 84–91; Landesco, *Organized Crime in Chicago*, 868–70.

47. Fred D. Pasley, *Al Capone: the Biography of a Self-made Man* (Garden City, N.Y., 1930), 9–14; Emmet Dedmon, *Fabulous Chicago* (New York, 1953), 289–90. Information on Colosimo's residence in 1897 is from *Precinct Lists*, Apr. 1897.

48. Landesco, *Organized Crime in Chicago*, 850–57.

49. Henry Barrett Chamberlain, "Crime as a Business in Chicago," *Bulletin of the Chicago Crime Commission* (Oct. 1, 1919), 1. Information on residence is from *Precinct Lists*, Nov. 1912.

50. *Chicago Daily News*, May 12, 1920; Dedmon, *Fabulous Chicago*, 290–91; Peterson, *Barbarians in Our Midst*, 108–9.

51. Lloyd Wendt and Herman Kogan, *Lords of the Levee: The Story of Bathhouse John and Hinky Dink* (Indianapolis, 1943), 340–41; Virgil W. Peterson, "Chicago: Shades of Capone," *Annals*, CCCXLVII (May 1963), 31–32.

52. Michele Pantaleone, *The Mafia and Politics* (London, 1966), 38–39 (see also the preface to the English edition written by Denis Mack Smith, 17–18); Peterson, *Barbarians in Our Midst*, 135. Denis Mack Smith examines the origins and growth of the Mafia in Sicily in his recent *A History of Sicily. Medieval Sicily: 800–1713* (London, 1968); and *Modern Sicily: After 1713* (London, 1968).

53. Among others, Ed Reid, *Mafia* (rev. ed.; New York, 1964), Chap. II.

54. Margaret Carlyle, *The Awakening of Southern Italy* (London, 1962), 13; also Carlo Sforza, *The Real Italians* (New York, 1942), Chaps. V and IX.

55. Harold Ross, "Crime and the Native Born Sons of European Immigrants," AICLC, XXVIII (Mar.-Apr. 1938), 202–9. Significantly, Italian residents of Latin American countries apparently indicated no propensity to indulge in crime for profit.

56. Alex Gottfried, *Boss Cermak of Chicago: A Study of Political Leadership* (Seattle, 1962), 68–70, 86, 268–69.

57. Italian "White Hand" Society, *Studies, Action and Results*, 27.

CHAPTER 6

1. Edith Abbott and Sophonisba P. Breckinridge, *The Delinquent Child and the Home* (New York, 1912), 55; Constantine M. Panunzio, *The Soul of an Immigrant* (New York, 1922), 231.

2. Commonwealth of Massachusetts, *The Problem of Immigration in Massachusetts. Report of the Commission on Immigration* (Boston, 1914), 202–7, presented an examination of the various institutions mentioned here among Greeks, Italians, Jews, Lithuanians, Poles, and Syrians in Massachusetts. Robert E. Park, "Foreign Language Press and Social Progress," NCSW (1920), XLVII, 494.

3. Luigi Carnovale, *Il Giornalismo degli emigrati italiani nel Nord America* (Chicago, 1909), 34; also 33, 74, 77.

4. *L'Italia,* July 14, 1894.

5. See Chicago Public Library Omnibus Project, *Bibliography of Foreign Language Newspapers and Periodicals Published in Chicago* (Chicago, 1942), 70–74, for a list of Chicago's Italian-language newspapers. Even with the Project, it is impossible to determine accurately the number of Italian-language journals published in the city. *Il Corriere dell'Italia* (1888), and *L'America* (1906), for example, are not included in the *Bibliography.*

6. *L'Italia,* Apr. 7, 1894; Apr. 30, 1887; Jan. 28, Mar. 24, June 23, 1888.

7. *Ibid.,* Apr. 30, 1892. Unless otherwise indicated, "circulation" indicates number of subscribers and not readers. The usual formula to estimate a paper's readership is to multiply the subscription rate by 4.

8. N. W. Ayer and Son, *American Newspaper Annual, 1915* (Philadelphia, 1915); and *Annual, 1921; La Tribuna Italiana Transatlantica,* Feb. 8, 1908.

9. In the municipal elections of 1906, for example, the paper focused on the campaign in the Nineteenth Ward (in Mastero-Valerio's words, "our ward").

10. Ayer, *American Newspaper Annual* for 1905 and 1908–21; *La Tribuna Italiana Transatlantica,* Mar. 17, 1906.

11. Interview with Mr. Egisto Clemente, Apr. 29, 1964; see also *La Parola del Popolo,* Feb. 17, 1908.

12. From a statement made by Bertelli in 1924, reprinted in Fort Velona, "Genesi del movimento socialista democratico e della *Parola del Popolo,*" *La Parola del Popolo. Cinquantesimo Anniversario, 1908–1958,* IX (Dec. 1958-Jan. 1959), 25–26.

13. See, for example, *La Parola dei Socialisti,* June 19, 1909; statement by Bertelli, quoted in Velona, "Genesi del movimento socialista democratico e della *Parola del Popolo,*" 26; Mario De Ciampis, "Storia del movimento socialista rivoluzionario italiano. Lavoratori Industriali del Mondo," 155.

14. *La Tribuna Italiana Transatlantica*, Feb. 15, 1908 and interview with Mr. Egisto Clemente, May 2, 1964.

15. Humbert S. Nelli, "The Role of the 'Colonial' Press in the Italian-American Community of Chicago, 1886-1921," unpublished Ph.D. dissertation, University of Chicago, 1965, Chap. VI, "Attitudes Toward Italy, 1886-1921."

16. Interview with Mr. Egisto Clemente, Apr. 29, 1964; Chicago Public Library Omnibus Project, *Bibliography*, 70-74; Ayer, *American Newspaper Annual*, 1910-21.

17. *La Fiaccola* (Protestant paper), Dec. 19, 1912; Oct. 28, 1920.

18. *La Tribuna Italiana Transatlantica*, Feb. 1, 1908; *La Parola del Popolo*, Sept. 3, 1921.

19. Robert F. Foerster, *The Italian Emigration of Our Times* (Cambridge, Mass., 1919), 396; Frank Luther Mott, *American Journalism: A History of Newspapers in the United States Through 250 Years, 1690 to 1940* (New York, 1941), 595; interviews with Mr. Vincent Coco, former editor of *L'Italia*, July 28, 1964, and Mrs. Oscar Durante, Apr. 8, 1964; Robert E. Park, *The Immigrant Press and Its Control* (New York, 1922), 343-44.

20. *La Parola dei Socialisti*, May 24, Aug. 23 and 30, Sept. 13 and 27, Nov. 1, 1913.

21. See Mott, *American Journalism*, Chaps. XXIV, XXX and XXXVII, for a discussion of trends, techniques, and problems of the American press during the period after 1892.

22. Interview with Mr. Vincent Coco, July 28, 1964.

23. *L'Italia*, July 14, 1894; Jan. 2, 1895; Oct. 13, 1918.

24. *Ibid.*, Jan. 19, 1901; Mar. 25, 1905; *Il Messaggiere Italo-Americano*, July 5, 1888; *La Tribuna Italiana Transatlantica*, Aug. 12, 1905.

25. *Chicago Herald*, Aug. 21, 1887; "Among the Foreign-Born," *Bulletin* (subsequently *Interpreter*), I (Dec. 1922), 10; The Mary McDowell Papers, located at the Chicago Historical Society.

26. William E. Davenport, "The Exodus of a Latin People," *Charities*, XII (May 7, 1904), 466, and Edward C. Banfield, *The Moral Basis of a Backward Society* (Glencoe, Ill., 1958), 16-17.

27. J. S. McDonald, "Italy's Rural Social Structure and Emigration," *Occidente*, XII (Sept.-Oct. 1956), 444-46; Daniel L. Horowitz, *The Italian Labor Movement* (Cambridge, Mass., 1963), 12.

28. J. Owen Stalson, *Marketing Life Insurance: Its History in America* (Cambridge, Mass., 1942), 446-49; Josef M. Baernreither, *English Associations of Working Men* (London, 1889), Chap. I.

29. Frank O. Beck, "The Italian in Chicago," *Bulletin of the Department of Public Welfare, City of Chicago*, II (Feb. 1919), 23; Giovanni E. Schiavo, *The Italians in Chicago: A Study in Americanization* (Chicago, 1928), 55-57; Robert E. Park and Herbert A. Miller, *Old World Traits Transplanted* (New York, 1921), 124-37.

30. State of Illinois, *Report of the Health Insurance Commission* (Springfield, 1919), 524, 527-28.

31. "Le Società Italiane all'estero," *Bollettino del Ministero degli Affari Esteri* (Apr. 1898), 64–69; "Le Società Italiane all'estero nel 1908," *Boll. Emig.*, No. 24 (1908), 96–99; Illinois, *Report of the Health Insurance Commission*, 524.

32. Illinois, *Report of the Health Insurance Commission*, 524; Beck, "The Italian in Chicago," 23; Luigi Provana del Sabbione, "Condizioni della Emigrazione nel R. Distretto consolare in Chicago," *Boll. Emig.*, No. 1 (1913), 29; interview with Mr. Vincent E. Ferrara, Jan. 20, 1967; Caroline F. Ware, *Greenwich Village, 1920–1930: A Comment on American Civilization in the Post-War Years* (New York, 1935), 155.

33. Illinois, *Report of the Health Insurance Commission*, 530–31.

34. "Le Società Italiane negli Stati Uniti del America del Nord nel 1910," *Boll. Emig.*, No. 4 (1912), 23; The Italian "White Hand" Society in Chicago, Illinois, *Studies, Action and Results* (Chicago, 1908), 22; *Italo-American National Union Bulletin*, Mar. 1927, 2; Schiavo, *Italians in Chicago*, 57–58.

35. *L'Italia*, Oct. 14, 1893; Vincent Massari, "La Federazione Colombiana nella Storia degli Italo-Americani," *La Parola del Popolo. Cinquantesimo Anniversario, 1908–1958*, 258–66; *Numero Ricordo per la Inaugurazione della Grande Loggia ed Istallazione del Grande Concilio dell'Illinois* [of the Order Sons of Italy in America], Nov. 9, 1924 (Chicago, 1924).

36. Illinois, *Report of the Health Insurance Commission*, 124, 443–82.

37. Spencer L. Kimball, *Insurance and Public Policy, 1835–1959* (Madison, 1960), 50–51, 112, 156–57; interviews with Mr. Vincent E. Ferrara, Jan. 20, 1967, and Mr. George J. Spatuzza (Grand Venerable, Order Sons of Italy in America, Grand Lodge of the State of Illinois), July 21, 1966.

38. Morton Keller, *The Life Insurance Enterprise, 1885–1910. A Study in the Limits of Corporate Power* (Cambridge, Mass., 1963), 11.

39. Interview with Mr. Vincent E. Ferrara, Jan. 20, 1967.

40. *La Tribuna Italiana Transatlantica*, Apr. 28, 1906; *L'Italia*, Dec. 5, 1908; Oct. 10, 1920; Schiavo, *Italians in Chicago*, 59.

41. "Our Alpine Gun Club," copy of a speech delivered in 1942 at the Golden Jubilee celebration of the Alpine Gun Club; interview with Mr. Roy Marcucci, Secretary of the Alpine Gun Club, Aug. 12, 1966; "Le Società Italiane all'estero," 64–67; "Le Società Italiane all'estero nel 1908," 96–97.

42. "Le Società Italiane all'estero nel 1908," 96–99; "Le Società Italiane negli Stati Uniti del America del Nord nel 1910," 23; *L'Italia*, May 31, 1914. On Italian political clubs see *L'Italia*, Sept. 29, 1894; Jan. 12, 1895; Jan. 16, 1897; Sept. 15, 1900; Feb. 22, 1908; Dec. 16, 1911; Feb. 24, 1912; Feb. 1, 1914.

43. *La Tribuna Italiana Transatlantica*, Aug. 13, 1907; Jan. 4—Mar. 7, 1908; *La Parola dei Socialisti*, Mar. 5, 1908; May 31, June 28, Nov. 22, 1913; Jan. 10, 1914.

44. For full documentation of the material presented in this and following paragraphs, see Nelli, "The Role of the 'Colonial' Press in the Italian-American Community of Chicago, 1886–1921," 75–79.

45. Tito Chiovendo, "Le Provincie interne dell'Argentina," *Bollettino degli Affari Esteri*, No. 11 (1914), 128.

46. Caroline F. Ware, "Cultural Groups in the United States," *The Cultural Approach to History*, ed. C. F. Ware (New York, 1940), 62–65.

47. *La Tribuna Italiana Transatlantica*, June 18, 1904.

48. *Ibid.*, Jan. 14, 1905; Nov. 9, 1907; Feb. 29, 1908; *L'Italia*, Nov. 1, 1890. Other Catholic groups resented Irish control of the Church in the United States. See Colman J. Barry, *The Catholic Church and German Americans* (Milwaukee, 1953); John P. Walsh, "The Catholic Church in Chicago and Problems of an Urban Society, 1893–1915," unpublished Ph.D. dissertation, University of Chicago, 1948.

49. A. Di Domenica, "The Sons of Italy in America," *Missionary Review of the World*, XLI (Mar. 1918), 193.

50. Laurence Franklin, "The Italian in America: What He Has Been, What He Shall Be," *Catholic World*, LXXI (Apr. 1900), 72–73.

51. D. Lynch, "The Religious Condition of Italians in New York," *America*, X (Mar. 21, 1914), 558. At least 25 articles appeared in *America, American Ecclesiastical Review*, and *Catholic World*, during the years between 1900 and 1921.

52. *La Fiaccola* (Protestant paper), Sept. 10, 1914; Sept. 19, 1912.

53. Aurelio Palmieri, "Italian Protestantism in the United States," *Catholic World*, CVII (May 1918), 177–89. Antonio Mangano, *Sons of Italy: A Social and Religious Study of the Italians in America* (New York, 1917), presents a useful bibliography—books, articles, pamphlets, leaflets—on Protestant efforts to convert Italian immigrants.

54. Jane Katherine Hackett, "A Survey of Presbyterian Work with Italians in the Presbytery of Chicago," unpublished M.A. thesis, Presbyterian College of Christian Education, Chicago, 1943; Antonio F. Scorza, "Pastor's Twentieth Anniversary at the Moody Italian Mission, 1914–1934," pamphlet dated Chicago, Sept. 9, 1934, 3–4.

55. Scorza, "Pastor's Twentieth Anniversary at the Moody Italian Mission, 1914–1934," 3; Palmerio Chessa, "A Survey Study of the Evangelical Work Among Italians in Chicago," unpublished B.Div. thesis, Presbyterian Theological Seminary, Chicago, 1934, 15; *La Fiaccola* (Protestant paper), Sept. 6, 1917.

56. Schiavo, *Italians in Chicago*, 79, for the De Carlo estimate; Chessa, "A Survey Study of the Evangelical Work Among Italians in Chicago," 11–18; *La Fiaccola* (Protestant paper), Sept. 14, 1916; U.S. Bureau of the Census, *Fifteenth Census of the United States, 1930. Population*, II, 316.

57. Philip M. Rose, *The Italians in America* (New York, 1922), 120; Mangano, *Sons of Italy*, 55, 186–88, 193–94.

58. *La Tribuna Italiana Transatlantica,* Sept. 21, 1907; *L'Italia,* July 27, 1919.

59. P. Mathew Titus, "A Study of Protestant Charities in Chicago with Special Reference to Neighborhood Houses and Social Settlements," unpublished Ph.D. dissertation, University of Chicago, 1939; Louise C. Wade, *Graham Taylor: Pioneer for Social Justice, 1851–1938* (Chicago, 1964), 126; Olivet Institute, *Annual Report* (for years 1910–17); interview with Mr. Wallace Heistad, Aug. 11, 1966.

60. *Hull House Year Book, 40th Year* (devoted to a "historical sketch of the foundation and development of each department" of the settlement); Hull House Boys' Club, Official Registration Book, in the Urban Historical Collection at the University of Illinois at Chicago Circle.

61. Howard B. Grose, *Aliens or Americans?* (New York, 1906), 256; *Literary Digest,* XLVII (Oct. 11, 1913), 636.

62. *La Fiaccola* (Protestant paper), Aug. 26, 1920; Joseph Schuyler, *Northern Parish; A Sociological and Pastoral Study* (Chicago, 1960), 228.

63. *L'Italia,* Oct. 20, 1890; *Il Progresso Italo-Americano,* Apr. 30, 1895; *La Tribuna Italiana Transatlantica,* Oct. 27, 1906; *La Fiaccola* (Protestant paper), Jan. 30, 1913; *Il Proletario,* Sept. 15, 1911; *La Parola dei Socialisti,* Sept. 27, 1913.

64. *New World,* Aug. 22, 1903.

65. *Ibid.,* Sept. 14, 1901; July 11, Aug. 8, 1903; *Chicago Tribune,* Aug. 16, 1901; *Chicago Chronicle,* July 24, 1905.

66. *L'Italia,* Nov. 1, 1890; *La Tribuna Italiana Transatlantica,* Jan. 14, 1905; Oct. 27, 1906; Feb. 29, 1908; Henry J. Browne, "The 'Italian Problem' in the Catholic Church of the United States, 1880–1900," *United States Catholic Historical Society: Historical Records and Studies,* XXXV (1946), 46–72.

67. These and following statements on Italian parishes in the city are based on the following sources: Province of St. John the Baptist (Western Province), *Missionary Fathers of St. Charles (Scalabrini Fathers) 75th Anniversary* (N.P., N.D.); *Diamond Jubilee of the Archdiocese of Chicago* (Desplaines, Ill., 1920); *The Official Catholic Directory* (1886–1920); and parish histories, including *Assumption Church Diamond Jubilee, 1881–1956* (Chicago, 1956), *St. Anthony of Padua Souvenir Book* (for dedication of a new church building, Aug. 20, 1961), *Our Lady of Pompei Golden Jubilee, 1911–1961* (Chicago, 1961); and newspaper files of the *New World* located at the offices of that paper.

68. Father Dunne replied in equally offensive terms to Mastro-Valerio and "his wretched newspaper" in *Memoirs of Zi Pre* (St. Louis, 1914), 22–27.

69. Joseph M. Sorrentino, "Religious Conditions in Italy," *America,* XII (Oct. 17, 1914), 6–7.

70. Andrew Shipman, "Emigration," *Official Report of the Second*

*American Catholic Missionary Congress, 1913* (Chicago, 1914), 154–71; *Assumption Church Diamond Jubilee; St. Anthony of Padua Souvenir Book; Missionary Fathers of St. Charles (Scalabrini Fathers) 75th Anniversary; Diamond Jubilee of the Archdiocese of Chicago; New World,* Aug. 28, 1903; Sept. 9, 1905; Feb. 12, 1910; *L'Italia,* Mar. 8, 1914; Dec. 30, 1917.

71. *New World,* June 17, 1899; *La Tribuna Italiana Transatlantica,* Sept. 9, 1906; *La Fiaccola* (Protestant paper), Sept. 12, 1912.

72. Kate Gertrude Prindeville, "Italy in Chicago," *Catholic World,* LXXVI (July 1903), 456–57; W. H. Agnew, "Pastoral Care of Italian Children in America. Some Plain Facts about the Condition of Our Italian Children," AER, XLVII (Mar. 1913), 264; Sister Ann Edward Scanlon, "The Catholic Church in Chicago, 1900–1910: A Study in Church Population, Educational and Charitable Contributions," unpublished paper located in the files of *New World.*

73. Parish records of the churches discussed in the text.

74. Marvin Reuel Schafer, "The Catholic Church in Chicago, Its Growth and Administration," unpublished Ph.D. dissertation, University of Chicago, 1929. Schafer based his study on examination of yearly parish reports to the Archdiocese (reports which are no longer available), interviews with parish priests, and visits to various national parishes in the city. Concerning the reliability of Catholic census figures, which critics of the Church frequently claimed to be "padded," he found that "every priest that I have talked with concerning the matter has stated that his report is conservative, and when asked as to the number in his parish the number which he offers for 'publication' is considerably less than he judges that actual number to be. Further, assessments are laid against his parish for the support of Catholic missions, the local hierarchy and Peter's Pence in proportion to the number of souls reported. All these tend to keep estimates conservative" (12, 14–15).

75. Interview with Mr. Vincent E. Ferrara, Jan. 20, 1967; Italian parish records. One reason for marriage outside the ethnic group, pointed out Mr. Ferrara, was that "Italian girls of the community lacked social graces."

76. City of Chicago, Policemen's Annuity and Benefit Fund, Official Records.

77. Illinois, *Report of the Health Insurance Commission,* 530–31.

78. In contrast to Catholic churches, which remained in core areas and served succeeding waves of immigrants, Protestant churches generally departed with their parishioners and moved to the outer parts of the city and its suburbs. J. DuBois Hunter, "Church and Immigrant," study (dated 1913) of the religious situation in the Seventeenth Ward, in the Chicago Commons Papers, Chicago Historical Society.

79. Robert E. Park, "Immigrant Heritages," NCSW (1921), 495.

CHAPTER 7

1. *L'Italia,* May 7, 1916; Sept. 30, 1917; *La Tribuna Italiana Trans-atlantica,* Nov. 10, 1917; Mar. 16, 1918; *Il Progresso Italo-Americano,* Dec. 24, 1917; Apr. 28, 1918.

2. *La Fiaccola* (Protestant paper), May 5, 1917. That many Italian-Americans were as unwilling to contribute money as they were to offer their lives is clear from press complaints about immigrant reluctance to buy (Italian) government bonds. *L'Italia,* Dec. 1, 1918; *La Fiaccola,* Mar. 18, 1920.

3. Illinois Military and Naval Department, *Roster of the Illinois National Guard and Illinois Naval Militia as Organized When Called by the President for World War Service, 1917* (Springfield, 1929 [?]), and *Roll of Honor, Record of Burial Places of Soldiers, Sailors, Marines and Army Nurses of All Wars of the United States Buried in the State of Illinois,* Vol. I (Springfield, 1929); *La Tribuna Italiana Transatlantica,* May 19, 1917; June 15, 1918; *L'Italia,* Feb. 10, Sept. 15, 1918.

4. Graham Taylor, "Local Board 39, Chicago" (typewritten summary of Board activities and attitudes of ethnic groups toward war service), in the Chicago Commons Papers, Chicago Historical Society; Philip M. Rose, *The Italians in America* (New York, 1922), 97; George Creel, *How We Advertised America* (New York, 1922), 176; *Chicago Daily News Almanac and Year-Book,* 1919 (Chicago, 1918), 836–42.

5. Robert F. Foerster, *The Italian Emigration of Our Times* (Cambridge, Mass., 1919), 399.

6. *L'Italia,* Oct. 16, 1921.

7. Local Community Research Committee, *Chicago Communities,* Vol. III, "Lower North Side," Document 27; Paul Frederick Cressey, "Population Succession in Chicago: 1898–1930," AJS, XLIV (July 1938), 67.

8. These and other comments on location of Italians in the city during the period 1920–30 are based on Ernest W. Burgess and Charles Newcomb, eds., *Census Data of the City of Chicago, 1920* (Chicago, 1931); and *Census Data of the City of Chicago, 1930* (Chicago, 1933); city directories for the years from 1920 to 1930; and precinct voter lists.

9. Judy Scheim, "Austin," History Research Paper, University of Illinois, Chicago Circle, 1967.

10. Chicago Plan Commission, *Forty-four Cities in the City of Chicago* (Chicago, 1942), 32–34, 51–76; Local Community Research Committee, *Chicago Communities,* Vol. VI, "West Englewood," Document 1a; also Documents 1, 3, 7, 7a; "East Side," Documents 1, 1a, 5, 8, 9; U.S. Bureau of the Census, *Fifteenth Census of the United States, 1930. Population,* II, 316.

11. Vivien M. Palmer, *Study of the Development of Chicago's North-*

*side* (unpublished study prepared for the United Charities of Chicago, Dec. 1932), 88–100; Local Community Research Committee, *Chicago Communities*, Vol. III, "Lower North Side," Document 18 and Vol. VI, "Hamlin Park," Document 15.

12. This situation was noted as early as 1916 by the City Superintendent of Schools in his *Report of the Chicago School Census, 1916* (Chicago, 1916), 4. On the national trend from city to suburb during the 'twenties see Harlan Paul Douglass, *The Suburban Trend* (New York, 1925).

13. *Diamond Jubilee of the Archdiocese of Chicago* (Desplaines, Ill., 1920), 570, 604–6; Province of St. John the Baptist (Western Province), *Missionary Fathers of St. Charles (Scalabrini Fathers) 75th Anniversary* (N.P., N.D.), 27–29; *Chicago Chronicle*, July 24, 1905; *La Tribuna Italiana Transatlantica*, Aug. 5, 12, 1905; *Il Proletario*, Aug. 11, 1909; *La Parola dei Socialisti*, Nov. 8, 1913.

14. Virgil W. Peterson, *A Report on Chicago Crime for 1966* (Chicago, 1967), 99–100; *A Report on Chicago Crime for 1967* (Chicago, 1968), 81–89; "Our Supreme President [Bulger] Candidate for Mayor of Melrose Park," and "Our Supreme President Elected Mayor of Melrose Park," *Italo-American National Union Bulletin*, Apr. and May 1933; *Chicago Daily News*, Aug. 21, 23, 1967.

15. This and material following are based on: Illinois Bell Telephone Company, *Suburban Alphabetical Telephone Directory* for the years from 1920 to 1929; R. L. Polk & Co., *Chicago City Directory, 1923* (Chicago, 1923) and *Chicago City Directory, 1928–1929* (Chicago, 1928); "Salerno Dies, Co-founder of Biscuit Firm," *Chicago Tribune*, Jan. 22, 1968; Francis Borrelli, "The Italian Residents of Chicago," *Chicago Herald and Examiner*, Oct. 1927; a scrapbook of three articles, Chicago Historical Society, six pp.; biographical sketches presented in Lisi Cipriani, comp., *Selected Directory of the Italians in Chicago, 1933–1934* (Chicago, 1933), 1–25; and Giovanni E. Schiavo, *The Italians in Chicago: A Study in Americanization* (Chicago, 1928), 157–203.

16. Lisi Cipriani, *Selected Directory of the Italians in Chicago. Issue 1930* (Chicago, 1930).

17. Elmer L. Irey and William J. Slocum, *The Tax Dodgers: The Inside Story of the T-Men's War with America's Political and Underworld Hoodlums* (Garden City, N.Y., 1949), 48. Irey directed the investigation that resulted in the conviction of Al Capone for income tax evasion in 1931.

18. Edward Dean Sullivan, *Chicago Surrenders* (New York, 1930), 205; John Landesco, "Prohibition and Crime," *Annals*, CLXIII (Sept. 1932), 125.

19. *Chicago American*, May 15, 1920; *Chicago Tribune*, May 15, 1920; *Avanti!*, May 22, 1920; Virgil W. Peterson, *Barbarians in Our Midst: A History of Chicago Crime and Politics* (Boston, 1952), 109.

20. John Landesco, "Prohibition and Crime," 120.

21. John Landesco, *Organized Crime in Chicago: Part III of the Illinois Crime Survey* (Chicago, 1929), 910–11, 916–18.

22. Lloyd Wendt and Herman Kogan, *Big Bill of Chicago* (Indianapolis, 1953), 238–39; Alson J. Smith, *Syndicate City: The Chicago Crime Cartel and What to Do About It* (Chicago, 1954), 36–37; Irey and Slocum, *The Tax Dodgers*, 165; Walter Noble Burns, *The One-way Ride: The Red Trail of Chicago Gangland from Prohibition to Jake Lingle* (Garden City, N.Y., 1931), 112.

23. *Chicago Tribune*, May 20, 1924; *Chicago Daily News*, Nov. 17, 1924; National Commission on Law Observance and Enforcement, *Publications, Vol. IV. Report on Prosecution* (Washington, 1931), 372.

24. File of newspaper articles on criminal activities in Chicago during the 1920's, maintained by the Chicago Crime Commission. None of the events discussed in the text received passing mention in the city's Italian-language press.

25. Landesco, *Organized Crime in Chicago*, 929–30; Denis Tilden Lynch, *Criminals and Politicians* (New York, 1932), 120–21; *Al Capone and Chicago's Gang Wars* (Chicago, 1931), 10–36.

26. Fred D. Pasley, *Al Capone; The Biography of a Self-made Man* (New York, 1930); William H. Stuart, *The Twenty Incredible Years* (Chicago, 1935), 193.

27. Pasley, *Al Capone*, 38–40; *This Is Cicero* (Cicero, N.D.), 1–3; Walter Spelman, *The Town of Cicero* (Cicero, 1923), 11–12.

28. John H. Lyle, *The Dry and Lawless Years* (Englewood Cliffs, N.J., 1960), 76–78; *Chicago Tribune*, Apr. 1, 2, 1924.

29. Pasley, *Al Capone*, 62; Lyle, *The Dry and Lawless Years*, 80; Eliot Ness, *The Untouchables* (New York, 1957), 227; Robert Ross, *The Trial of Al Capone* (Chicago, 1933). For a defense of Cermak's lack of action against Capone see Alex Gottfried, *Boss Cermak of Chicago: A Study of Political Leadership* (Seattle, 1962), 140–43.

30. Frank J. Wilson (as told to Howard Whitman), "How We Caught Al Capone," *Chicago Tribune Sunday Magazine*, June 14, 1959; Herbert Asbury, *Gem of the Prairie: An Informal History of the Chicago Underworld* (New York, 1940), 346–47; *Al Capone and Chicago's Gang Wars*, 1.

31. Landesco, *Organized Crime in Chicago*, 1046.

32. Lloyd Lewis and Henry Justin Smith, *Chicago: The History of Its Reputation* (New York, 1929), 436; Landesco, *Organized Crime in Chicago*, 1077–79. Repeal of the Eighteenth Amendment in 1933 doomed the bootlegging business and removed the major source of "syndicate" income. Years before this, however, the organization had discovered a lucrative new field of criminal exploitation and profit—labor and business racketeering. Gordon L. Hostetter and Thomas Quinn Beesley, *It's a Racket* (Chicago, 1929); Fred D. Pasley, *Muscling In* (New York, 1931).

33. Pasley, *Al Capone*, 59; Burns, *The One-way Ride*, 225; Edward D. Sullivan, *Rattling the Cup on Chicago Crime* (New York, 1929), 175–79.

34. Herbert Asbury, *The Great Illusion: An Informal History of Prohibition* (Garden City, N.Y., 1950), 291; Frederick Lewis Allen, *Only Yesterday: An Informal History of the Nineteen-Twenties* (New York, 1931), 220.

35. Based on examination of Chicago's Italian-language press during the Torrio-Capone era and interview with former *L'Italia* editor Vincent Coco, July 28, 1964.

36. Mary Borden, "Chicago Revisited," *Harper's Magazine*, CLXII (Apr. 1931), 542; Burns, *The One-way Ride*, 32.

37. *L'Italia*, Feb. 4, 11, 18, 25, 1923; *La Tribuna Italiana Transatlantica*, Feb. 3, 10, 17, 24, Mar. 3, 1923.

38. *Precinct Lists* and Election Returns for the Feb. 27, 1923 primary; Stuart, *Twenty Incredible Years*, 121, 186, 337–38.

39. Among the variety of appointive offices held by Italians during the 1920's were: Clerk, Office of the State's Attorney; Assistant United States District Attorney; Member, Board of Local Improvements; Chief of the Contract Division, City Engineer's Office; Chief Clerk, Office of the Prosecuting Attorney; Assistant Prosecuting Attorney; and Assistant Corporation Counsel.

40. Lynch, *Criminals and Politicians*, 111, 113; *La Tribuna Italiana Transatlantica*, Nov. 22, 1924.

41. *Bulletin of the Chicago Crime Commission* (Mar. 1, 1924), 42–43; *Chicago Tribune*, Dec. 31, 1935.

42. Municipal Voters' League of Chicago, *Report for the Thirty-third Year* (Chicago, 1929), 14–15; Pasley, *Al Capone*, 247; Election Returns, Feb. 26, 1929; *Chicago Tribune*, Dec. 30, 31, 1935; Sept. 6, 1948; U.S. Senate, Special Committee to Investigate Organized Crime in Interstate Commerce, *Third Interim Report*, 82nd Cong., 1st Sess., 1951, 59.

43. *La Tribuna Italiana Transatlantica*, Nov. 15, 1924; Carroll Hill Wooddy, *The Chicago Primary of 1926: A Study in Election Methods* (Chicago, 1926), 137–38, 153, 157, 208–10; Stuart, *Twenty Incredible Years*, 190, 360; *L'Italia*, Mar. 25, 1928.

44. Asbury, *Gem of the Prairie*, 341; *Precinct Lists* and Election Returns, Nov. 4, 1924.

45. Lloyd Wendt and Herman Kogan, *Lords of the Levee: The Story of Bathhouse John and Hinky Dink* (Indianapolis, 1943), 344–45.

46. *Precinct Lists* and Election Returns, Apr. 5, 1927; Stuart, *Twenty Incredible Years*, 315–17; Wendt and Kogan, *Big Bill of Chicago*, 268–69; "What 'Big Bill's' Victory Means," *Literary Digest*, XCIII (Apr. 16, 1927), 5.

47. *Chicago Daily News*, Apr. 6, 1927; *Chicago Tribune*, Apr. 6, 1927; William Allen White, "They Can't Beat My Big Boy," *Collier's*, LXXIX (June 18, 1927), 46–47; Elmer Davis, "Portrait of an

Elected Person," *Harper's Magazine*, CLV (July 1927), 182–83; Nels Anderson, "Democracy in Chicago: Big Bill Thompson, Friend of the Plain People," *Century*, CXV (Nov. 1927), 73.

48. *Chicago Daily News*, Apr. 4, 1927; Charles E. Merriam, *Chicago, a More Intimate View of Urban Politics* (New York, 1929), 289–90; George C. Hoffmann, "Big Bill Thompson, His Mayoral Campaigns and Voting Strength," unpublished M.A. thesis, University of Chicago, 1956, 34–42.

49. Stuart, *Twenty Incredible Years*, 317.

50. Hoffmann, "Big Bill Thompson, His Mayoral Campaigns and Voting Strength," 30–32; Wendt and Kogan, *Big Bill of Chicago*, 206–13; Wooddy, *The Chicago Primary of 1926; Chicago Tribune*, Feb. 12, 1927.

51. Gottfried, *Boss Cermak of Chicago*, 147–52; Hoffmann, "Big Bill Thompson, His Mayoral Campaigns and Voting Strength," 43–45.

52. Lewis and Smith, *Chicago*, 469; *Chicago Daily News*, Aug. 27, 1930; Apr. 1, 1931; *Chicago Tribune*, Apr. 2, 1931; *People v. Serritella*, 272 Ill. Appellate Ct. (1933), 616.

53. Gottfried, *Boss Cermak of Chicago*, Chap. XI.

54. Arthur W. Thurner, "The Impact of Ethnic Groups on the Democratic Party in Chicago, 1920–1928," unpublished Ph.D. dissertation, University of Chicago, 1966, 344, 329; John M. Allswang, "The Political Behavior of Chicago's Ethnic Groups, 1918–1932," unpublished Ph.D. dissertation, University of Pittsburgh, 1967; J. Joseph Huthmacher, *Massachusetts People and Politics, 1919–1933* (Cambridge, Mass., 1959); David Burner, *The Politics of Provincialism: The Democratic Party in Transition, 1918–1932* (New York, 1968), emphasizes New York City.

55. Allswang, "The Political Behavior of Chicago's Ethnic Groups, 1918–1932," 54–55, 57.

56. Gottfried, *Boss Cermak of Chicago*, 218–21, 234–35.

57. Burgess and Newcomb, *Census Data of the City of Chicago* for 1920 and 1930; Chicago Plan Commission, *Chicago Land Use Survey*, Vol. II. *Land Use in Chicago* (Chicago, 1943); City of Chicago, Board of Election Commissioners, Official Ward Maps.

58. Edith Abbott, *The Tenements of Chicago, 1908–1935* (Chicago, 1936), 97, noted the reluctance of many older people to leave the Italian district, in sharp contrast to the more venturesome and ambitious younger adults who preferred Columbus Park and Oak Park to the Near West Side. She did not recognize, however, the variety among remaining residents of the Italian district and the reasons for their staying there.

59. Alice Hamilton, "Witchcraft in West Polk Street," *American Mercury*, X (Jan. 1927), 71.

60. Anna Zaloha, "A Study of the Persistence of Italian Customs Among 143 Families of Italian Descent Members of Social Clubs at Chicago Commons," unpublished M.A. thesis, Northwestern University,

1937, 160–61. (I examined the carbon copy of this thesis, deposited in the Chicago Commons Papers, Chicago Historical Society.)

61. Copy of an unpublished and undated autobiographical essay written by Mr. E. L. Hicks, Principal of the Jackson School; it covers the period between Feb. 1, 1927, and the end of 1930 (in the possession of the author).

62. John Landesco, "The Life History of a Member of the '42' Gang," AICLC, XXIII (Mar.-Apr. 1933), 964–98. For a probing and sensitive examination of the origins of the "42" Gang, its activities during the late 'twenties and early 'thirties, and the life histories and family backgrounds of gang members, see the MS prepared by John Landesco, in the Landesco Papers, University of Chicago Library, "The Forty-two Gang: A Study of a Neighborhood Criminal Group."

63. Anthony Sorrentino, unpublished autobiography.

64. Frederic M. Thrasher, The Gang: A Study of 1,313 Gangs in Chicago (rev. ed.; Chicago, 1936); Clifford R. Shaw et al., Delinquency Areas: A Study of the Geographic Distribution of School Truants, Juvenile Delinquents and Adult Offenders in Chicago (Chicago, 1929); Harvey Warren Zorbaugh, The Gold Coast and the Slum: A Sociological Study of Chicago's Near North Side (Chicago, 1929), 154–57.

65. Chicago Public Library Omnibus Project, Bibliography of Foreign Language Newspapers and Periodicals Published in Chicago (Chicago, 1942), 71–74; N. W. Ayer and Son, American Newspaper Annual for the years 1920–69.

66. Schiavo, The Italians in Chicago, 58–59, 65; interview, July 21, 1966, with Mr. George J. Spatuzza, Grand Venerable, Order Sons of Italy in America, Grand Lodge of the State of Illinois (he has held that position since the late 1920's); interview, Jan. 20, 1967, with Mr. Vincent E. Ferrara, Supreme Secretary, Italo-American National Union (since 1925).

67. L'Italia, Feb. 10, 17, Mar. 17, 24, 1929; La Tribuna Italiana Transatlantica, Feb. 16, 23, 1929.

68. Schiavo, The Italians in Chicago, 118; Caroline F. Ware, "Cultural Groups in the United States," The Cultural Approach to History, ed. C. F. Ware (New York, 1940), 63; L'Italia, July 27, 1920; Aug. 31, 1924; Feb. 6, 1927; Mar. 25, 1928; Apr. 21, 1929; La Tribuna Italiana Transatlantica, Jan. 13, 1923; Apr. 5, 1924; Feb. 12, 1927. On Apr. 20, 1924, L'Italia interpreted the Johnson-Reed Act for its readers: "Italians are not wanted in America." This Act became law on May 26, 1924, but articles opposing it appeared in L'Italia and other Chicago Italian-language papers throughout 1924.

69. Gaetano Salvemini and George La Piana, What to Do with Italy (New York, 1943), Chap. III; Edward Corsi, "Italian Immigrants and Their Children," Annals, CCXXIII (Sept. 1942), 105.

70. Schiavo, The Italians in Chicago, 119; interviews with Mr. Vincent

Coco, former editor of *L'Italia,* July 28, 1964; Mr. Vincent E.
Ferrara, Jan. 20, 1967; Mr. George J. Spatuzza, July 21, 1966; and
Mr. Peter Fosco, General Secretary-Treasurer, International Hod
Carriers', Building and Common Laborers' Union of America, Aug.
6, 1967.

71. "Fascismo in America," *Interpreter,* II (May, 1923), 6; *La Parola
del Popolo,* Aug. 4, 1923; interview, July 28, 1964, with Mr. Vincent
Coco; "Il movimento fascista fra gli italiani d'America," *La Parola
del Popolo. Cinquantesimo Anniversario,* IX (Dec. 1958-Jan. 1959),
69–72; Marcus Duffield, "Mussolini's American Empire: The Fascist
Invasion of the United States," *Harper's Magazine,* CLIX (Nov.
1929), 662; John P. Diggins, "The Italo-American Fascist Opposition," JAH, LIV (Dec. 1967), 587.

72. Local Community Research Committee, *Chicago Communities,* Vol.
III, "The Lower North Side," Document 30 (exerpts from the notes
of Harvey Warren Zorbaugh). A similar situation existed during the
decade in other American cities. See, for example, Caroline F. Ware,
*Greenwich Village, 1920–1930: A Comment on American Civiliza-
tion in the Post-War Years* (Boston, 1935), 156–57.

73. Local Community Research Committee, *Chicago Communities,* Vol.
III, "The Lower North Side," Document 27. An observer of the
same Italian colony in 1924 speculated about the future of the
settlement. "It is difficult to predict the changes which will occur
in the Italian district in the next few years. Whether it will become
as predominantly Colored as it has been German, Irish, Swedish,
and Italian in turn, cannot at this time be foretold." Esther Crockett
Quaintance, "Rents and Housing Conditions in the Italian District
of the Lower North Side of Chicago, 1924," unpublished M.A.
thesis, University of Chicago, 1925, 47. This population shift did
take place during the following thirty years. Depression in the
1930's and housing shortages during and immediately after World
War II slowed the pace of Italian dispersion from the ethnic district;
since the 1950's it has again accelerated. St. Philip Benizi Church
and the "Southern" colony it once served, for example, no longer
exist.

74. The survey referred to in the text grew out of a course in U.S. Urban
History which I taught at the University of Illinois at Chicago Circle
during the summers of 1966 and 1967. It covered the areas bounded
by Harrison, Morgan and Loomis streets and Roosevelt Road.
Student interviewers and I prepared a three-page questionnaire
focusing on community and personal life. The response of neighborhood residents to college students who asked questions about
their ethnic background, property ownership, residence, church
membership, education, reading habits, political attitudes, employment, and organizational activities—among other things—was, almost without exception, friendly and open. In addition to the
information requested, several interviewees volunteered autobio-

graphical statements about their experiences as immigrants, or experiences told them by their immigrant parents. We found that young people continue to leave the area at the first opportunity. In 1967 one Near West Side teenager expressed amazement to a student interviewer over the construction of townhouses on West Flournoy Street near Loomis, and of the movement of university professors and other middle-class Americans into the neighborhood. To his surprise, university personnel moved even into older houses and apartments. As soon as he could, he confided, he planned to move to a suburb, just as his brothers and sisters had done before him.

# A Note on Sources

Since the works relevant to various topics have been cited in footnotes, their mention here is superfluous. This bibliographical note will describe instead the major unpublished sources and a few of the most important (and often neglected) printed materials used in the study, and their location, in the hope that this information will prove to be of value to others interested in examining the adjustment of immigrant groups to urban America.

Much valuable and virtually untapped material is located in city and county agencies and departments. I will not attempt to list all sources in all the offices I visited, but only the most pertinent to this book. Information on Italian purchase of property throughout Chicago was obtained through examination of plat maps, found at City Hall in the Bureau of Maps and Plats, and Real Estate Conveyances, in the Office of the Recorder of Deeds at the County Building. Also in City Hall are the Board of Election Commissioners, with official precinct voter registration lists, ward maps and manuscripts of official election returns (the last-named at the Board's warehouse on the South Side); the Civil Service Commission, with records of employment by various city agencies of policemen, firemen, laborers and supervisory personnel; the Retirement Board of the Policemen's Annuity and Benefit Fund, with information on date and place of birth, parentage, religious preferences, residences, marriages and deaths of policemen. While the Police Department did not open its files to me, much of the information contained there appears in the records of the Policeman's Annuity and Benefit

Fund and the Civil Service Commission. For crime statistics I used
the Municipal Reference Library's copies of the printed yearly reports
of the Superintendent of Police to the City Council. For other specific
and detailed data I preferred to go to the particular department or
agency willing to open its records to me, and my job in this respect was
somewhat simplified because in Chicago the county and city offices are
located in one huge building in the Loop. Together, the above sources
provided a wealth of information on residential mobility, public employment, economic status, ethnic intermarriage, crime, political activities and voting patterns.

Italian national parishes in the Chicago area permitted me to examine
their records, which give an indication of members' religious preferences, intermarriages and involvement in church activities. Since these
records often list addresses of members, they can be used as an additional resource in measuring residential mobility. Parish histories, anniversary brochures and jubilee books focus on highlights within local
areas and provide peripheral information about ethnic activities, church
attendance, parish growth and community services provided by various
churches. The *New World*, the official newspaper of the Archdiocese
of Chicago, offered its files and some unpublished studies of the Catholic
Church of Chicago, thus facilitating a deeper understanding of church
relations with ethnic groups, including Italians.

The Chicago Historical Society contains city directories, suburban
telephone directories, school censuses, reports of federal, state and local
governments and private agencies, fire insurance atlases, land use maps,
and a number of ward maps. Maps and photographs (of which the
Society owns an excellent collection) are a valuable source for urban
history, for they show the physical makeup—and the changes over the
passage of years—of buildings, blocks, and even of sections of the city.
During the period of my research, the Society obtained the Chicago
Commons Papers, which include yearly reports and special studies of
social and economic conditions in the area, as well as the records of
Graham Taylor's activities during World War I in a local draft board.
(While the Commons Papers contain a great deal of useful material
on ethnic groups in the community served by the settlement house, I
found the Graham Taylor Papers at Newberry Library of less value.)
Other sources include the Mary McDowell Papers, with a few items of
value, and the Local Community Research Committee's *Chicago Communities*, a bound, typescript manuscript of interviews and research
gathered by the Research Committee of the University of Chicago during the 1920's and based on Chicago's community areas; unfortunately,
only six of these volumes are available, and the information elicited by

the interviewers is not verified in any way. I have used data from the Committee's manuscript only in combination with other sources, and have benefited from its illustrative material and pungent quotations, as well as from observations of trained sociologists like Harvey Warren Zorbaugh. The Society offers a microfilm copy of the Foreign Language Press Survey, and the manuscript population census schedules (on microfilm) for the federal censuses up to and including 1880 (the 1890 manuscript schedules were destroyed by fire). Papers from the Citizens' Association of Chicago and the Municipal Voters' League, including the League's Minute Book, provide material on reform efforts and middle class reformers. There are also pamphlets and other campaign publications used by reform groups in their struggles against ward bosses.

The Urban Historical Collection of the University of Illinois at Chicago Circle offers some Hull House records and papers; among the most useful for this study was the Hull House Boys' Club Official Registration Book, listing names, ages, ethnic origins, home addresses, and, if not in school, occupations, of all members of the club for 1907. This Collection contains also the papers of the Juvenile Protective Association, with much information about woman and child labor and violation of city and state ordinances.

I made use of the Chicago Crime Commission's records (which include copies of Police Department correspondence), its extensive files of newspaper clippings relating to crime, and its printed annual reports. These materials were indispensable when I examined Italians in crime and politics during the 1920's.

The Charles E. Merriam Papers, the John Landesco Papers and the Ernest W. Burgess Papers at the University of Chicago offered additional information on politics and crime. Landesco's manuscript detailing interviews with members of an Italian neighborhood criminal gang was of particular value. His meticulous study, *Organized Crime in Chicago: Part III of the Illinois Crime Survey* (Chicago, 1929), deserves special mention. Based on research in police department records, interviews with criminals and public officials, and careful examination of newspapers, the volume is a basic source on criminal operations in the Chicago metropolitan area from 1900 to 1928.

I visited with and talked to officers of the Italo-American National Union, the Order Sons of Italy in America, Grand Lodge of the State of Illinois, and the Alpine Gun Club, all of whom opened their organizations' records to me. Information prior to 1930 is rather sparse, but includes copies of speeches, pamphlets, monthly journals, proceedings of conventions, and—from the Sons of Italy—a membership list. Among the unions which permitted me to examine their papers were the Inter-

national Hod Carriers', Building and Common Laborers' Union, the
Amalgamated Clothing Workers' Union, and the Chicago Typographical
Union, Local No. 16. While in each case there were only a few items
relating to my areas of research, they added to the total, reinforcing
some ideas and raising questions about others.

I was indeed fortunate in obtaining permission to make a xerox copy
of an unpublished autobiography in which Anthony Sorrentino recorded
his experiences as an immigrant youth in an Italian colony on the Near
West Side; and of an autobiographical statement dating from the late
1920's prepared by an elementary school principal describing the problems faced in attempting to teach in a deteriorating neighborhood within
the (Italian) West Side, and of the extracurricular—and generally
illegal—activities of students and former students. I interviewed scores
of immigrants and the sons and daughters of immigrants, ethnic group
leaders, social settlement workers, juvenile delinquency officers, and
workers in rehabilitation programs. Material from a few of the more
valuable sessions is quoted in the text or cited in footnotes, although
information obtained verbally about a period so far in the past (in terms
of the human life span) cannot be accepted unquestioningly. It is
inevitable that recollections should blur, that attitudes be altered to
conform to present criteria, that opinions held five decades ago become
unconsciously modified by subsequent events. I have made use of such
reminiscences only when verified by other sources.

The foreign-language press is an excellent source of information on
immigrant colony life, including contemporary attitudes; for a detailed
examination of Chicago's Italian-language newspapers, see my dissertation. Since the press was geared to the needs and problems of newly
arrived immigrants, it provides an inaccurate picture of long-term residents and of second-generation—that is, American-born—inhabitants.
Other materials must be used to fill these gaps.

# Index